Qt5 C++ GUI Programming Cookbook
Second Edition

Practical recipes for building cross-platform GUI applications, widgets, and animations with Qt 5

Lee Zhi Eng

BIRMINGHAM - MUMBAI

Qt5 C++ GUI Programming Cookbook
Second Edition

Commissioning Editor: Richa Tripathi
Acquisition Editor: Alok Dhuri
Content Development Editor: Akshita Billava
Technical Editor: Abin Sebastian
Copy Editor: Safis Editing
Project Coordinator: Ulhas Kambali
Proofreader: Safis Editing
Indexer: Tejal Daruwale Soni
Graphics: Tom Scaria
Production Coordinator: Deepika Naik

First published: July 2016
Second edition: March 2019

Production reference: 1220319

Published by Packt Publishing Ltd.
Livery Place
35 Livery Street
Birmingham
B3 2PB, UK.

ISBN 978-1-78980-382-2

www.packtpub.com

`mapt.io`

Mapt is an online digital library that gives you full access to over 5,000 books and videos, as well as industry leading tools to help you plan your personal development and advance your career. For more information, please visit our website.

Why subscribe?

- Spend less time learning and more time coding with practical eBooks and Videos from over 4,000 industry professionals

- Improve your learning with Skill Plans built especially for you

- Get a free eBook or video every month

- Mapt is fully searchable

- Copy and paste, print, and bookmark content

Packt.com

Did you know that Packt offers eBook versions of every book published, with PDF and ePub files available? You can upgrade to the eBook version at `www.packt.com` and as a print book customer, you are entitled to a discount on the eBook copy. Get in touch with us at `customercare@packtpub.com` for more details.

At `www.packt.com`, you can also read a collection of free technical articles, sign up for a range of free newsletters, and receive exclusive discounts and offers on Packt books and eBooks.

Contributors

About the author

Lee Zhi Eng is a self-taught programmer who worked as an artist and programmer at several game studios before becoming a part-time lecturer for two years at a university, teaching game development subjects related to Unity and Unreal Engine. He has not only taken part in various projects related to games, interactive apps, and virtual reality, but has also participated in multiple projects that are more oriented toward software and system development. When he is not writing code, he enjoys traveling, photography, and exploring new technologies.

About the reviewer

Nibedit Dey is a technopreneur with a multidisciplinary technology background. He holds a bachelor's degree in biomedical engineering and a master's degree in digital design and embedded systems. Before starting his entrepreneurial journey, he worked for L&T and Tektronix for several years in different research and development roles. He has been using C++ to build complex software-based systems for the last eight years.

Packt is searching for authors like you

If you're interested in becoming an author for Packt, please visit `authors.packtpub.com` and apply today. We have worked with thousands of developers and tech professionals, just like you, to help them share their insight with the global tech community. You can make a general application, apply for a specific hot topic that we are recruiting an author for, or submit your own idea.

Table of Contents

Preface

The continuous growth of the computer software market has led us to a very competitive and challenging era. Not only does your software need to be functional and easy to use, it must also look appealing and professional to the users. In order to gain the upper hand and a competitive advantage over other software products on the market, the look and feel of your product is of the utmost importance and should be taken care of early in the production stage. In this book, we will teach you how to create functional, appealing, and user-friendly software using the Qt 5 development platform.

Who this book is for

This book intended for those who want to develop software using Qt 5. If you want to improve the visual quality and content presentation of your software application, this book is for you.

What this book covers

Chapter 1, *Look-and-Feel Customization with Qt Designer*, shows how to design your program's user interface using both Qt Designer and Qt Quick Designer.

Chapter 2, *Event Handling – Signals and Slots*, covers topics related to the signals and slots mechanism provided by Qt 5, which allows you to handle your program's event callbacks with ease.

Chapter 3, *States and Animations with Qt and QML*, explains how to animate your user interface widgets by empowering the state machine framework and the animation framework.

Chapter 4, *QPainter and 2D Graphics*, covers how to draw vector shapes and bitmap images on screen using Qt's built-in classes.

Chapter 5, *OpenGL Implementation*, demonstrates how to render 3D graphics in your program by integrating OpenGL in your Qt project.

Chapter 6, *Using Network and Managing Large Documents*, shows how to set up an FTP file server, then create a program that helps you to transfer files to and from the file server.

Chapter 7, *Threading Basics – Asynchronous Programming*, covers how to create multi-threading processes in your Qt 5 application and run them simultaneously to process heavy calculations.

Chapter 8, *Building a Touch Screen Application with Qt 5*, explains how to create a program that works on a touchscreen device.

Chapter 9, *XML Parsing Made Easy*, shows how to process data in the XML format and use it together with the Google Geocoding API to create a simple address finder.

Chapter 10, *Conversion Library*, covers how to convert between different variable types, image formats, and video formats using Qt's built-in classes as well as third-party programs.

Chapter 11, *Accessing Databases with SQL Driver and Qt*, explains how to connect your program to a SQL database using Qt.

Chapter 12, *Developing Web Applications Using Qt Web Engine*, covers how to use the web rendering engine provided by Qt and develop programs that empower the web technology.

Chapter 13, *Performance Optimization*, shows how to optimize your Qt 5 application and speed up its processing.

To get the most out of this book

This book intended for those who are just starting out with C++, QML, and Qt 5. It would help if you already understand the C++ programming language. However, it is okay if you do not, because through our step-by-step examples, you will be able to master the language in no time. There are many sub-versions of Qt 5; please make sure that the version you're installing to your computer is at least Qt 5.10 or later so that the code is compatible with the book.

Download the example code files

You can download the example code files for this book from your account at www.packtpub.com. If you purchased this book elsewhere, you can visit www.packtpub.com/support and register to have the files emailed directly to you.

You can download the code files by following these steps:

1. Log in or register at `www.packtpub.com`.
2. Select the **SUPPORT** tab.
3. Click on **Code Downloads & Errata**.
4. Enter the name of the book in the **Search** box and follow the onscreen instructions.

Once the file is downloaded, please make sure that you unzip or extract the folder using the latest version of:

- WinRAR/7-Zip for Windows
- Zipeg/iZip/UnRarX for Mac
- 7-Zip/PeaZip for Linux

The code bundle for the book is also hosted on GitHub at `https://github.com/PacktPublishing/Qt5-CPP-GUI-Programming-Cookbook-Second-Edition`. We also have other code bundles from our rich catalog of books and videos available at `https://github.com/PacktPublishing/`. Check them out!

Download the color images

We also provide a PDF file that has color images of the screenshots/diagrams used in this book. You can download it here: `http://www.packtpub.com/sites/default/files/downloads/9781789803822_ColorImages.pdf`.

Code in Action

Visit the following link to check out videos of the code being run: `http://bit.ly/2TrFE2i`

Conventions used

There are a number of text conventions used throughout this book.

`CodeInText`: Indicates code words in text, database table names, folder names, filenames, file extensions, pathnames, dummy URLs, user input, and Twitter handles. Here is an example: "This happens because we specifically tell the selector to apply the style to all the widgets with a class called `QPushButton`."

A block of code is set as follows:

```
html, body, #map {
  height: 100%;
  margin: 0;
  padding: 0
}
```

When we wish to draw your attention to a particular part of a code block, the relevant lines or items are set in bold:

```
int main(int argc, char *argv[]) {
    QApplication a(argc, argv);
    MainWindow w;
    w.show();
    printText("A", 100);
    printText("B", 100);
    return a.exec();
}
```

Any command-line input or output is written as follows:

```
$ mkdir css
$ cd css
```

Bold: Indicates a new term, an important word, or words that you see onscreen. For example, words in menus or dialog boxes appear in the text like this. Here is an example: "Once you are done with that, open up Qt Creator and create a new **Qt Widgets Application** project."

 Warnings or important notes appear like this.

 Tips and tricks appear like this.

Sections

In this book, you will find several headings that appear frequently (*Getting ready, How to do it..., How it works..., There's more...,* and *See also*). To give clear instructions on how to complete a recipe, use these sections as follows:

Getting ready

This section tells you what to expect in the recipe and describes how to set up any software or any preliminary settings required for the recipe.

How to do it...

This section contains the steps required to follow the recipe.

How it works...

This section usually consists of a detailed explanation of what happened in the previous section.

There's more...

This section consists of additional information about the recipe in order to make you moreknowledgeable about the recipe.

See also

This section provides helpful links to other useful information for the recipe.

Get in touch

Feedback from our readers is always welcome.

General feedback: Email `feedback@packtpub.com` and mention the book title in the subject of your message. If you have questions about any aspect of this book, please email us at `questions@packtpub.com`.

Errata: Although we have taken every care to ensure the accuracy of our content, mistakes do happen. If you have found a mistake in this book, we would be grateful if you would report this to us. Please visit www.packtpub.com/submit-errata, selecting your book, clicking on the Errata Submission Form link, and entering the details.

Piracy: If you come across any illegal copies of our works in any form on the internet, we would be grateful if you would provide us with the location address or website name. Please contact us at copyright@packtpub.com with a link to the material.

If you are interested in becoming an author: If there is a topic that you have expertise in and you are interested in either writing or contributing to a book, please visit authors.packtpub.com.

Reviews

Please leave a review. Once you have read and used this book, why not leave a review on the site that you purchased it from? Potential readers can then see and use your unbiased opinion to make purchase decisions, we at Packt can understand what you think about our products, and our authors can see your feedback on their book. Thank you!

For more information about Packt, please visit packtpub.com.

Look-and-Feel Customization with Qt Designer

1

We will cover the following recipes in this chapter:

- Using style sheets with Qt Designer
- Customizing basic style sheets
- Creating a login screen using style sheets
- Using resources in style sheets
- Customizing properties and sub-controls
- Styling in **Qt Modeling Language** (**QML**)
- Exposing the QML object pointer to C++

Introduction

Qt 5 allows us to easily design our program's user interface through a method most people are familiar with. Qt not only provides us with a powerful user interface toolkit, called **Qt Designer**, which enables us to design our user interface without writing a single line of code, but it also allows advanced users to customize their user interface components through a simple scripting language called **Qt Style Sheets**.

Technical requirements

The technical requirements for this chapter include Qt 5.11.2 MinGW 32 bit, Qt Creator 4.8.2, and Windows 10.

All the code used in this chapter can be downloaded from the following GitHub repository, at: `https://github.com/PacktPublishing/Qt5-CPP-GUI-Programming-Cookbook-Second-Edition/tree/master/Chapter01`.

Check out the following video to see the code in action: `http://bit.ly/2TqQJ3I`

Using style sheets with Qt Designer

In this example, we will learn how to change the look and feel of our program and make it look more professional by using style sheets and resources. Qt allows you to decorate your **graphical user interfaces** (**GUIs**) using a style sheet language called Qt Style Sheets, which is very similar to **Cascading Style Sheets** (**CSS**), used by web designers to decorate their websites.

How to do it...

Let's get started by learning how to create a new project and get ourselves familiar with the Qt Designer:

1. Open up **Qt Creator** and create a new project. If this is the first time you have used Qt Creator, you can either click the big button, which reads **+ New Project**, or simply go to **File | New File or Project**.
2. Select **Application** under the **Projects** window, and select **Qt Widgets Application**.
3. Click the **Choose...** button at the bottom. A window will pop out and ask you to insert the project name and its location.
4. Click **Next** several times, and click the **Finish** button to create the project. We will stick with the default settings for now. Once the project has been created, the first thing you will see is the panel with tons of big icons on the left side of the window, which is called the mode selector panel; we will discuss this more later in the *How it works...* section.
5. You will see all your source files listed on the sidebar panel which is located next to the mode selector panel. This is where you can select which file you want to edit, which in this case is `mainwindow.ui`, because we are about to start designing the program's UI.

6. Double-click the `mainwindow.ui` file, and you will see an entirely different interface appear out of nowhere. Qt Creator actually helped you to switch from the script editor to the UI editor (Qt Designer) because it detected the `.ui` extension on the file you're trying to open.

7. You will also notice that the highlighted button on the mode selector panel has changed from the **Edit** button to the **Design** button. You can switch back to the script editor or change to any other tools by clicking one of the buttons located in the upper half of the mode selector panel.

8. Let's go back to the Qt Designer and look at the `mainwindow.ui` file. This is basically the main window of our program (as the filename implies) and it's empty by default, without any widget on it. You can try to compile and run the program by pressing the Run button (the green arrow button) at the bottom of the mode selector panel, and you will see an empty window pop up once the compilation is complete.

9. Let's add a push button to our program's UI by clicking on the **Push Button** item in the **Widget Box** (under the **Buttons** category) and dragging it to your main window in the form editor. Keep the push button selected, and now you will see all the properties of this button inside the **Property Editor** on the right side of your window. Scroll down to the middle and look for a property called **styleSheet**. This is where you apply styles to your widget, which may or may not inherit to its children or grandchildren recursively, depending on how you set your style sheet. Alternatively, you can right-click on any widget in your UI at the form editor and select **Change styleSheet...** from the pop-up menu.

10. You can click on the input field of the **styleSheet** property to directly write the style sheet code, or click on the **...** button beside the input field to open up the **Edit Style Sheet** window, which has a bigger space for writing longer code for style sheets. At the top of the window, you can find several buttons, such as **Add Resource**, **Add Gradient**, **Add Color**, and **Add Font**, that can help you to kickstart your coding if you can't remember the properties' names. Let's try to do some simple styling with the **Edit Style Sheet** window.

11. Click **Add Color** and choose a color.

12. Pick a random color from the color picker window; let's say, a pure red color. Then click **OK**.

13. A line of code has been added to the text field on the **Edit Style Sheet** window, which in my case is as follows:

```
color: rgb(255, 0, 0);
```

14. Click the **OK** button and the text on your push button should have changed to red.

How it works...

Let's take a bit of time to get familiar with Qt Designer's interface before we start learning how to design our own UI:

The explanation for the preceding screenshot is as follows:

1. **Menu bar**: The menu bar houses application-specific menus that provide easy access to essential functions such as creating new projects, saving files, undoing, redoing, copying, and pasting. It also allows you to access development tools that come with Qt Creator, such as the compiler, debugger, and profiler.
2. **Widget Box**: This is where you can find all the different types of widget provided by Qt Designer. You can add a widget to your program's UI by clicking one of the widgets from the **Widget Box** and dragging it to the form editor.

3. **Mode selector**: The mode selector is a side panel that places shortcut buttons for easy access to different tools. You can quickly switch between the script editor and form editor by clicking the **Edit** or **Design** buttons on the mode selector panel, which is very useful for multitasking. You can also easily navigate to the debugger and profiler tools in the same speed and manner.

4. **Build shortcuts**: The build shortcuts are located at the bottom of the mode selector panel. You can build, run, and debug your project easily by pressing the shortcut buttons here.

5. **Form editor**: The form editor is where you edit your program's UI. You can add different widgets to your program by selecting a widget from the **Widget Box** and dragging it to the form editor.

6. **Form toolbar**: From here, you can quickly select a different form to edit. Click the drop-down box located on top of the **Widget Box** and select the file you want to open with Qt Designer. Beside the drop-down box are buttons to switch between the different modes of the form editor, and also buttons to change the layout of your UI.

7. **Object Inspector**: The **Object Inspector** lists all the widgets within your current `.ui` file. All the widgets are arranged according to their parent-child relationship in the hierarchy. You can select a widget from the **Object Inspector** to display its properties in the **Property Editor**.

8. **Property Editor**: The **Property Editor** will display all the properties of the widget you selected from either the **Object Inspector** window or the form editor window.

9. **Action Editor** and the **Signals & Slots Editor**: This window contains two editors, the **Action Editor** and the **Signals & Slots Editor**, which can be accessed from the tabs beneath the window. The **Action Editor** is where you create actions that can be added to a menu bar or toolbar in your program's UI.

10. **Output panes**: Output panes consist of several different windows that display information and output messages related to script compilation and debugging. You can switch between different output panes by pressing the buttons that carry a number before them, such as **1 Issues**, **2 Search Results**, or **3 Application Output**.

There's more...

In the previous section, we discussed how to apply style sheets to Qt Widgets through C++ coding. Although that method works really well, most of the time, the person who is in charge of designing the program's UI is not the programmer, but rather a UI designer who specializes in designing user-friendly UI. In this case, it's better to let the UI designer design the program's layout and style sheet with a different tool and not mess around with the code. Qt provides an all-in-one editor called **Qt Creator**.

Qt Creator consists of several different tools, such as script editor, compiler, debugger, profiler, and UI editor. The UI editor, which is also called **Qt Designer**, is the perfect tool for designers to design their program's UI without writing any code. This is because Qt Designer adopted the *what you see is what you get* approach by providing an accurate visual representation of the final result, which means whatever you design with Qt Designer will turn out exactly the same visually when the program is compiled and run.

The similarities between Qt Style Sheets and CSS are as follows:

- This is how a typical piece of CSS code looks:

```
h1 { color: red; background-color: white;}
```

- This is how Qt Style Sheets look, which is almost the same as the preceding CSS:

```
QLineEdit { color: red; background-color: white;}
```

As you can see, both of them contain a selector and a declaration block. Each declaration contains a property and a value, separated by a colon. In Qt, a style sheet can be applied to a single widget by calling the `QObject::setStyleSheet()` function in C++ code. Consider the following, for example:

```
myPushButton->setStyleSheet("color : blue");
```

The preceding code will turn the text of a button with the `myPushButton` variable name to blue. You can achieve the same result by writing the declaration in the style sheet property field in Qt Designer. We will discuss Qt Designer more in the following *Customizing basic style sheets* section.

Qt Style Sheets also supports all the different types of selectors defined in the CSS2 standard, including the universal selector, type selector, class selector, and ID selector, which allows us to apply styling to a very specific individual widget or group of widgets. For instance, if we want to change the background color of a specific line-edit widget with the usernameEdit object name, we can do this by using an ID selector to refer to it:

```
QLineEdit#usernameEdit { background-color: blue }
```

 To learn about all the selectors available in CSS2 (which are also supported by Qt Style Sheets), please refer to this document: http://www. w3.org/TR/REC-CSS2/selector.html.

Customizing basic style sheets

In the previous recipe, you learned how to apply a style sheet to a widget with Qt Designer. Let's go crazy and push things further by creating a few other types of widgets and change their style properties to something bizarre for the sake of learning.

This time, however, we will not apply the style to every single widget one by one, but we will learn to apply the style sheet to the main window and let it inherit down the hierarchy to all the other widgets, so that the style sheet is easier to manage and maintain in the long run.

How to do it...

In the following example, we will format different types of widgets on the canvas and add some code to the style sheet to change its appearance:

1. Remove the style sheet from PushButton by selecting it and clicking the small arrow button beside the **styleSheet** property. This button will revert the property to the default value, which in this case is the empty style sheet.
2. Add a few more widgets to the UI by dragging them one by one from the **Widget Box** to the form editor. I've added a line edit, combo box, horizontal slider, radio button, and a check box.

3. For the sake of simplicity, delete the **menuBar**, **mainToolBar**, and the **statusBar** from your UI by selecting them from the **Object Inspector**, right-click, and choose **Remove**. Now, your UI should look similar to this:

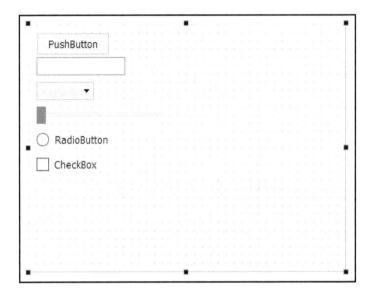

4. Select the main window from either the form editor or the **Object Inspector**, then right-click and choose **Change styleSheet...** to open up the **Edit Style Sheet** window. Insert the following into the style sheet:

```
border: 2px solid gray;
border-radius: 10px;
padding: 0 8px;
background: yellow;
```

5. You will see a bizarre-looking UI with everything covered in yellow with a thick border. This is because the preceding style sheet does not have a selector, which means the style will apply to the children widgets of the main window all the way down the hierarchy. To change that, let's try something different:

```
QPushButton {
    border: 2px solid gray;
    border-radius: 10px;
    padding: 0 8px;
    background: yellow;
}
```

6. This time, only `PushButton` will get the style described in the preceding code, and all other widgets will return to the default styling. You can try to add a few more push buttons to your UI and they will all look the same:

7. This happens because we specifically tell the selector to apply the style to all the widgets with the `QPushButton` class. We can also apply the style to just one of the push buttons by mentioning its name in the style sheet, as in the following code:

```
QPushButton#pushButton_3 {
  border: 2px solid gray;
  border-radius: 10px;
  padding: 0 8px;
  background: yellow;
}
```

8. Once you understand this method, we can add the following code to the style sheet:

```
QPushButton {
    color: red;
    border: 0px;
    padding: 0 8px;
    background: white;
}
```

```
QPushButton#pushButton_2 {
    border: 1px solid red;
    border-radius: 10px;
}
```

9. This code basically changes the style of all the push buttons, as well as some properties of the pushButton_2 button. We keep the style sheet of pushButton_3 as it is. Now the buttons will look like this:

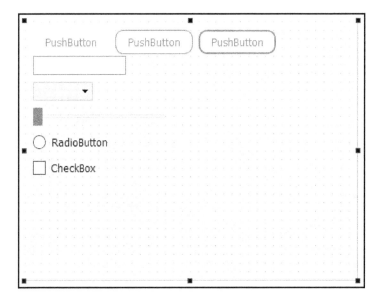

10. The first set of style sheets will change all widgets of the QPushButton type to a white rectangular button with no border and red text. The second set of style sheets changes only the border of a specific QPushButton widget called pushButton_2. Notice that the background color and text color of pushButton_2 remain white and red, respectively, because we didn't override them in the second set of style sheets, hence it will return to the style described in the first set of style sheets since it's applicable to all the QPushButton widgets. The text of the third button has also changed to red because we didn't describe the **Color** property in the third set of style sheets.

11. Create another set of style sheets that use the universal selector, using the following code:

```
* {
  background: qradialgradient(cx: 0.3, cy: -0.4, fx: 0.3, fy:
  -0.4, radius: 1.35, stop: 0 #fff, stop: 1 #888);
  color: rgb(255, 255, 255);
  border: 1px solid #ffffff;
}
```

12. The universal selector will affect all the widgets, regardless of their type. Therefore, the preceding style sheet will apply a nice gradient color to all the widgets' backgrounds and set their text to white with a one-pixel solid outline that is also white. Instead of writing the name of the color (that is, white), we can use the `rgb` function (`rgb(255, 255, 255)`) or hex code (`#ffffff`) to describe the color value.

13. As before, the preceding style sheet will not affect the push buttons because we have already given them their own styles, which will override the general style described in the universal selector. Just remember that in Qt, the style that is more specific will ultimately be used when there is more than one style with an influence on a widget. This is how the UI will look now:

How it works...

If you are ever involved in web development using HTML and CSS, Qt's style sheet works exactly the same way as CSS. Style sheets provide the definitions to describe the presentation of the widgets – what the colors are for each element in the widget group, how thick the border should be, and so on and so forth. If you specify the name of the widget to the style sheet, it will change the style of the particular `PushButton` widget with the name you provide. None of the other widgets will be affected and will remain as the default style.

To change the name of a widget, select the widget from either the form editor or the **Object Inspector** and change the property called **objectName** in the property window. If you have used the ID selector previously to change the style of the widget, changing its object name will break the style sheet and lose the style. To fix this problem, simply change the object name in the style sheet as well.

Creating a login screen using style sheets

Next, we will learn how to put all the knowledge we've learned in the previous example together and create a fake graphical login screen for an imaginary operating system. Style sheets are not the only thing you need to master in order to design a good UI. You will also need to learn how to arrange the widgets neatly using the layout system in Qt Designer.

How to do it...

Let's get started by following these steps:

1. We need to design the layout of the graphical login screen before we start doing anything. Planning is very important in order to produce good software. The following is a sample layout design I made to show you how I imagine the login screen will look. Just a simple line drawing like this is sufficient as long as it conveys the message clearly:

```
Monday, 25-10-2015 3:14 PM                                    ↻  ⏻

                        MyOS Logo

                ┌─────────────────────────────────┐
                │  Username:  [                  ] │
                │                                  │
                │  Password:  [                  ] │
                │                                  │
                │  [            Login            ] │
                └─────────────────────────────────┘
```

2. Go back to Qt Designer again.
3. We will be placing the widgets at the top panel first, then the logo and the login form beneath it.
4. Select the main window and change its width and height from 400 and 300 to 800 and 600, respectively, because we'll need a bigger space in which to place all the widgets.
5. Click and drag a label under the **Display Widgets** category from the **Widget Box** to the form editor.
6. Change the **objectName** property of the label to `currentDateTime` and change its **text** property to the current date and time just for display purposes, such as `Monday, 25-10-2015 3:14 PM`.
7. Click and drag a `PushButton` under the **Buttons** category to the form editor. Repeat this process once more because we have two buttons on the top panel. Rename the two buttons `restartButton` and `shutdownButton`.
8. Select the main window and click the small icon button on the form toolbar that says Lay Out Vertically when you mouse over it. You will see the widgets are automatically arranged on the main window, but it's not exactly what we want yet.
9. Click and drag a **Horizontal Layout** widget under the **Layouts** category to the main window.

10. Click and drag the two push buttons and the text label into the horizontal layout. You will see the three widgets being arranged in a horizontal row, but vertically they are located in the middle of the screen. The horizontal arrangement is almost correct, but the vertical position is totally off.

11. Click and drag a **Vertical Spacer** from the **Spacers** category and place it beneath the **Horizontal Layout** we created previously in *step 9* (under the red rectangular outline). All the widgets are pushed to the top by the spacer.

12. Place a **Horizontal Spacer** between the text label and the two buttons to keep them apart. This will ensure the text label always sticks to the left and the buttons align to the right.

13. Set both the **Horizontal Policy** and **Vertical Policy** properties of the two buttons to **Fixed** and set the **minimumSize** property to 55 x 55. Set the **text** property of the buttons to empty, as we will be using icons instead of text. We will learn how to place an icon in the button widgets in the following *Using resources in style sheets* section.

14. Your UI should look similar to this:

Next, we will be adding the logo using the following steps:

1. Add a **Horizontal Layout** between the top panel and the **Vertical Spacer** to serve as a container for the logo.

2. After adding the **Horizontal Layout**, you will find the layout is way too thin in height (almost zero height) to be able to add any widgets to it. This is because the layout is empty and it's being pushed by the vertical spacer under it into zero height. To solve this problem, we can set its **vertical margin** (either **layoutTopMargin** or **layoutBottomMargin**) to be temporarily bigger until a widget is added to the layout.

3. Add a **Label** to the **Horizontal Layout** that you just created and rename it logo. We will learn more about how to insert an image into the label to use it as a logo in the following *Using resources in style sheets* section. For now, just empty out the **text** property and set both its **Horizontal Policy** and **Vertical Policy** properties to **Fixed**. Set the **minimumSize** property to 150 x 150.

4. Set the vertical margin of the layout back to zero if you haven't already done so.

5. The logo now appears to be invisible, so we will just place a temporary style sheet to make it visible until we add an image to it in the following *Using resources in style sheets* section. The style sheet is really simple:

```
border: 1px solid;
```

6. Your UI should look similar to this:

Now, let's create the login form using the following steps:

1. Add a **Horizontal Layout** between the logo's layout and the **Vertical Spacer**. Set the **layoutTopMargin** property to a large number (that is, `100`), so that you can add a widget to it more easily.
2. Add a **Vertical Layout** inside the **Horizontal Layout** you just created. This layout will be used as a container for the login form. Set its **layoutTopMargin** to a number lower than that of the horizontal layout (that is, `20`) so that we can place widgets in it.
3. Right-click the **Vertical Layout** you just created and choose **Morph into** | **QWidget**. The **Vertical Layout** is being converted into an empty widget. This step is essential because we will be adjusting the width and height of the container for the login form. A layout widget does not contain any properties for width and height, but only margins, due to the fact that a layout will expand toward the empty space surrounding it, which makes sense, considering that it does not have any size properties. After you have converted the layout to a `QWidget` object, it will automatically inherit all the properties from the widget class, and so we are now able to adjust its size to suit our needs.

4. Rename the `QWidget` object, which we just converted from the layout, to `loginForm` and change both its **Horizontal Policy** and **Vertical Policy** properties to **Fixed**. Set the **minimumSize** parameter to `350 x 200`.

5. Since we already placed the `loginForm` widget inside the **Horizontal Layout**, we can now set its **layoutTopMargin** property back to zero.

6. Add the same style sheet as for the logo to the `loginForm` widget to make it visible temporarily, except this time we need to add an ID selector in front, so that it will only apply the style to `loginForm` and not its children widgets:

```
#loginForm { border: 1px solid; }
```

7. Your UI should look something like this:

We are not done with the login form yet. Now that we have created the container for the login form, it's time to put more widgets into the form:

1. Place two horizontal layouts into the login form container. We need two layouts: one for the username field and another for the password field.
2. Add a **Label** and a **Line Edit** to each of the layouts you just added. Change the **text** property of the upper label to Username: and the one beneath to Password:. Rename the two line edits to username and password, respectively.
3. Add a push button beneath the password layout and change its **text** property to Login. Rename it to loginButton.
4. You can add a Vertical Spacer between the password layout and the Login button to distance them slightly. After the Vertical Spacer has been placed, change its sizeType property to Fixed and change the Height to 5.
5. Select the loginForm container and set all its margins to 35. This is to make the login form look better by adding some space to all its sides.
6. Set the **Height** property of the Username, Password, and loginButton widgets to 25 so that they don't look so cramped.
7. Your UI should look something like this:

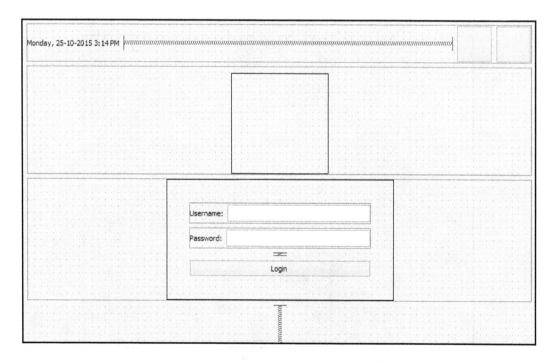

We're not done yet! As you can see, the login form and the logo are both sticking to the top of the main window due to the **Vertical Spacer** beneath them. The logo and the login form should be placed at the center of the main window instead of the top. To fix this problem, use the following steps:

1. Add another **Vertical Spacer** between the top panel and the logo's layout, which will counter the spacer at the bottom that balances out the alignment.
2. If you think that the logo is sticking too close to the login form, you can add a **Vertical Spacer** between the logo's layout and the login form's layout. Set its **sizeType** property to **Fixed** and the **Height** property to 10.
3. Right-click the top panel's layout and choose **Morph into | QWidget**. Rename it topPanel. The layout has to be converted into **QWidget** because we cannot apply style sheets to a layout, as it doesn't have any properties other than margins.
4. There is a little bit of a margin around the edges of the main window—we don't want that. To remove the margins, select the **centralWidget** object from the **Object Inspector** window, which is right under the **MainWindow** panel, and set all the margin values to zero.
5. Run the project by clicking the Run button (with the green arrow icon) to see what your program looks like. If everything went well, you should see something like this:

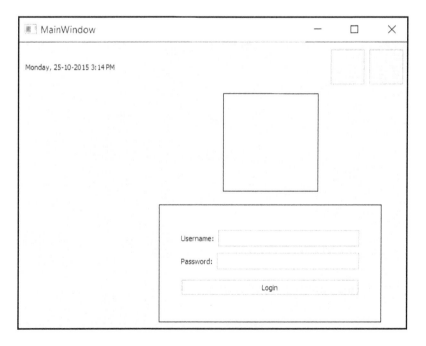

6. Let's decorate the UI using style sheets! Since all the important widgets have been given an object name, it's easier for us to apply the style sheets to it from the main window, since we will only write the style sheets to the main window and let them inherit down the hierarchy tree.

7. Right-click on **MainWindow** from the **Object Inspector** window and choose **Change styleSheet....**

8. Add the following code to the style sheet:

```
#centralWidget { background: rgba(32, 80, 96, 100); }
```

9. The background of the main window changes its color. We will learn how to use an image for the background in the following *Using resources in style sheets* section. So the color is just temporary.

10. In Qt, if you want to apply styles to the main window itself, you must apply them to its **centralWidget**, instead of the main window because the window is just a container.

11. Add a nice gradient color to the top panel:

```
#topPanel {
    background-color: qlineargradient(spread:reflect, x1:0.5,
y1:0, x2:0, y2:0, stop:0 rgba(91, 204, 233, 100), stop:1
rgba(32, 80, 96, 100));
}
```

12. Apply the black color to the login form and make it look semi-transparent. We will also make the corners of the login form container slightly rounded by setting the `border-radius` property:

```
#loginForm {
 background: rgba(0, 0, 0, 80);
 border-radius: 8px;
}
```

13. Apply styles to the general types of widgets:

```
QLabel { color: white; }
QLineEdit { border-radius: 3px; }
```

14. The preceding style sheets will change all the labels' texts to a white color, which includes the text on the widgets as well because, internally, Qt uses the same type of label on the widgets that have text on them. Also, we made the corners of the line edit widgets slightly rounded.

15. Apply style sheets to all the push buttons on our UI:

```
QPushButton {
    color: white;
    background-color: #27a9e3;
    border-width: 0px;
    border-radius: 3px;
}
```

16. The preceding style sheet changes the text of all the buttons to a white color, then sets its background color to blue, and makes its corners slightly rounded as well.

17. To push things even further, we will make it so that the color of the push buttons changes when we mouse over it, using the `hover` keyword:

```
QPushButton:hover { background-color: #66c011; }
```

18. The preceding style sheet will change the background color of the push buttons to green when we mouse over them. We will talk more about this in the following *Customizing properties and sub-controls* section.

19. You can further adjust the size and margins of the widgets to make them look even better. Remember to remove the border line of the login form by removing the style sheet that we applied directly to it earlier in *step 6*.

20. Your login screen should look something like this:

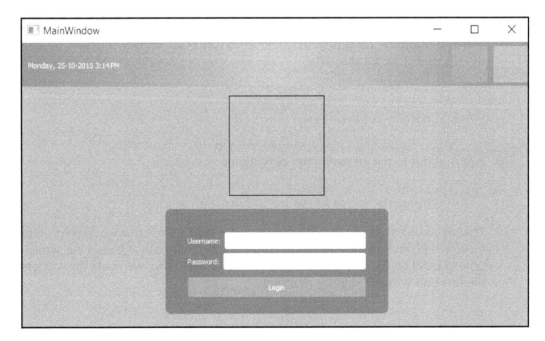

How it works...

This example focuses more on the layout system of Qt. Qt's layout system allows our application GUI to automatically arrange itself within the given space by arranging the children objects of each widget. The spacer items used in the preceding example help to push the widgets contained in a layout outward to create spacing along the width of the spacer item.

To locate a widget to the middle of the layout, put two spacer items to the layout: one on the left side of the widget and one on the right side of the widget. The widget will then be pushed to the middle of the layout by the two spacers.

Using resources in style sheets

Qt provides us with a platform-independent resource system that allows us to store any type of files in our program's executable for later use. There is no limit to the types of files we can store in our executable – images, audio, video, HTML, XML, text files, binary files, and so on are all permitted.

The resource system is really useful for embedding resource files (such as icons and translation files) into the executable so that it can be accessed by the application at any time. To achieve this, we must tell Qt which files we want to add to its resource system in the .qrc file and Qt will handle the rest during the build process.

How to do it

To add a new .qrc file to our project, go to **File** | **New File or Project**. Then, select **Qt** under the **Files and Classes** category and select **Qt Resources File**. After that, give it a name (that is, resources) and click the **Next** button followed by the **Finish** button. The .qrc file will now be created and automatically opened by Qt Creator. You don't have to edit the .qrc file directly in XML format as Qt Creator provides you the user interface to manage your resources.

To add images and icons to your project, you need to make sure that the images and icons are being placed in your project's directory. While the .qrc file is opened in Qt Creator, click the **Add** button, followed by **Add Prefix** button. The **prefix** is used to categorize your resources so that they can be better managed when you have a ton of resources in your project:

1. Rename the prefix you just created to /icons.
2. Create another prefix by clicking **Add**, followed by **Add Prefix**.
3. Rename the new prefix to /images.
4. Select the /icon prefix and click **Add**, followed by **Add Files**.
5. A file selection window will appear; use that to select all the icon files. You can select multiple files at a time by holding the *Ctrl* key on your keyboard while clicking on the files to select them. Click **Open** once you're done.
6. Select the /images prefix and click the **Add** button, followed by the **Add Files** button. The file-selection window will pop up again, and this time we will select the background image.
7. Repeat the preceding steps, but this time we will add the logo image to the /images prefix. Don't forget to save once you're done by pressing *Ctrl + S*. Your .qrc file should now look like this:

8. Go back to the mainwindow.ui file; let's make use of the resources we have just added to our project. Select the restart button located on the top panel. Scroll down the **Property Editor** until you see the **icon** property. Click the little button with a drop-down arrow icon and click **Choose Resources** from its menu.

9. The **Select Resource** window will pop up. Click on the icons prefix on the left panel and select the restart icon on the right panel. Press **OK**.

10. A tiny icon will appear on the button. The icon looks very tiny because the default icon size is set to 16 x 16. Change the **iconSize** property to 50 x 50 and you will see the icon appear bigger. Repeat the preceding steps for the shutdown button, except this time, choose the shutdown icon instead.

11. The two buttons should now look like this:

12. Let's use the image we added to the resource file as our logo. Select the logo widget and remove the style sheet that we added earlier to render its outline.

13. Scroll down the **Property Editor** until you see the **pixmap** property.

14. Click the little drop-down button behind the **pixmap** property and select **Choose Resources** from the menu. Select the logo image and click **OK**. The logo size no longer follows the dimension you set previously; it follows the actual dimension of the image instead. We cannot change its dimension because this is simply how the **pixmap** property works.

15. If you want more control over the logo's dimension, you can remove the image from the **pixmap** property and use a style sheet instead. You can use the following code to apply an image to the icon container:

```
border-image: url(:/images/logo.png);
```

16. To obtain the path of the image, right-click the image's name on the file list window and choose **Copy path**. The path will be saved to your operating system's clipboard and now you can just paste it into the preceding style sheet. Using this method will ensure that the image fits the dimensions of the widget that you applied the style to. Your logo should now appear like that in the following screenshot:

17. Apply the wallpaper image to the background using a style sheet. Since the background dimension will change according to the window size, we cannot use **pixmap** here. Instead, we will use the `border-image` property in a style sheet. Right-click the main window and select **Change styleSheet...** to open up the **Edit Style Sheet** window. We will add a new line under the style sheet of the **centralWidget**:

```
#centralWidget {
    background: rgba(32, 80, 96, 100);
    border-image: url(:/images/login_bg.png);
}
```

18. It's really that simple and easy! Your login screen should now look like this:

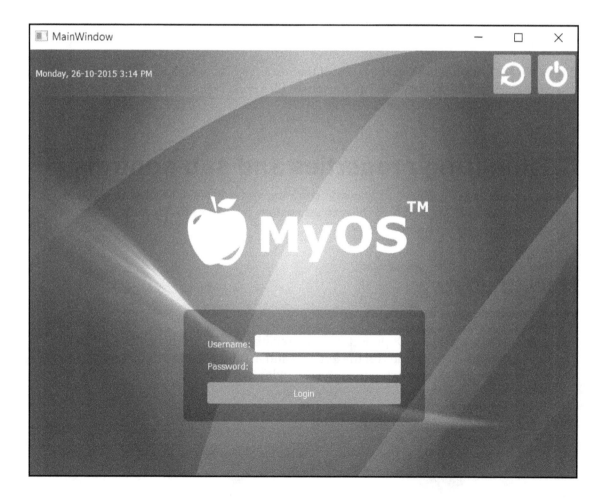

How it works...

The resource system in Qt stores binary files, such as images and translation files, in the executable when it gets compiled. It reads the resource collection files (.qrc) in your project to locate the files that need to be stored in the executable and include them in the build process. A .qrc file looks something like this:

```
<!DOCTYPE RCC><RCC version="1.0">
<qresource>
<file>images/copy.png</file>
<file>images/cut.png</file>
<file>images/new.png</file>
<file>images/open.png</file>
<file>images/paste.png</file>
<file>images/save.png</file>
</qresource>
</RCC>
```

It uses the XML format to store the paths of the resource files, which are relative to the directory that contains them. The listed resource files must be located in the same directory as the .qrc file, or one of its subdirectories.

Customizing properties and sub-controls

Qt's style sheet system enables us to create stunning and professional-looking UIs with ease. In this example, we will learn how to set custom properties to our widgets and use them to switch between different styles.

How to do it...

Let's follow these steps to customize widget properties and sub-controls:

1. Let's create a new Qt project. I have prepared the UI for this purpose. The UI contains three buttons on the left side and a **Tab Widget** with three pages located on the right side, as shown in the following screenshot:

2. The three buttons are blue because I've added the following style sheet to the main window (not to the individual button):

```
QPushButton {
    color: white;
    background-color: #27a9e3;
    border-width: 0px;
    border-radius: 3px;
}
```

3. I will explain what pseudo-states are in Qt by adding the following style sheet to the main window, which you might be familiar with:

```
QPushButton:hover {
    color: white;
    background-color: #66c011;
    border-width: 0px;
    border-radius: 3px;
}
```

4. We used the preceding style sheet in the previous *Creating a login screen using style sheets* recipe, to make the buttons change color when there is a mouse-over event. This is made possible by Qt Style Sheet's pseudo-state, which in this case is the word hover separated from the QPushButton class by a colon. Every widget has a set of generic pseudo-states, such as active, disabled, and enabled, and also a set of pseudo states that are applicable to their widget type. For example, states such as open and flat are available for QPushButton, but not for QLineEdit. Let's add the pressed pseudo-state to change the buttons' color to yellow when the user clicks on it:

```
QPushButton:pressed {
    color: white;
    background-color: yellow;
    border-width: 0px;
    border-radius: 3px;
}
```

5. **Pseudo-states** allow the users to load a different set of style sheets based on the condition that applies to it. Qt pushes this concept further by implementing dynamic properties in Qt Style Sheets. This allows us to change the style sheet of a widget when a custom condition has been met. We can make use of this feature to change the style sheet of our buttons based on a custom condition that we can set using custom properties in Qt. First, we will add this style sheet to our main window:

```
QPushButton[pagematches=true] {
    color: white;
    background-color: red;
    border-width: 0px;
    border-radius: 3px;
}
```

6. This changes the push button's background color to red if the pagematches property returns true. Obviously, this property does not exist in the QPushButton class. However, we can add it to our buttons using QObject::setProperty():

- In your mainwindow.cpp source code, add the following code right after ui->setupUi(this):

```
ui->button1->setProperty("pagematches", true);
```

- The preceding code will add a custom property called `pagematches` to the first button and set its value as `true`. This will make the first button turn red by default.
- After that, right-click on the **Tab Widget** and choose **Go to slot....** A window will then pop up; select the **currentChanged(int)** option from the list and click **OK**. Qt will generate a slot function for you, which looks something like this:

```
private slots:
void on_tabWidget_currentChanged(int index);
```

- The slot function will be called whenever we change the page of the **Tab Widget**. We can then decide what we want it to do by adding our code into the slot function. To do that, open up `mainwindow.cpp` and you will see the function's declaration there. Let's add some code to the function:

```
void MainWindow::on_tabWidget_currentChanged(int
index) {
    // Set all buttons to false
    ui->button1->setProperty("pagematches", false);
    ui->button2->setProperty("pagematches", false);
    ui->button3->setProperty("pagematches", false);

    // Set one of the buttons to true
    if (index == 0)
        ui->button1->setProperty("pagematches", true);
    else if (index == 1)
        ui->button2->setProperty("pagematches", true);
    else
        ui->button3->setProperty("pagematches", true);

    // Update buttons style
    ui->button1->style()->polish(ui->button1);
    ui->button2->style()->polish(ui->button2);
    ui->button3->style()->polish(ui->button3);
}
```

7. The preceding code sets the `pagematches` properties of all three buttons to `false` when the **Tab Widget** switches its current page. Be sure to reset everything before we decide which button should change to red.
8. Check the `index` variable supplied by the event signal, which will tell you the index number of the current page. Set the `pagematches` property of one of the buttons to `true`, based on the index number.

9. Refresh the style of all three buttons by calling `polish()`. You may also want to add the following header to `mainwindow.h`:

```
#include <QStyle>
```

10. Build and run the project. You should now see the three buttons changing to red whenever you switch the **Tab Widget** to a different page. Also, the buttons will change to green when there is a mouse-over, as well as change to yellow when you click on them:

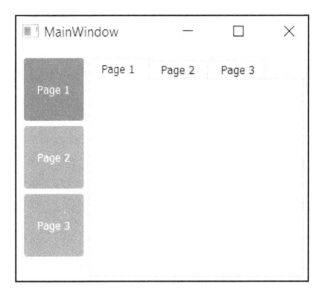

How it works...

Qt provides users the freedom of adding their own custom properties to any type of widget. Custom properties are very useful if you want to change a particular widget when a special condition is met, where Qt doesn't provide such a context by default. This allows the user to extend the usability of Qt and makes it a flexible tool for customized solutions. For example, if we have a row of buttons on our main window and we need one of them to change its color depending on which page the **Tab Widget** is currently showing, there is no way the buttons would know when they should change their color, because Qt itself has no built-in context for this type of situation. To solve this issue, Qt gives us a method to add our own properties to the widgets, which uses a generic function called `QObject::setProperty()`. To read the custom property, we can use another function called `QObject::property()`.

Next, we will talk about sub-controls in Qt Style Sheets. Often, a widget is not just a single object, but a combination of more than one object or control, used to form a more complex widget. These objects are called **sub-controls**.

For example, a spin box widget contains an input field, a down button, an up button, an up arrow, and a down arrow, which is quite complicated compared to some other widgets. In this case, Qt grants us more flexibility by allowing us to change every sub-control using a style sheet if we wanted to. We can do so by specifying the name of the sub-control behind the widget's class name, separated by a double colon. For instance, if I want to change the image of the down button to a spin box, I can write my style sheet as follows:

```
QSpinBox::down-button {
    image: url(:/images/spindown.png);
    subcontrol-origin: padding;
    subcontrol-position: right bottom;
}
```

That will only apply the image to the down button of my spin box, and not to any other parts of the widget. By combining custom properties, pseudo-states, and sub-controls, Qt provides us with a very flexible method to customize our user interface.

 Visit the following link to learn more about pseudo-states and sub-controls in Qt:
http://doc.qt.io/qt-5.12/stylesheet-reference.html.

Styling in Qt Modeling Language (QML)

Qt Meta Language or **Qt Modeling Language** (**QML**) is a JavaScript-inspired user interface markup language used by Qt to design user interfaces. Qt provides you with **Qt Quick Components** (widgets powered by the QML technology) to easily design touch-friendly UI without C++ programming. We will learn more about how to use QML and Qt Quick Components to design our program's UI by following the steps given in the following section.

How to do it...

Let's follow these steps to learn about styling in QML:

1. Create a new project by going to **File | New File or Project**. Select **Application** under the **Projects** category and choose **Qt Quick Application - Empty**.

2. Press the **Choose...** button, which will bring you to the next window. Insert a name for your project and click the **Next** button again.

3. Another window will appear and ask you to choose the minimum Qt version required. Pick the latest version installed on your computer and click **Next**.

4. Click **Next** again, followed by **Finish**. Qt Creator will now create a new project for you.

5. There are some differences between a QML project and a C++ Qt project. You will see a main.qml file inside the project resource. This .qml file is the UI description file written using the QML mark-up language. If you double-click the main.qml file, Qt Creator will open up the script editor and you will see something like this:

```
import QtQuick 2.5
import QtQuick.Window 2.2
Window {
    visible: true
    width: 640
    height: 480
    title: qsTr("Hello World")
}
```

6. This file tells Qt to create an empty window with 640 x 480 resolution and a window title that says Hello World.

7. If you open up the main.cpp file in your project, you will see this line of code:

```
QQmlApplicationEngine engine;
engine.load(QUrl(QStringLiteral("qrc:/main.qml")));
```

8. The preceding code tells Qt's QML engine to load the `main.qml` file when the program starts. If you want to load the other `.qml` file, you know where to look for the code.

9. If you build the project now, all you get is an empty window. To add in UI elements, let's first create a **QtQuick UI File** by going to **File | New File or Project** and selecting **QtQuick UI File** under the **Files and Classes | Qt** category:

10. Enter the component name as `Main`, followed by the component form name as `MainForm`. Click **Next**, followed by **Finish**:

11. A new file called `MainForm.ui.qml` has been added to your project resources. Try to open the `MainForm.ui.qml` file by double-clicking on it, if it hasn't been automatically opened by Qt Designer (UI editor) upon creation. You will see a completely different UI editor compared to the C++ project we did in all previous recipes. This editor is also called the **Qt Quick Designer**; it is specially designed for editing QML-based UIs only.

12. When `main.qml` is loaded by the QML engine, it will also import `MainForm.ui.qml` into the UI, since `MainForm` is being called in the `main.qml` file. Qt will check whether `MainForm` is a valid UI by searching for its `.qml` file based on the naming convention. The concept is similar to the C++ project we did in all our previous recipes; the `main.qml` file acts like the `main.cpp` file and `MainForm.ui.qml` acts like the `MainWindow` class. You can also create other UI templates and use them in `main.qml`. Hopefully, this comparison will make it easier to understand how QML works.

13. Open up `MainForm.ui.qml`. You should see only one item listed on the **Navigator** window: **Item**. The **Item** item is basically the base layout of the window, which shouldn't be deleted. It is similar to the **centralWidget** we used in the previous section.

14. The canvas is really empty at the moment, let's drag a **Mouse Area** and **Text** items, to the canvas from the **QML Types** panel on the left. Resize the **Mouse Area** to fill the entire canvas. Also, make sure that both **Mouse Area** and **Text** items are being placed under the **Item** item in the **Navigator** panel, as in the following screenshot:

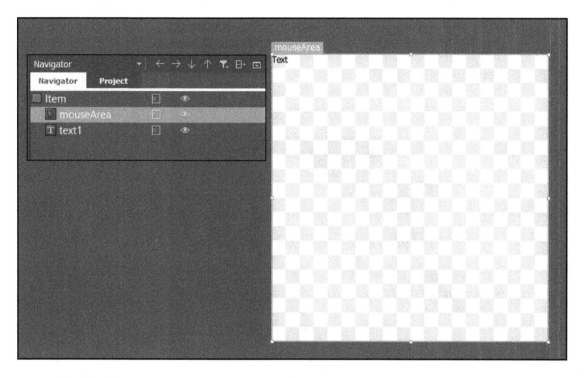

15. The **Mouse Area** item is an invincible item that gets triggered when the mouse is clicking on it, or when a finger is touching it (for mobile platforms). The **Mouse Area** item is also used in a button component, which we will be using in a while. The **Text** item is self-explanatory: it is a label that displays a block of text on the application.

16. On the **Navigator** window, we can hide or show an item by clicking on the icon, beside the item, that resembles an eye. When an item is hidden, it will not show on the canvas nor the compiled application. Just like the widgets in a C++ Qt project, Qt Quick Components are arranged in a hierarchy based on the parent-child relationship. All the child items will be placed under the parent item with an indented position. In our case, you can see the **Mouse Area** and **Text** items are positioned slightly to the right compared to the **Item** item, because they are both the children of the **Item** item. We can rearrange the parent-child relationship, as well as their position in the hierarchy, by using a click-and-drag method from the **Navigator** window. You can try clicking on the **Text** item and dragging it on top of the mouse area. You will then see that the **Text** item changes its position and is now located beneath the mouse area with a wider indentation:

17. We can rearrange them by using the arrow buttons located on top of the **Navigator** window, as shown in the preceding screenshot. Anything that happens to the parent item will also affect all its children, such as moving the parent item, and hiding and showing the parent item.

You can pan around the canvas view by holding the middle mouse button (or mouse scroll) while moving your mouse around. You can also zoom in and out by scrolling your mouse while holding the Ctrl key on your keyboard. By default, scrolling your mouse will move the canvas view up and down. However, if your mouse cursor is on top of the horizontal scroll bar of the canvas, scrolling the mouse will move the view to the left and right.

18. Delete both the **Mouse Area** and **Text** items as we will be learning how to create a user interface from scratch using QML and Qt Quick.

19. Set the **Item** item's size to 800 x 600, as we're going to need a bigger space for the widgets.

20. Copy the images we used in the previous C++ project, the *Using resources in style sheets* recipe, over to the QML project's folder, because we are going recreate the same login screen, with QML.

21. Add the images to the resource file so that we can use them for our UI.

22. Open up Qt Quick Designer and switch to the **Resources** window. Click and drag the background image directly to the canvas. Switch over to the **Layout** tab on the **Properties** pane and click the fill anchor button, indicated here by a red circle. This will make the background image always stick to the window size:

23. Click and drag a **Rectangle** component from the **Library** window to the canvas. We will use this as the top panel for our program.

24. For the top panel, enable the top anchor, left anchor, and right anchor so that the panel sticks to the top of the window and follows its width. Make sure all the margins are set to zero.

25. Go to the **Color** property of the top panel and select the **Gradient** mode. Set the first color to `#805bcce9` and the second color to `#80000000`. This will create a half-transparent panel with a blue gradient.

26. Add a **Text** widget to the canvas and make it a child of the top panel. Set its **text** property to the current date and time (for example, **Monday, 26-10-2015 3:14 PM**) for display purposes. Then, set the **text color** to **white**.

27. Switch over to the **Layout** tab and enable top anchor and left anchor so that the text widget will always stick to the top-left corner of the screen.

28. Add a **Mouse Area** to the screen and set its size to `50 x 50`. Then, make it a child of the top panel by dragging it on top of the top panel in the **Navigator** window.

29. Set the color of the mouse area to blue (`#27a9e3`) and set its radius to `2` to make its corners slightly rounded. Enable the top anchor and right anchor to make it stick to the top-right corner of the window. Set the top anchor's margin to `8` and the right anchor's margin to `10` to create some space.

30. Open up the **Resources** window and drag the shutdown icon to the canvas. Make it a child of the **Mouse Area** item we created a moment ago. Then, enable the fill anchor to make it fit the size of the mouse area.

31. Phew, that's a lot of steps! Now your items should be arranged as follows on the navigator window:

32. The parent-child relationship and the layout anchors are both very important to keep the widgets in the correct positions when the main window changes its size. Your top panel should look something like this:

33. Let's work on the login form. Add a new **Rectangle** to the canvas by dragging it from the **Library** window. Resize the rectangle to `360 x 200` and set its radius to `15`.

34. Set its color to `#80000000`, which will change it to black with 50% transparency.

35. Enable the vertical center anchor and the horizontal center anchor to make the rectangle always align to the center of the window. Then, set the **margin** of the vertical center anchor to `100` so that it moves slightly lower to the bottom, so that we have the space to place the logo. The following screenshot illustrates the settings of the **Anchors**:

36. Add the text objects to the canvas. Make them children of the login form (**Rectangle** widget) and set their **text** property to `Username:` and `Password:`. Change their **text color** to **white** and position them accordingly. We don't need to set a margin this time because they will follow the rectangle's position.

37. Add two text input objects to the canvas and place them next to the text widgets we just created. Make sure the text input are also the children of the login form. Since the text input don't contain any background color property, we need to add two rectangles to the canvas to use as their background.

38. Add two rectangles to the canvas and make each of them a child of one of the text input we just created. Set the **radius** property to 5 to give them some rounded corners. After that, enable **fill anchors** on both of the rectangles so that they will follow the size of the text input widgets.

39. Let's create the login button beneath the password field. Add a mouse area to the canvas and make it a child of the login form. Resize it to your preferred dimension and move it into place.

40. Since the mouse area does not contain any background color property, we need to add a **Rectangle** widget and make it a child of the mouse area. Set the color of the rectangle to blue (#27a9e3) and enable the fill anchor so that it fits nicely with the mouse area.

41. Add a text object to the canvas and make it a child of the login button. Change its text color to white and set its **text** property to `Login`. Finally, enable the horizontal center anchor and the vertical center anchor to align it to the center of the button.

42. You will now get a login form that looks pretty similar to the one we made in the C++ project:

43. It's time to add the logo, which is actually very simple. Open up the **Resources** window and drag the logo image to the canvas.
44. Make it a child of the login form and set its size to `512 x 200`.
45. Position it on top of the login form and you're done.
46. This is what the entire UI looks like when compiled. We have successfully recreated the login screen from the C++ project, but this time we did it with QML and Qt Quick:

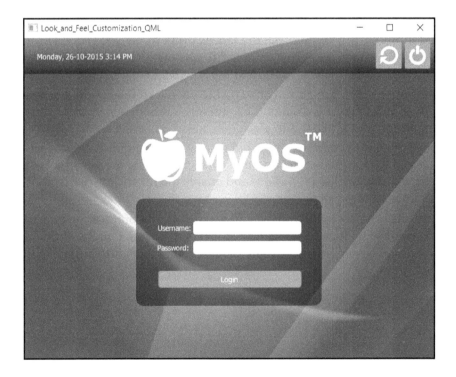

How it works...

Qt Quick editor uses a very different approach for placing widgets in the application compared to the form editor. The user can decide which method is best suited to their purposes. The following screenshot shows what the Qt Quick Designer looks like:

We will now look at the various elements of the editor's UI:

1. **Navigator**: The **Navigator** window displays the items in the current QML file as a tree structure. It's similar to the object operator window in the other Qt Designer we used in the previous *Using style sheets with Qt Designer* section.

2. **Library**: The **Library** window displays all the Qt Quick Components or Qt Quick Controls available in QML. You can click and drag it to the canvas window to add to your UI. You can also create your own custom QML components and display it here.

3. Resources: The Resources window displays all the resources in a list that can then be used in your UI design.

4. Imports: The Imports window allows you to import different QML modules into your current QML file, such as a Bluetooth module, a WebKit module, or a positioning module, to add additional functionality to your QML project.

5. Properties pane: Similar to the Property Editor we used in previous recipe, the Properties pane in QML Designer displays the properties of the selected item. You can also change the properties of the items in the code editor.

6. anvas: The canvas is the working area where you create QML components and design applications.

7. tate pane: The State pane displays the different states in the QML project, describing UI configurations, such as the UI controls, their properties and behavior, and the available actions.

8. onnections: This panel is where you set the signal handlers for each QML component in your canvas, which empowers the signals and slots mechanism provided by Qt.

Exposing the QML object pointer to C++

Sometimes, we want to modify the properties of a QML object through C++ scripting, such as changing the text of a label, hiding/showing the widget, or changing its size. Qt's QML engine allows you to register your QML objects to C++ types, which automatically exposes all its properties.

How to do it...

We want to create a label in QML and change its text occasionally. In order to expose the label object to C++, we can do the following steps:

1. Create a C++ class called `MyLabel` that extends from the `QObject` class in `mylabel.h`:

```
class MyLabel : public QObject {
Q_OBJECT
public:
    // Object pointer
    QObject* myObject;
    explicit MyLabel(QObject *parent = 0);

    // Must call Q_INVOKABLE so that this function can be used
```

```
in QML
    Q_INVOKABLE void SetMyObject(QObject* obj);
}
```

2. In the `mylabel.cpp` source file, define a function called `SetMyObject()` to save the object pointer. This function will later be called in QML in `mylabel.cpp`:

```
void MyLabel::SetMyObject(QObject* obj) {
    // Set the object pointer
    myObject = obj;
}
```

3. In `main.cpp`, include the `MyLabel` header and register it to the QML engine using the
`qmlRegisterType()` function:

```
include "mylabel.h"
int main(int argc, char *argv[]) {
    // Register your class to QML
    qmlRegisterType<MyLabel>("MyLabelLib", 1, 0, "MyLabel");
}
```

4. Notice that there are four parameters you need to declare in `qmlRegisterType()`. Besides declaring your class name (`MyLabel`), you also need to declare your library name (`MyLabelLib`) and its version (1.0), which will be used to import your class to QML.

5. Map the QML engine to our label object in QML and import the class library we defined earlier in *step 3* by calling `import MyLabelLib 1.0` in our QML file. Notice that the library name and its version number have to match the one you declared in `main.cpp`, otherwise it will throw an error. After declaring `MyLabel` in QML and setting its ID as `mylabels`, call `mylabel.SetMyObject(myLabel)` to expose its pointer to C/C++ right after the label is initialized:

```
import MyLabelLib 1.0
ApplicationWindow {
    id: mainWindow
    width: 480
    height: 640
    MyLabel {
        id: mylabel
    }
    Label {
        id: helloWorldLabel
        text: qsTr("Hello World!")
        Component.onCompleted: {
```

```
                    mylabel.SetMyObject(hellowWorldLabel);
            }
        }
    }
```

6. Wait until the label is fully initiated before exposing its pointer to C/C++, otherwise you may cause the program to crash. To make sure it's fully initiated, call the `SetMyObject()` function within `Component.onCompleted` and not in any other functions or event callbacks. Now that the QML label has been exposed to C/C++, we can change any of its properties by calling the `setProperty()` function. For instance, we can set its visibility to `true` and change its text to `Bye bye world!`:

```
// QVariant automatically detects your data type
myObject->setProperty("visible", QVariant(true));
myObject->setProperty("text", QVariant("Bye bye world!"));
```

7. Besides changing the properties, we can also call its functions by calling the following:

```
QMetaObject::invokeMethod():
QVariant returnedValue;
QVariant message = "Hello world!";
QMetaObject::invokeMethod(myObject, "myQMLFunction",
Q_RETURN_ARG(QVariant, returnedValue), Q_ARG(QVariant,
message));
qDebug() << "QML function returned:" <<
returnedValue.toString();
```

8. Or, simply, we can call the `invokedMethod()` function with only two parameters if we do not expect any values to be returned from it:

```
QMetaObject::invokeMethod(myObject, "myQMLFunction");
```

How it works...

QML is designed in such a way that it can be expanded through C++ code. The classes in the Qt QML module permit QML objects to be used and operate from C++, and the capability of the QML engine's united with Qt's meta-object system allows C++ functionality to be called directly from QML. To add some C++ data or usage to QML, it should come forward from a QObject-derived class. QML object types could be instituted from C++ and supervised to access their properties, appeal their methods, and get their signal alerts. This is possible because all QML object types are executed using QObject-derived classes, allowing the QML engine to forcibly load and inspect objects through the Qt meta-object system.

Event Handling - Signals and Slots

2

In this chapter, we will cover the following recipes:

- New signals and slots syntax
- UI events with signals and slots
- Asynchronous programming made easier
- Function callbacks

Introduction

The signals and slots mechanism in Qt 5 is one of its most important features. It's a method that allows communication between objects, which is a crucial part of a program's graphical user interface. A signal can be emitted from any `QObject` objects or its subclasses, which will then trigger any slot functions of any objects that are connected to the signal.

Compared to callbacks (which Qt 5 also support), the signals and slots mechanism is comparably more fluid and flexible for the programmer to use. The signals and slots mechanism is both type safe and not strongly coupled to the processing function, which makes it better than the callback's implementation.

A signal of an arbitrary class can trigger any private slots of an unrelated class that is going to be invoked, which is not possible with callbacks.

Technical requirements

The technical requirements for this chapter include Qt 5.11.2 MinGW 32 bit, Qt Creator 4.8.2, and Windows 10.

All the code used in this chapter can be downloaded from the following GitHub link: `https://github.com/PacktPublishing/Qt5-CPP-GUI-Programming-Cookbook-Second-Edition/tree/master/Chapter02`.

Check out the following video to see the code in action: `http://bit.ly/2FozGKA`

New signals and slots syntax

The signals and slots mechanism has gone through some changes in the recent version of Qt, most notably its coding syntax. Qt 5 continues to support the older syntax for future releases, but there is no mention of how long it will be before it will be dropped completely. Therefore, it's better for us to start learning the new syntax before that day comes.

How to do it...

Let's get started by following these steps:

1. Let's create a **Qt Widgets Application** project and open up `mainwindow.ui`.
2. Drag and drop a **PushButton** from the **Widget Box** to the UI canvas:

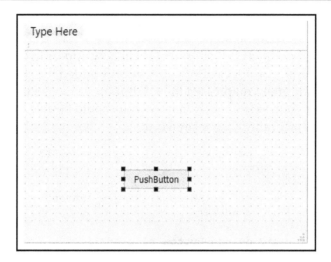

3. Right-click on the **PushButton** and select **Go to slot**. A window will appear:

4. You will see a list of built-in slot functions available for the push button. Let's select the **clicked()** option and press **OK**. A slot function called `on_pushButton_clicked()` will now appear in both `mainwindow.h` and `mainwindow.cpp`. Qt Creator automatically added the slot function to your source code after you pressed the **OK** button on the **Go to slot** window. If you check out your `mainwindow.h` now, you should be able to see an extra function under the `private slots` keyword:

```
class MainWindow : public QMainWindow {
    Q_OBJECT
public:
    explicit MainWindow(QWidget *parent = 0);
    ~MainWindow();
private slots:
    void on_pushButton_clicked();
private:
    Ui::MainWindow *ui;
};
```

5. The same goes for `mainwindow.cpp`, where the `on_pushButton_clicked()` function has been added for you:

```
void MainWindow::on_pushButton_clicked()
{
}
```

6. Now, let's add a `QMessageBox` header to the top of your source file:

```
#include <QMessageBox>
```

7. Then, add the following code within the `on_pushButton_clicked()` function:

```
void MainWindow::on_pushButton_clicked() {
    QMessageBox::information(this, "Hello", "Button has been
clicked!");
}
```

8. Now, build and run the project. Then, click on the push button; you should see that a message box pops out:

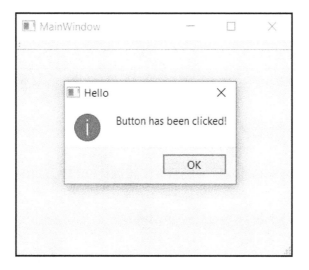

9. Next, we want to create our own signals and slots functions. Go to **File | New File or Project**, then create a new **C++ Class** under the **Files and Classes** category:

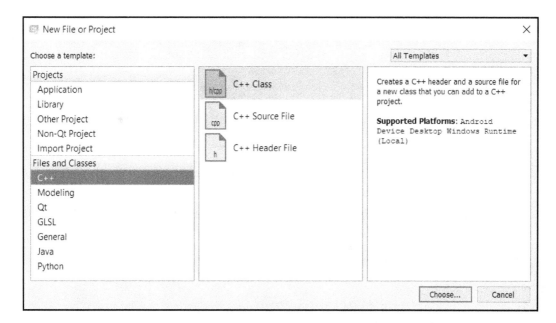

10. Then, we need to name our class `MyClass` and make sure that the base class is **QObject**:

11. Once you have created the class, open up `myclass.h` and add the following code, which is highlighted here for clarity:

```
#include <QObject>
#include <QMainWindow>
#include <QMessageBox>
class MyClass : public QObject {
    Q_OBJECT
public:
    explicit MyClass(QObject *parent = nullptr);
signals:
public slots:
    void doSomething();
};
```

12. Then, open up `myclass.cpp` and implement the `doSomething()` slot function. We'll copy the message box function from the previous example:

```
#include "myclass.h"

MyClass::MyClass(QObject *parent) : QObject(parent) {}
void MyClass::doSomething() {
    QMessageBox::information(this, "Hello", "Button has been
clicked!");
}
```

13. Now, open up `mainwindow.h` and include the `myclass.h` header at the top:

```
#ifndef MAINWINDOW_H
#define MAINWINDOW_H

#include "myclass.h"

namespace Ui {
class MainWindow;
}
```

14. Also, declare a `doNow()` signal in `myclass.h`:

```
signals:
    void doNow();

private slots:
    void on_pushButton_clicked();
```

15. After that, open up `mainwindow.cpp` and define a `MyClass` object. Then, we'll connect the `doNow()` signal that we created in the previous step with our `doSomething()` slot function:

```
MainWindow::MainWindow(QWidget *parent) : QMainWindow(parent),
ui(new Ui::MainWindow) {
    ui->setupUi(this);
    MyClass* myclass = new MyClass;
    connect(this, &MainWindow::doNow, myclass,
&MyClass::doSomething);
}
```

16. Then, we have to change the code of the `on_pushButton_clicked()` function to something like this:

```
void MainWindow::on_pushButton_clicked() {
    emit doNow();
}
```

17. If you build and run the program now, you will get a result that is similar to what's shown in the previous example. However, we have placed the message box code in the `MyClass` object instead of in `MainWindow`.

How it works...

In the good old days, we would typically connect a signal to a slot like this:

```
connect(
    sender, SIGNAL(valueChanged(QString)),
    receiver, SLOT(updateValue(QString))
);
```

However, things have changed slightly since then. In the new syntax, the `SIGNAL` and `SLOT` macros are now gone, and you must specify the type of your object, as shown in the following code:

```
connect(
    sender, &Sender::valueChanged,
    receiver, &Receiver::updateValue
);
```

The new syntax also allows you to connect a signal directly to a function instead of `QObject`:

```
connect(
    sender, &Sender::valueChanged, myFunction
);
```

Additionally, you can also connect your signal to a lambda expression. We will talk more about this in the *Asynchronous programming made easier* recipe.

UI events with signals and slots

In the previous example, we demonstrated the use of signals and slots on a push button. Now, let's explore the signals and slots that are available in other common widget types.

How to do it...

To learn how to use signals and slots with UI events, follow these steps:

1. Let's create a new **Qt Widgets Application** project.
2. Drag and drop a **Push Button**, **Combo Box**, **Line Edit**, **Spin Box**, and **Slider** from the **Widget Box** into your UI canvas:

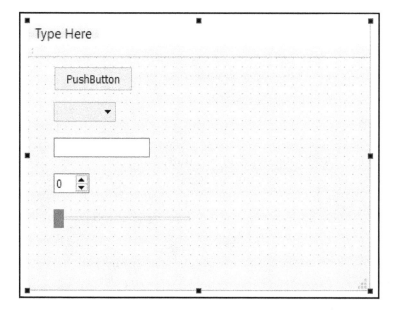

3. Then, right-click on the push button and select `clicked()` and press the **OK** button to proceed. A slot function will be created for you by Qt Creator:

4. Repeat the previous step, but this time, select the next selection until every function in `QAbstractButton` has been added to the source code:

```
void on_pushButton_clicked();
void on_pushButton_clicked(bool checked);
void on_pushButton_pressed();
void on_pushButton_released();
void on_pushButton_toggled(bool checked);
```

5. Next, repeat the same steps again on the combo box until all the slot functions available under the `QComboBox` class have been added to the source code:

```
void on_comboBox_activated(const QString &arg1);
void on_comboBox_activated(int index);
void on_comboBox_currentIndexChanged(const QString &arg1);
void on_comboBox_currentIndexChanged(int index);
void on_comboBox_currentTextChanged(const QString &arg1);
void on_comboBox_editTextChanged(const QString &arg1);
void on_comboBox_highlighted(const QString &arg1);
void on_comboBox_highlighted(int index);
```

6. The same goes for `lineEdit`, all of which are under the `QLineEdit` class:

```
void on_lineEdit_cursorPositionChanged(int arg1, int arg2);
void on_lineEdit_editingFinished();
void on_lineEdit_returnPressed();
void on_lineEdit_selectionChanged();
void on_lineEdit_textChanged(const QString &arg1);
void on_lineEdit_textEdited(const QString &arg1);
```

7. After that, add the slot functions from the `QSpinBox` class for our spin box widget as well, which is relatively short:

```
void on_spinBox_valueChanged(const QString &arg1);
void on_spinBox_valueChanged(int arg1);
```

8. Lastly, repeat the same step for our slider widget, which yields similar results:

```
void on_horizontalSlider_actionTriggered(int action);
void on_horizontalSlider_rangeChanged(int min, int max);
void on_horizontalSlider_sliderMoved(int position);
void on_horizontalSlider_sliderPressed();
void on_horizontalSlider_sliderReleased();
void on_horizontalSlider_valueChanged(int value);
```

9. Once you're done with that, open up `mainwindow.h` and add the `QDebug` header, as highlighted in the following code:

```
#ifndef MAINWINDOW_H
#define MAINWINDOW_H

#include <QMainWindow>
#include <QDebug>

namespace Ui {
class MainWindow;
}
```

10. Let's implement the slot functions for our push button:

```
void MainWindow::on_pushButton_clicked() {
    qDebug() << "Push button clicked";
}
void MainWindow::on_pushButton_clicked(bool checked) {
    qDebug() << "Push button clicked: " << checked;
}
void MainWindow::on_pushButton_pressed() {
    qDebug() << "Push button pressed";
}
```

```
void MainWindow::on_pushButton_released() {
    qDebug() << "Push button released";
}
void MainWindow::on_pushButton_toggled(bool checked) {
    qDebug() << "Push button toggled: " << checked;
}
```

11. If you build and run the project now, and then click on the push button, you will see that a different status gets printed out but at a slightly different timing. This is due to different signals being emitted at different actions during the whole clicking process:

```
Push button pressed
Push button released
Push button clicked
Push button clicked: false
```

12. Next, we will move on to the combo box. Since the default combo box is empty, let's add some options to it by double-clicking on it from `mainwindow.ui` and adding the options that are shown in the pop-up window:

13. Then, let's implement the slot functions for the combo box in `mainwindow.cpp`:

```
void MainWindow::on_comboBox_activated(const QString &arg1) {
    qDebug() << "Combo box activated: " << arg1;
}
void MainWindow::on_comboBox_activated(int index) {
    qDebug() << "Combo box activated: " << index;
}
void MainWindow::on_comboBox_currentIndexChanged(const QString
&arg1) {
    qDebug() << "Combo box current index changed: " << arg1;
```

```
}
void MainWindow::on_comboBox_currentIndexChanged(int index) {
    qDebug() << "Combo box current index changed: " << index;
}
```

14. We will continue to implement the rest of the slot functions for the combo box:

```
void MainWindow::on_comboBox_currentTextChanged(const QString
&arg1) {
    qDebug() << "Combo box current text changed: " << arg1;
}
void MainWindow::on_comboBox_editTextChanged(const QString
&arg1) {
    qDebug() << "Combo box edit text changed: " << arg1;
}
void MainWindow::on_comboBox_highlighted(const QString &arg1) {
    qDebug() << "Combo box highlighted: " << arg1;
}
void MainWindow::on_comboBox_highlighted(int index) {
    qDebug() << "Combo box highlighted: " << index;
}
```

15. Build and run the project. Then, try click on the combo box, hover over the other options, and select an option by clicking on it. You should see similar results to the following in your debug output:

```
Combo box highlighted: 0
Combo box highlighted: "Option One"
Combo box highlighted: 1
Combo box highlighted: "Option Two"
Combo box highlighted: 2
Combo box highlighted: "Option Three"
Combo box current index changed: 2
Combo box current index changed: "Option Three"
Combo box current text changed: "Option Three"
Combo box activated: 2
Combo box activated: "Option Three"
```

16. Next, we will move on to line edit and implement its slot functions, as shown in the following code:

```
void MainWindow::on_lineEdit_cursorPositionChanged(int arg1,
int arg2) {
    qDebug() << "Line edit cursor position changed: " << arg1
<< arg2;
}
void MainWindow::on_lineEdit_editingFinished() {
    qDebug() << "Line edit editing finished";
```

```
}
void MainWindow::on_lineEdit_returnPressed() {
    qDebug() << "Line edit return pressed";
}
```

17. We will continue to implement the rest of the slot functions of line edit:

```
void MainWindow::on_lineEdit_selectionChanged() {
    qDebug() << "Line edit selection changed";
}
void MainWindow::on_lineEdit_textChanged(const QString &arg1) {
    qDebug() << "Line edit text changed: " << arg1;
}
void MainWindow::on_lineEdit_textEdited(const QString &arg1) {
    qDebug() << "Line edit text edited: " << arg1;
}
```

18. Build and run the project. Then, click on the line edit and type `Hey`. You should see results similar to the following appearing on the debug output panel:

```
Line edit cursor position changed: -1 0
Line edit text edited: "H"
Line edit text changed: "H"
Line edit cursor position changed: 0 1
Line edit text edited: "He"
Line edit text changed: "He"
Line edit cursor position changed: 1 2
Line edit text edited: "Hey"
Line edit text changed: "Hey"
Line edit cursor position changed: 2 3
Line edit editing finished
```

19. After that, we need to implement the slot functions for the spin box widget, as shown in the following code:

```
void MainWindow::on_spinBox_valueChanged(const QString &arg1){
    qDebug() << "Spin box value changed: " << arg1;
}
void MainWindow::on_spinBox_valueChanged(int arg1) {
    qDebug() << "Spin box value changed: " << arg1;
}
```

20. Try to build and run the program. Then, click the arrow buttons on the spin box, or directly edit the value in the box – you should get something similar to this:

```
Spin box value changed: "1"
Spin box value changed: 1
Spin box value changed: "2"
```

```
Spin box value changed: 2
Spin box value changed: "3"
Spin box value changed: 3
Spin box value changed: "2"
Spin box value changed: 2
Spin box value changed: "20"
Spin box value changed: 20
```

21. Lastly, we'll implement the slot functions for the horizontal slider widget:

```
void MainWindow::on_horizontalSlider_actionTriggered(int
action) {
    qDebug() << "Slider action triggered" << action;
}
void MainWindow::on_horizontalSlider_rangeChanged(int min, int
max) {
    qDebug() << "Slider range changed: " << min << max;
}
void MainWindow::on_horizontalSlider_sliderMoved(int position)
{
    qDebug() << "Slider moved: " << position;
}
```

22. Continue to implement the slot function for the slider, as shown in the following code:

```
void MainWindow::on_horizontalSlider_sliderPressed() {
    qDebug() << "Slider pressed";
}
void MainWindow::on_horizontalSlider_sliderReleased() {
    qDebug() << "Slider released";
}
void MainWindow::on_horizontalSlider_valueChanged(int value) {
    qDebug() << "Slider value changed: " << value;
}
```

23. Build and run the program. Then, click and drag the slider to the left and right – you should be seeing results that are similar to the following:

```
Slider pressed
Slider moved: 1
Slider action triggered 7
Slider value changed: 1
Slider moved: 2
Slider action triggered 7
Slider value changed: 2
Slider moved: 3
Slider action triggered 7
```

```
Slider value changed: 3
Slider moved: 4
Slider action triggered 7
Slider value changed: 4
Slider released
```

How it works...

Almost every widget has a set of slot functions associated with its usage or purpose. For example, a push button will start emitting signals that trigger the slot functions associated with it when it's pressed or released. These expected behaviors that define the widget have slot functions that get called when the user triggers an action. As programmers, all we need to do is implement the slot functions and tell Qt what to do when these slot functions are being triggered.

Asynchronous programming made easier

Since the signals and slots mechanism is asynchronous in nature, we can make use of it for things other than user interfaces. In programming terms, an asynchronous operation is a process that works independently, allowing the program to continue its operation without waiting for the process to complete, which may stall the whole program.

Qt 5 allows you to make use of its signals and slots mechanism to easily achieve asynchronous processes without much effort. This is even more true after Qt 5 introduced the new syntax for signals and slots, which allows a signal to trigger a normal function instead of a slot function from a `QObject`.

In the following example, we will further explore this opportunity and learn how we can improve our program's efficiency by using asynchronous operations through the signals and slots mechanism that's provided by Qt 5.

How to do it...

To learn how to achieve asynchronous operations using the signals and slots mechanism, let's follow this example:

1. Create a **Qt Console Application** project:

2. This type of project will only provide a `main.cpp` file for you, instead of `mainwindow.h` and `mainwindow.cpp`, like our previous example projects. Let's open up `main.cpp` and add the following headers to it:

```
#include <QNetworkAccessManager>
#include <QNetworkReply>
#include <QDebug>
```

3. Then, add the following code to our `main()` function. We will be using the `QNetworkAccessManager` class to initiate a `GET` request to the following web URL:

```
int main(int argc, char *argv[]) {
    QCoreApplication a(argc, argv);

    QString *html = new QString;
    qDebug() << "Start";

    QNetworkAccessManager manager;
    QNetworkRequest req(QUrl("http://www.dustyfeet.com"));
    QNetworkReply* reply = manager.get(req);
```

4. Then, we use C++11's lambda expression to connect `QNetworkReply` signals to inline functions:

```
QObject::connect(reply, &QNetworkReply::readyRead,
[reply, html]() {
    html->append(QString(reply->readAll()));
});

QObject::connect(reply, &QNetworkReply::downloadProgress,
[reply](qint64 bytesReceived, qint64 bytesTotal) {
    qDebug() << "Progress: " << bytesReceived << "bytes /" <<
bytesTotal << "bytes";
});
```

5. We can also use a lambda expression with `connect()` to call a function that is not under a `QObject` class:

```
QObject::connect(reply, &QNetworkReply::finished,
[=]() {
    printHTML(*html);
});

return a.exec();
}
```

6. Lastly, we define the `printHTML()` function, as shown in the following code:

```
void printHTML(QString html) {
    qDebug() << "Done";
    qDebug() << html;
}
```

7. If you build and run the program now, you will see that it's functional even without declaring any slot function. Lambda expressions make declaring a slot function optional, but this is only recommended if your code is really short:

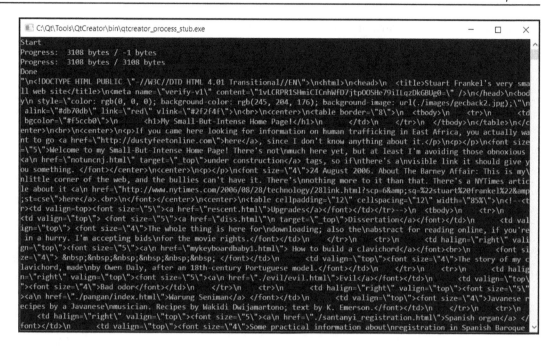

How it works...

The preceding example is a very simple application that showcases the use of lambda expressions to connect a signal with a lambda function or a regular function without declaring any slot function, and thus does not need to be inherited from a `QObject` class. This is especially useful for calling asynchronous processes that are not under UI objects.

Lambda expressions are functions that get defined within another function anonymously, which is quite similar to the anonymous functions in JavaScript. The format of a lambda function looks like this:

```
[captured variables](arguments) {
    lambda code
}
```

You can insert variables into a lambda expression by placing them into the captured variables part, like we did in the example project in this recipe. We capture the `QNetworkReply` object called `reply`, and the `QString` object called `html`, and put them in our lambda expression.

Then, we can use these variables within our lambda code, as shown in the following code:

```
[reply, html]() {
    html->append(QString(reply->readAll()));
}
```

The argument part is similar to an ordinary function, where you input values to the arguments and use them within your lambda code. In this case, the values of bytesReceived and bytesTotal are coming from the downloadProgress signal:

```
QObject::connect(reply, &QNetworkReply::downloadProgress,
[reply](qint64 bytesReceived, qint64 bytesTotal) {
    qDebug() << "Progress: " << bytesReceived << "bytes /" << bytesTotal <<
"bytes";
});
```

You can also capture all variables that are used in your function using the equals sign. In this case, we captured the html variable without specifying it in the captured variable area:

```
[=]() {
    printHTML(*html);
}
```

Function callbacks

Even though Qt 5 supports the signals and slots mechanism, some of the features in Qt 5 still use function callbacks, such as keyboard input, window resize, graphics painting, and others. Since these events only need to be implemented once, there is no need to use the signals and slots mechanism.

How to do it...

Let's get started by following this example:

1. Create a Qt Widgets Application project, open up mainwindow.h, and add the following headers:

```
#include <QDebug>
#include <QResizeEvent>
#include <QKeyEvent>
#include <QMouseEvent>
```

2. Then, declare these functions in `mainwindow.h`:

```
public:
    explicit MainWindow(QWidget *parent = 0);
    ~MainWindow();

    void resizeEvent(QResizeEvent *event);
    void keyPressEvent(QKeyEvent *event);
    void keyReleaseEvent(QKeyEvent *event);
    void mouseMoveEvent(QMouseEvent *event);
    void mousePressEvent(QMouseEvent *event);
    void mouseReleaseEvent(QMouseEvent *event);
```

3. After that, open up `mainwindow.cpp` and add the following code to the class constructor:

```
MainWindow::MainWindow(QWidget *parent) : QMainWindow(parent),
ui(new Ui::MainWindow) {
    ui->setupUi(this);
    this->setMouseTracking(true);
    ui->centralWidget->setMouseTracking(true);
}
```

4. Then, define the `resizeEvent()` and `keyPressedEvent()` functions:

```
void MainWindow::resizeEvent(QResizeEvent *event) {
    qDebug() << "Old size:" << event->oldSize() << ", New
size:" << event->size();
}

void MainWindow::keyPressEvent(QKeyEvent *event) {
    if (event->key() == Qt::Key_Escape) {
        this->close();
    }
    qDebug() << event->text() << "has been pressed";
}
```

5. Continue to implement the rest of the functions:

```
void MainWindow::keyReleaseEvent(QKeyEvent *event) {
    qDebug() << event->text() << "has been released";
}

void MainWindow::mouseMoveEvent(QMouseEvent *event) {
    qDebug() << "Position: " << event->pos();
}

void MainWindow::mousePressEvent(QMouseEvent *event) {
```

```
        qDebug() << "Mouse pressed:" << event->button();
}

void MainWindow::mouseReleaseEvent(QMouseEvent *event) {
    qDebug() << "Mouse released:" << event->button();
}
```

6. Build and run the program. Then, try and move the mouse around, rescale the main window, press some random keys on your keyboard, and finally press the *Esc* key on your keyboard to close the program. You should be seeing debug texts similar to the ones that are being printed out on the application output window:

```
Old size: QSize(-1, -1) , New size: QSize(400, 300)
Old size: QSize(400, 300) , New size: QSize(401, 300)
Old size: QSize(401, 300) , New size: QSize(402, 300)
Position: QPoint(465,348)
Position: QPoint(438,323)
Position: QPoint(433,317)
"a" has been pressed
"a" has been released
"r" has been pressed
"r" has been released
"d" has been pressed
"d" has been released
"\u001B" has been pressed
```

How it works...

Qt 5 objects, especially the main window, has a dozen of built-in callbacks that exist as virtual functions. These functions can be overridden to perform your intended behavior when called. Qt 5 may invoke these callback functions when its expected condition has been met, such as a keyboard button has been pressed, the mouse cursor has been moved, the window has been resized, and so on.

The functions that we declared in the `mainwindow.h` file are virtual functions that are built into the `QWidget` class. We are just overriding it with our own code to define its new behavior when it's called.

Do take note that you must call `setMouseTracking(true)` for both **MainWindow** and **centralWidget** for the `mouseMoveEvent()` callback to work.

States and Animations with Qt and QML

This chapter will cover the following recipes:

- Property animation in Qt
- Using easing curves to control property animation
- Creating an animation group
- Creating a nested animation group
- State machines in Qt
- States, transitions, and animations in QML
- Animating widget properties using animators
- Sprite animation

Introduction

Qt provides an easy way to animate widgets or any other objects that inherit the `QObject` class through its powerful animation framework. The animation can be used either on its own or together with the state machine framework, which allows different animations to be played based on the current active state of the widget. Qt's animation framework also supports grouped animation, which allows you to move more than one graphics item simultaneously or move them in sequence, one after the other.

Technical requirements

The technical requirements for this chapter include Qt 5.11.2 MinGW 32-bit, Qt Creator 4.8.2, and Windows 10.

All of the code that's used in this chapter can be downloaded from the following GitHub link: `https://github.com/PacktPublishing/Qt5-CPP-GUI-Programming-Cookbook-Second-Edition/tree/master/Chapter03`.

Check out the following video to see the code in action: `http://bit.ly/2ToKkpU`

Property animation in Qt

In this example, we will learn how to animate our **Graphical User Interface** (**GUI**) elements using Qt's property animation class, a part of its powerful animation framework that allows us to create fluid looking animation with minimal effort.

How to do it...

In the following example, we will create a new widget project and animate the push button by changing its properties:

1. Let's create a new `Qt Widgets Application` project. After that, open up `mainwindow.ui` with Qt Designer and place a button on the main window, as shown here:

2. Open up `mainwindow.cpp` and add the following line of code at the beginning of the source code:

```
#include <QPropertyAnimation>
```

3. After that, open up `mainwindow.cpp` and add the following code to the constructor:

```
QPropertyAnimation *animation = new
QPropertyAnimation(ui->pushButton, "geometry");
animation->setDuration(10000);
animation->setStartValue(ui->pushButton->geometry());
animation->setEndValue(QRect(200, 200, 100, 50));
animation->start();
```

How it works...

One of the more common methods to animate a GUI element is through the property animation class provided by Qt, known as the `QPropertyAnimation` class. This class is part of the animation framework and it makes use of the timer system in Qt to change the properties of a GUI element over a given duration.

What we are trying to accomplish here is to animate the button from one position to another while, at the same time, enlarging the button size along the way. By including the `QPropertyAnimation` header in our source code in *step 2*, we will be able to access the `QPropertyAnimation` class provided by Qt and make use of its functionalities.

The code in *step 3* basically creates a new property animation and applies it to the **push button** we just created in Qt Designer. We specifically request that the property animation class changes the geometry properties of the push button and sets its duration to 3,000 milliseconds (3 seconds).

Then, the start value of the animation is set to the initial geometry of the push button because, obviously, we want it to start from where we initially place the button in Qt Designer. The end value is then set to what we want it to become; in this case, we will move the button to a new position at `x: 200` and `y: 200` while changing its size to `width: 100` and `height: 50` along the way.

After that, call `animation | start()` to start the animation. Compile and run the project. You should see the button start to move slowly across the main window while expanding in size a bit at a time, until it reaches its destination. You can change the animation duration and the target position and scale by altering the values in the preceding code. It is really that simple to animate a GUI element using Qt's property animation system!

There's more...

Qt provides us with several different sub-systems to create animations for our GUI, including timer, timeline, animation framework, state machine framework, and graphics view framework:

- **Timer**: Qt provides us with repetitive and single-shot timers. When the timeout value is reached, an event callback function will be triggered through Qt's signal-and-slot mechanism. You can make use of a timer to change the properties (color, position, scale, and so on) of your GUI element within a given interval to create an animation.

- **Timeline**: Timeline calls a slot periodically to animate a GUI element. It is quite similar to a repetitive timer, but instead of doing the same thing all of the time when the slot is triggered, timeline provides a value to the slot to indicate its current frame index so that you can do different things (such as offset to a different space of the sprite sheet) based on the given value.

- **Animation framework**: The animation framework makes animating a GUI element easy by allowing its properties to be animated. The animations are controlled by using easing curves. Easing curves describe a function that controls what the speed of the animation should be, resulting in different acceleration and deceleration patterns. The types of easing curve supported by Qt include linear, quadratic, cubic, quartic, sine, exponential, circular, and elastic.

- **State machine framework**: Qt provides us with classes for creating and executing state graphs, which allow each GUI element to move from one state to another when triggered by signals. The state graph in the state machine framework is hierarchical, which means every state can also be nested inside of other states.

- **Graphics view framework**: The graphics view framework is a powerful graphics engine for visualizing and interacting with a large number of custom-made 2D graphical items. You can use the graphics view framework to draw your GUI and have them animated in a totally manual way if you are an experienced programmer.

By making use of all of the powerful features we've mentioned here, we're able to create an intuitive and modern GUI with ease. In this chapter, we will look into the practical approaches to animating GUI elements using Qt.

Using easing curves to control property animation

In this example, we will learn how to make our animation more interesting by utilizing easing curves. We will still use the previous source code, which uses the property animation to animate a push button.

How to do it...

In the following example, we will learn how to add an easing curve to our animation:

1. Define an easing curve and add it to the property animation before calling the start() function:

```
QPropertyAnimation *animation = new
QPropertyAnimation(ui->pushButton, "geometry");
animation->setDuration(3000);
animation->setStartValue(ui->pushButton->geometry());
animation->setEndValue(QRect(200, 200, 100, 50));

QEasingCurve curve;
curve.setType(QEasingCurve::OutBounce);
animation->setEasingCurve(curve);
animation->start();
```

2. Call the setLoopCount() function to set how many loops you want it to repeat for:

```
QPropertyAnimation *animation = new
QPropertyAnimation(ui->pushButton, "geometry");
animation->setDuration(3000);
```

```
animation->setStartValue(ui->pushButton->geometry());
animation->setEndValue(QRect(200, 200, 100, 50));

QEasingCurve curve;
curve.setType(EasingCurve::OutBounce);
animation->setEasingCurve(curve);
animation->setLoopCount(2);
animation->start();
```

3. Call `setAmplitude()`, `setOvershoot()`, and `setPeriod()` before applying the easing curve to the animation:

```
QEasingCurve curve;
curve.setType(QEasingCurve::OutBounce);
curve.setAmplitude(1.00);
curve.setOvershoot(1.70);
curve.setPeriod(0.30);
animation->setEasingCurve(curve);
animation->start();
```

How it works...

To let an easing curve control the animation, all you need to do is define an **easing curve** and add it to the property animation before calling the `start()` function. You can also try several other types of easing curve and see which one suits you best. Here is an example:

```
animation->setEasingCurve(QEasingCurve::OutBounce);
```

If you want the animation to loop after it has finished playing, you can call the `setLoopCount()` function to set how many loops you want it to repeat for or set the value to `-1` for an infinite loop:

```
animation->setLoopCount(-1);
```

There are several parameters that you can set to refine the easing curve before applying it to the property animation. These parameters include **amplitude**, **overshoot**, and **period**:

- **Amplitude**: The higher the amplitude, the higher the bounce or elastic spring effect that will be applied to the animation.
- **Overshoot**: Some curve functions will produce an overshoot (exceeding its final value) curve due to a damping effect. By adjusting the overshoot value, we are able to increase or decrease this effect.
- **Period**: Setting a small period value will give a high frequency to the curve. A large period will give it a small frequency.

These parameters, however, are not applicable to all curve types. Please refer to the Qt documentation to see which parameter is applicable to which curve type.

There's more...

While the **property animation** works perfectly fine, sometimes it feels a little boring to look at a GUI element being animated at a constant speed. We can make the animation look more interesting by adding an **easing curve** to control the motion. There are many types of easing curve that you can use in Qt, and here are some of them:

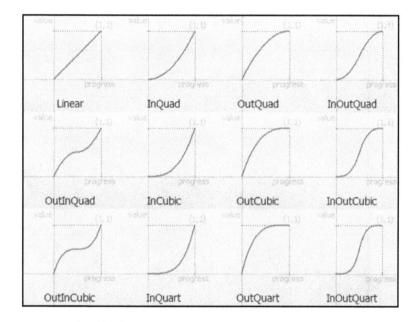

As you can see from the preceding diagram, each easing curve produces a different ease-in and ease-out effect.

For the full list of easing curves available in Qt, please refer to the Qt documentation at `http://doc.qt.io/qt-5/qeasingcurve.html#Type-enum`.

Creating an animation group

In this example, we will learn how to use an animation group to manage the states of the animations contained in the group.

How to do it...

Let's create an animation group by following these steps:

1. We will use the previous example but, this time, we will add two more push buttons to the main window, as shown in the following screenshot:

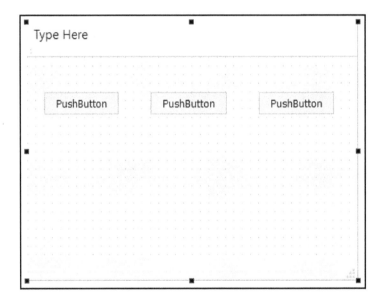

2. Define the animation for each of the push buttons in the main window's constructor:

```
QPropertyAnimation *animation1 = new
QPropertyAnimation(ui->pushButton, "geometry");
animation1->setDuration(3000);
animation1->setStartValue(ui->pushButton->geometry());
animation1->setEndValue(QRect(50, 200, 100, 50));

QPropertyAnimation *animation2 = new
QPropertyAnimation(ui->pushButton_2, "geometry");
animation2->setDuration(3000);
```

```
animation2->setStartValue(ui->pushButton_2->geometry());
animation2->setEndValue(QRect(150, 200, 100, 50));

QPropertyAnimation *animation3 = new
QPropertyAnimation(ui->pushButton_3, "geometry");
animation3->setDuration(3000);
animation3->setStartValue(ui->pushButton_3->geometry());
animation3->setEndValue(QRect(250, 200, 100, 50));
```

3. Create an easing curve and apply the same curve to all three animations:

```
QEasingCurve curve;
curve.setType(QEasingCurve::OutBounce);
curve.setAmplitude(1.00);
curve.setOvershoot(1.70);
curve.setPeriod(0.30);

animation1->setEasingCurve(curve);
animation2->setEasingCurve(curve);
animation3->setEasingCurve(curve);
```

4. Once you have applied the easing curve to all three animations, we will then create an animation group and add all three animations to the group:

```
QParallelAnimationGroup *group = new QParallelAnimationGroup;
group->addAnimation(animation1);
group->addAnimation(animation2);
group->addAnimation(animation3);
```

5. Call the `start()` function from the animation group we just created:

```
group->start();
```

How it works...

Since we are using an **animation group** now, we no longer call the `start()` function from the individual animation. Instead, we will be calling the `start()` function from the animation group we just created. If you compile and run the example now, you will see all three buttons being played at the same time. This is because we are using the **parallel animation group**. You can replace it with a **sequential animation group** and run the example again:

```
QSequentialAnimationGroup *group = new QSequentialAnimationGroup;
```

This time, only a single button will play its animation at a time, while the other buttons will wait patiently for their turn to come. The priority is set based on which animation is added to the animation group first. You can change the animation sequence by simply rearranging the sequence of an animation that's being added to the group. For example, if we want button 3 to start the animation first, followed by button 2, and then button 1, the code will look like this:

```
group->addAnimation(animation3);
group->addAnimation(animation2);
group->addAnimation(animation1);
```

Since property animations and animation groups are both inherited from the QAbstractAnimator class, it means that you can also add an animation group to another animation group to form a more complex, nested animation group.

There's more...

Qt allows us to create multiple animations and group them into an animation group. A group is usually responsible for managing the state of its animations (that is, it decides when to start, stop, resume, and pause them). Currently, Qt provides two types of class for animation groups, QParallelAnimationGroup and QSequentialAnimationGroup:

- QParallelAnimationGroup: As its name implies, a parallel animation group runs all of the animations in its group at the same time. The group is deemed finished when the longest-lasting animation has finished running.
- QSequentialAnimationGroup: A sequential animation group runs its animations in sequence, meaning it will only run a single animation at a time and only play the next animation when the current one has finished.

Creating a nested animation group

One good example of using a **nested animation group** is when you have several parallel animation groups and you want to play the groups in a sequential order.

How to do it...

Let's follow these steps to create a nested animation group to play different animation groups in a sequential order:

1. We will use the UI from the previous example and add a few more buttons to the main window, like so:

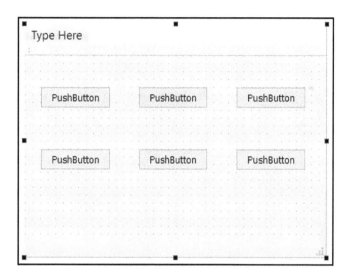

2. Create all of the animations for the buttons, and then create an **easing curve** and apply it to all of the animations:

```
QPropertyAnimation *animation1 = new
QPropertyAnimation(ui->pushButton, "geometry");
animation1->setDuration(3000);
animation1->setStartValue(ui->pushButton->geometry());
animation1->setEndValue(QRect(50, 50, 100, 50));

QPropertyAnimation *animation2 = new
QPropertyAnimation(ui->pushButton_2, "geometry");
animation2->setDuration(3000);
animation2->setStartValue(ui->pushButton_2->geometry());
animation2->setEndValue(QRect(150, 50, 100, 50));

QPropertyAnimation *animation3 = new
QPropertyAnimation(ui->pushButton_3, "geometry");
animation3->setDuration(3000);
animation3->setStartValue(ui->pushButton_3->geometry());
animation3->setEndValue(QRect(250, 50, 100, 50));
```

Next, apply the following code:

```
QPropertyAnimation *animation4 = new
QPropertyAnimation(ui->pushButton_4, "geometry");
animation4->setDuration(3000);
animation4->setStartValue(ui->pushButton_4->geometry());
animation4->setEndValue(QRect(50, 200, 100, 50));

QPropertyAnimation *animation5 = new
QPropertyAnimation(ui->pushButton_5, "geometry");
animation5->setDuration(3000);
animation5->setStartValue(ui->pushButton_5->geometry());
animation5->setEndValue(QRect(150, 200, 100, 50));

QPropertyAnimation *animation6 = new
QPropertyAnimation(ui->pushButton_6, "geometry");
animation6->setDuration(3000);
animation6->setStartValue(ui->pushButton_6->geometry());
animation6->setEndValue(QRect(250, 200, 100, 50));
```

Then, apply the following code:

```
QEasingCurve curve;
curve.setType(QEasingCurve::OutBounce);
curve.setAmplitude(1.00);
curve.setOvershoot(1.70);
curve.setPeriod(0.30);

animation1->setEasingCurve(curve);
animation2->setEasingCurve(curve);
animation3->setEasingCurve(curve);
animation4->setEasingCurve(curve);
animation5->setEasingCurve(curve);
animation6->setEasingCurve(curve);
```

3. Create two **animation groups**, one for the buttons in the upper column and another one for the lower column:

```
QParallelAnimationGroup *group1 = new QParallelAnimationGroup;
group1->addAnimation(animation1);
group1->addAnimation(animation2);
group1->addAnimation(animation3);

QParallelAnimationGroup *group2 = new QParallelAnimationGroup;
group2->addAnimation(animation4);
group2->addAnimation(animation5);
group2->addAnimation(animation6);
```

4. We will create yet another animation group, which will be used to store the two animation groups we created previously:

```
QSequentialAnimationGroup *groupAll = new
QSequentialAnimationGroup;
groupAll->addAnimation(group1);
groupAll->addAnimation(group2);
groupAll->start();
```

How it works...

What we are trying to do here is play the animation of the buttons in the upper column first, followed by the buttons in the lower column. Since both of the animation groups are **parallel animation groups**, the buttons belonging to the respective groups will be animated at the same time when the start() function is called.

This time, however, the group is a **sequential animation group**, which means only a single parallel animation group will be played at a time, followed by the other when the first one is finished. Animation groups are a very handy system that allows us to create very complex GUI animations with simple coding. Qt will handle the difficult part for us so that we don't have to.

State machines in Qt

A **state machines** can be used for many purposes but, in this chapter, we will only cover topics related to animation.

How to do it...

State machine is not that hard to achieve in Qt at all. Let's get started by following these steps:

1. We will set up a new user interface for our example program, which looks like this:

2. We will include some headers in our source code:

```
#include <QStateMachine>
#include <QPropertyAnimation>
#include <QEventTransition>
```

3. In our main window's constructor, add the following code to create a new **state machine** and two **states**, which we will be using later:

```
QStateMachine *machine = new QStateMachine(this);
QState *s1 = new QState();
QState *s2 = new QState();
```

4. We will define what we should do within each state, which, in this case, will be to change the label's **text**, as well as the button's **position** and **size**:

```
QState *s1 = new QState();
s1->assignProperty(ui->stateLabel, "text", "Current state: 1");
s1->assignProperty(ui->pushButton, "geometry", QRect(50, 200,
100, 50));

QState *s2 = new QState();
```

```
s2->assignProperty(ui->stateLabel, "text", "Current state: 2");
s2->assignProperty(ui->pushButton, "geometry", QRect(200, 50,
140, 100));
```

5. Once you are done with that, let's proceed by adding **event transition** classes to our source code:

```
QEventTransition *t1 = new QEventTransition(ui->changeState,
QEvent::MouseButtonPress);
t1->setTargetState(s2);
s1->addTransition(t1);

QEventTransition *t2 = new QEventTransition(ui->changeState,
QEvent::MouseButtonPress);
t2->setTargetState(s1);
s2->addTransition(t2);
```

6. Add all of the states we have just created to the **state machine** and define state 1 as the initial state. Then, call `machine->start()` to run the state machine:

```
machine->addState(s1);
machine->addState(s2);
machine->setInitialState(s1);
machine->start();
```

7. If you run the example program now, you will notice that everything works fine, except the button is not going through a smooth transition and it simply jumps instantly to the position and size we set previously. This is because we have not used a **property animation** to create a smooth transition.

8. Go back to the event transition step and add the following lines of code:

```
QEventTransition *t1 = new QEventTransition(ui->changeState,
QEvent::MouseButtonPress);
t1->setTargetState(s2);
t1->addAnimation(new QPropertyAnimation(ui->pushButton,
"geometry"));
s1->addTransition(t1);

QEventTransition *t2 = new QEventTransition(ui->changeState,
QEvent::MouseButtonPress);
t2->setTargetState(s1);
t2->addAnimation(new QPropertyAnimation(ui->pushButton,
"geometry"));
s2->addTransition(t2);
```

9. You can also add an **easing curve** to the animation to make it look more interesting:

```
QPropertyAnimation *animation = new
QPropertyAnimation(ui->pushButton, "geometry");
animation->setEasingCurve(QEasingCurve::OutBounce);
QEventTransition *t1 = new QEventTransition(ui->changeState,
QEvent::MouseButtonPress);
t1->setTargetState(s2);
t1->addAnimation(animation);
s1->addTransition(t1);

QEventTransition *t2 = new QEventTransition(ui->changeState,
QEvent::MouseButtonPress);
t2->setTargetState(s1);
t2->addAnimation(animation);
s2->addTransition(t2);
```

How it works...

There are two **push buttons** and a **label** on the main window layout. The button at the top-left corner will trigger the state change when pressed, while the label at the top-right corner will change its text to show which state we are currently in, and the button below will animate according to the current state. The `QEventTransition` classes define what will trigger the transition between one state and another.

In our case, we want the state to change from state 1 to state 2 when the **changeState** button (the one at the upper-left) is clicked. After that, we also want to change from state 2 back to state 1 when the same button is pressed again. This can be achieved by creating another **event transition** class and setting the target state back to state 1. Then, add these transitions to their respective states. Instead of just assigning the properties directly to the widgets, we tell Qt to use the property animation class to smoothly interpolate the properties toward the target values. It is that simple! There is no need to set the start value and end value, because we have already called the `assignProperty()` function, which has automatically assigned the end value.

There's more...

The **state machine framework** in Qt provides classes for creating and executing state graphs. Qt's event system is used to drive the state machines, where transitions between states can be triggered by using *signals*, and then the *slots* on the other end will be invoked by the signals to perform an action, such as playing an animation.

Once you understand the basics of state machines, you can use them to do other things as well. The state graph in the state machine framework is hierarchical. Just like the animation group in the previous section, states can also be nested inside of other states:

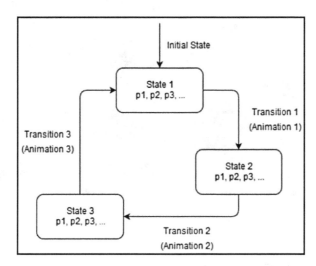

States, transitions, and animations in QML

If you prefer to work with QML instead of C++, Qt also provides similar features in Qt Quick that allow you to easily animate a GUI element with minimal lines of code. In this example, we will learn how to achieve this with QML.

How to do it…

Let's get started by following these steps to create a window that continuously changes its background color:

1. We will create a new **Qt Quick Application** project and set up our user interface, like so:

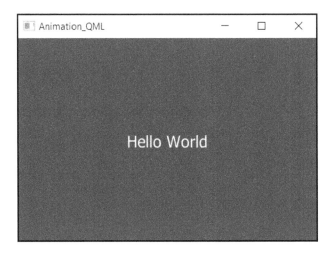

2. Here is what my main.qml file looks like:

```
import QtQuick 2.9
import QtQuick.Window 2.3
Window {
    visible: true
    width: 480;
    height: 320;
    Rectangle {
        id: background;
        anchors.fill: parent;
        color: "blue";
    }
    Text {
        text: qsTr("Hello World");
        anchors.centerIn: parent;
        color: "white";
        font.pointSize: 15;
    }
}
```

3. Add the **color animation** to the `Rectangle` object:

```
Rectangle {
    id: background;
    anchors.fill: parent;
    color: "blue";
    SequentialAnimation on color {
        ColorAnimation { to: "yellow"; duration: 1000 }
        ColorAnimation { to: "red"; duration: 1000 }
        ColorAnimation { to: "blue"; duration: 1000 }
        loops: Animation.Infinite;
    }
}
```

4. Add a number animation to the `text` object:

```
Text {
    text: qsTr("Hello World");
    anchors.centerIn: parent;
    color: "white";
    font.pointSize: 15;
    SequentialAnimation on opacity {
        NumberAnimation { to: 0.0; duration: 200}
        NumberAnimation { to: 1.0; duration: 200}
        loops: Animation.Infinite;
    }
}
```

5. Add another number animation to it:

```
Text {
    text: qsTr("Hello World");
    anchors.centerIn: parent;
    color: "white";
    font.pointSize: 15;
    SequentialAnimation on opacity {
        NumberAnimation { to: 0.0; duration: 200}
        NumberAnimation { to: 1.0; duration: 200}
        loops: Animation.Infinite;
    }
    NumberAnimation on rotation {
        from: 0;
        to: 360;
        duration: 2000;
        loops: Animation.Infinite;
    }
}
```

6. Define two states, one called the PRESSED state and another called the RELEASED state. Then, set the default state to RELEASED:

```
Rectangle {
    id: background;
    anchors.fill: parent;
    state: "RELEASED";
    states: [
        State {
            name: "PRESSED"
            PropertyChanges { target: background; color:
"blue"}
        },
        State {
            name: "RELEASED"
            PropertyChanges { target: background; color: "red"}
        }
    ]
}
```

7. After that, create a mouse area within the Rectangle object so that we can click on it:

```
MouseArea {
    anchors.fill: parent;
    onPressed: background.state = "PRESSED";
    onReleased: background.state = "RELEASED";
}
```

8. Add some transitions to the Rectangle object:

```
transitions: [
    Transition {
        from: "PRESSED"
        to: "RELEASED"
        ColorAnimation { target: background; duration: 200}
    },
    Transition {
        from: "RELEASED"
        to: "PRESSED"
        ColorAnimation { target: background; duration: 200}
    }
]
```

How it works...

The main window consists of a blue rectangle and static text that says **Hello World**. We want the background color to change from blue to yellow, then to red, and back to blue in a loop. This can be easily achieved by using the color animation type in QML. What we are doing at *step 3* is basically creating a sequential animation group within the Rectangle object, then creating three different color animations within the group, which will change the color of the object every 1,000 milliseconds (1 second). We also set the animations to loop infinitely.

In *step 4*, we want to use the number animation to animate the alpha value of the static text. We created another sequential animation group within the Text object and created two number animations to animate the alpha value from 0 to 1 and back. Then, we set the animations to loop infinitely.

Then, in *step 5*, we rotate the **Hello World** text by adding another number animation to it. In *step 6*, we wanted to make the Rectangle object change from one color to another when we click on it. When the mouse is released, the Rectangle object will change back to its initial color. To achieve that, first we need to define the two states, one called the PRESSED state and another called the RELEASED state. Then, we set the default state to RELEASED.

Now, when you compile and run the example, the background will instantly change color to blue when pressed and change back to red when the mouse is released. That works great, and we can further enhance it by giving it a little transition when switching color. This can be easily achieved by adding transitions to the Rectangle object.

There's more...

In QML, there are eight different types of property animation you can use, and these are as follows:

- **Anchor animation**: Animates changes in anchor values
- **Color animation**: Animates changes in color values
- **Number animation**: Animates changes in qreal-type values
- **Parent animation**: Animates changes in parent values
- **Path animation**: Animates an item along a path
- **Property animation**: Animates changes in property values
- **Rotation animation**: Animates changes in rotation values
- **Vector3d animation**: Animates changes in QVector3D values

Just like the C++ version, these animations can also be grouped together in an animation group to play the animations in sequence or in parallel. You can also control the animations using easing curves and determine when to play these animations using state machines, just like we did in the previous section.

Animating widget properties using animators

In this recipe, we will learn how to animate the properties of our GUI widgets using the animator feature that's provided by QML.

How to do it...

Animating QML objects is really easy if you perform the following steps:

1. Create a `Rectangle` object and add a scale animator to it:

```
Rectangle {
    id: myBox;
    width: 50;
    height: 50;
    anchors.horizontalCenter: parent.horizontalCenter;
    anchors.verticalCenter: parent.verticalCenter;
    color: "blue";
    ScaleAnimator {
        target: myBox;
        from: 5;
        to: 1;
        duration: 2000;
        running: true;
    }
}
```

2. Add a rotation animator and set the running value in the parallel animation group, but not in any of the individual animators:

```
ParallelAnimation {
    ScaleAnimator {
        target: myBox;
        from: 5;
        to: 1;
        duration: 2000;
```

```
        }
        RotationAnimator {
            target: myBox;
            from: 0;
            to: 360;
            duration: 1000;
        }
        running: true;
    }
```

3. Add an easing curve to the scale animator:

```
    ScaleAnimator {
        target: myBox;
        from: 5;
        to: 1;
        duration: 2000;
        easing.type: Easing.InOutElastic;
        easing.amplitude: 2.0;
        easing.period: 1.5;
        running: true;
    }
```

How it works...

The animator type can be used just like any other animation type. We want to scale a rectangle from a size of 5 to a size of 1 within 2,000 milliseconds (2 seconds). We created a blue `Rectangle` object and added a scale animator to it. We set the initial value to 5 and the final value to 1. Then, we set the animation duration to `2000` and set the running value to true so that it will be played when the program starts.

Just like the animation types, animators can also be put into groups (that is, parallel animation groups or sequential animation groups). An animation group will also be treated as an *animator* by QtQuick and be run on the scene graph's rendering thread whenever possible. In *step 2*, we want to group two different animators into a parallel animation group so that they run together at the same time.

We will keep the scale animator we created previously and add another rotation animator to rotate the `Rectangle` object. This time, set the running value in the parallel animation group, but not in any of the individual animators.

Just like the C++ version, QML also supports easing curves, and they can be easily applied to any of the animations or animator types.

There is something called animator in QML, which is different from the usual animation type, even though there is some similarity between them. Unlike regular animation types, animator types are directly operated on Qt Quick's scene graph, rather than the QML objects and their properties. The value of the QML property will not be changed while the animation is running, as it will only change once the animation is finished. The benefits of using the animator type is that it operates directly on the scene graph's rendering thread, which means its performance will be slightly better than running on the UI thread.

Sprite animation

In this example, we will learn how to create sprite animation in QML.

How to do it...

Let's make a horse run across our application window by following these steps:

1. We will need to add our sprite sheet to Qt's resource system so that it can be used in the program. Open up `qml.qrc` and click the **Add** | **Add Files** buttons. Select your sprite sheet image and save the resource file by pressing *Ctrl + S*.

2. Create a new empty window in `main.qml`:

```
import QtQuick 2.9
import QtQuick.Window 2.3
Window {
    visible: true
    width: 420
    height: 380
    Rectangle {
        anchors.fill: parent
        color: "white"
    }
}
```

3. Once you are done with that, we will start creating an `AnimatedSprite` object in QML:

```
import QtQuick 2.9
import QtQuick.Window 2.3
Window {
    visible: true;
    width: 420;
    height: 380;
    Rectangle {
        anchors.fill: parent;
        color: "white";
    }
```

Then, set the following:

```
AnimatedSprite {
        id: sprite;
        width: 128;
        height: 128;
        anchors.centerIn: parent;
        source: "qrc:///horse_1.png";
        frameCount: 11;
        frameWidth: 128;
        frameHeight: 128;
        frameRate: 25;
        loops: Animation.Infinite;
        running: true;
    }
}
```

4. Add a mouse area to the window and check for the `onClicked` event:

```
MouseArea {
    anchors.fill: parent;
    onClicked: {
        if (sprite.paused)
            sprite.resume();
        else
            sprite.pause();
    }
}
```

5. If you compile and run the example program now, you will see a little pony running in the middle of the window. How fun:

6. Next, we want to try and do something cool. We will make the horse run across the window and loop infinitely while playing its running animation! First, we need to remove `anchors.centerIn: parent` from QML and replace it with `x` and `y` values:

```
AnimatedSprite {
    id: sprite;
    width: 128;
    height: 128;
    x: -128;
    y: parent.height / 2;
    source: "qrc:///horse_1.png";
    frameCount: 11;
    frameWidth: 128;
    frameHeight: 128;
    frameRate: 25;
    loops: Animation.Infinite;
    running: true;
}
```

7. Add a number animation to the sprite object and set its properties, like this:

```
NumberAnimation {
    target: sprite;
    property: "x";
    from: -128;
    to: 512;
    duration: 3000;
    loops: Animation.Infinite;
    running: true;
}
```

8. If you compile and run the example program now, you will see the pony go crazy and start running across the window!

How it works...

In this recipe, we place the animated sprite object in the middle of the window and set its image source to the sprite sheet that we have just added to the project resource. Then, we count how many frames there are in the sprite sheet that belong to the running animation, which in this case is 11 frames. We also inform Qt regarding the dimension of each frame of the animation, which in this case is 128 x 128. After that, we set the frame rate to 25 to get a decent speed and then set it to loop infinitely. We then set the running value to true so that the animation will play by default when the program starts running.

Then, in *step 4*, we want to be able to pause the animation and resume it by clicking on the window. We simply check whether the sprite is currently paused when clicking on the mouse area. If the sprite animation is paused, then the animation resumes; otherwise, the animation is paused.

In *step 6*, we replace anchors.centerIn with x and y values so that the animated sprite object is not anchored to the center of the window, which would make it impossible to move around. Then, we create a number animation within the animated sprite to animate its x property. We set the start value to somewhere outside the window on the left side, and we set the end value to somewhere outside the window on the right side. After that, we set the duration to 3,000 milliseconds (3 seconds) and make it loop infinitely.

Lastly, we also set the running value to true so that it plays the animation by default when the program starts running.

There's more...

Sprite animation is used extensively, especially in game development. Sprites are used for character animation, particle animation, and even GUI animation. A sprite sheet consists of many images combined into one, which can then be chopped down and displayed on the screen, one at a time. The transitions between different images (or sprites) from the sprite sheet creates the illusion of animation, which we usually refer to as sprite animation. Sprite animation can be easily achieved in QML using the `AnimatedSprite` type.

In this example program, I am using a free and open source image that was created by **bluecarrot16** under the `CC-BY 3.0/GPL 3.0/GPL 2.0/OGA-BY 3.0` license. The image can be obtained legally at `http://opengameart.org/content/lpc-horse`.

QPainter and 2D Graphics

4

The list of topics covered in this chapter is as follows:

- Drawing basic shapes onscreen
- Exporting shapes to **Scalable Vector Graphics (SVG)** files
- Coordinate transformation
- Displaying images onscreen
- Applying image effects to graphics
- Creating a basic paint program
- Rendering a 2D canvas in QML

Introduction

In this chapter, we will learn how to render 2D graphics onscreen with Qt. Internally, Qt uses a low-level class called **QPainter** to render its widgets on the main window. Qt allows us to access and use the QPainter class for drawing vector graphics, text, 2D images, and even 3D graphics.

You can make use of the QPainter class to create your own custom widgets or to create programs that rely heavily on rendering computer graphics such as video games, photo editors, and 3D modeling tools.

Technical requirements

The technical requirements for this chapter include Qt 5.11.2 MinGW 32-bit, Qt Creator 4.8.2, and Windows 10

All the code used in this chapter can be downloaded from the GitHub repository for this chapter, at: `https://github.com/PacktPublishing/Qt5-CPP-GUI-Programming-Cookbook-Second-Edition/tree/master/Chapter04`.

Check out the following video to see the code in action: `http://bit.ly/2FrVYeq`

Drawing basic shapes onscreen

In this section, we will learn how to draw simple vector shapes (a line, a rectangle, a circle, and so on) and display text on the main window using the `QPainter` class. We will also learn how to change the drawing style of these vector shapes using the `QPen` class.

How to do it...

Let's follow the steps listed here to display basic shapes in our Qt window:

1. First, let's create a new `Qt Widgets Application` project.
2. Open up `mainwindow.ui` and remove the **menuBar**, **mainToolBar**, and **statusBar** objects so that we get a clean, empty main window. Right-click on the bar widgets and select **Remove Menu Bar** from the pop-up menu:

3. Then, open up `mainwindow.h` file and add the following code to include the `QPainter` header file:

```
#include <QMainWindow>
#include <QPainter>
```

4. Then, declare the `paintEvent()` event handler below the class destructor:

```
public:
    explicit MainWindow(QWidget *parent = 0);
    ~MainWindow();
    virtual void paintEvent(QPaintEvent *event);
```

5. Next, open up `mainwindow.cpp` file and define the `paintEvent()` event handler:

```
void MainWindow::paintEvent(QPaintEvent *event) {}
```

6. After that, we will add text to the screen using the `QPainter` class inside the `paintEvent()` event handler. We set the text font settings before drawing it on the screen at the position of (`20, 30`):

```
QPainter textPainter;
textPainter.begin(this);
textPainter.setFont(QFont("Times", 14, QFont::Bold));
textPainter.drawText(QPoint(20, 30), "Testing");
textPainter.end();
```

7. Then, we will draw a straight line that starts from (`50, 60`) and ends at (`100, 100`):

```
QPainter linePainter;
linePainter.begin(this);
linePainter.drawLine(QPoint(50, 60), QPoint(100, 100));
linePainter.end();
```

8. We can also easily draw a rectangle by calling the `drawRect()` function using a `QPainter` class. This time, however, we also apply a background pattern to the shape before drawing it:

```
QPainter rectPainter;
rectPainter.begin(this);
rectPainter.setBrush(Qt::BDiagPattern);
rectPainter.drawRect(QRect(40, 120, 80, 30));
rectPainter.end();
```

9. Next, declare a `QPen` class, set its color to red, and set its drawing style to `Qt::DashDotLine`. Then, apply the `QPen` class to `QPainter`, and draw an ellipse shape at (`80, 200`) with a horizontal radius of `50` and a vertical radius of `20`:

```
QPen ellipsePen;
ellipsePen.setColor(Qt::red);
```

```
ellipsePen.setStyle(Qt::DashDotLine);

QPainter ellipsePainter;
ellipsePainter.begin(this);
ellipsePainter.setPen(ellipsePen);
ellipsePainter.drawEllipse(QPoint(80, 200), 50, 20);
ellipsePainter.end();
```

10. We can also use the `QPainterPath` class to define a shape before passing it over to the `QPainter` class for rendering:

```
QPainterPath rectPath;
rectPath.addRect(QRect(150, 20, 100, 50));

QPainter pathPainter;
pathPainter.begin(this);
pathPainter.setPen(QPen(Qt::red, 1, Qt::DashDotLine,
Qt::FlatCap, Qt::MiterJoin));
pathPainter.setBrush(Qt::yellow);
pathPainter.drawPath(rectPath);
pathPainter.end();
```

11. You can also draw any other shapes by using `QPainterPath`, such as an ellipse:

```
QPainterPath ellipsePath;
ellipsePath.addEllipse(QPoint(200, 120), 50, 20);

QPainter ellipsePathPainter;
ellipsePathPainter.begin(this);
ellipsePathPainter.setPen(QPen(QColor(79, 106, 25), 5,
Qt::SolidLine, Qt::FlatCap, Qt::MiterJoin));
ellipsePathPainter.setBrush(QColor(122, 163, 39));
ellipsePathPainter.drawPath(ellipsePath);
ellipsePathPainter.end();
```

12. `QPainter` can also be used to draw an image file onto the screen. In the following example, we load an image file called `tux.png` and draw it on the screen at the (100, 150) position:

```
QImage image;
image.load("tux.png");

QPainter imagePainter(this);
imagePainter.begin(this);
imagePainter.drawImage(QPoint(100, 150), image);
imagePainter.end();
```

13. The final result should look something like this:

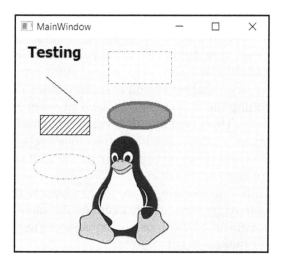

How it works...

If you want to draw something onscreen using QPainter, all you need to do is tell it what type of graphics it should be drawing (as in text, a vector shape, an image, a polygon) with the desired position and size. The QPen class determines what the outline of the graphic should look like, such as its color, line width, line style (solid, dashed, or dotted), cap style, join style, and so on. On the other hand, QBrush sets the style of the background of the graphics, such as the background color, pattern (solid color, gradient, dense brush, and crossing diagonal lines) and pixmap.

The options for the graphics should be set before calling a draw function (such as drawLine(), drawRect(), or drawEllipse()). If your graphics do not appear onscreen and you see warnings such as **QPainter::setPen: Painter not active** and **QPainter::setBrush: Painter not active** appearing on the application output window in Qt Creator, it means that the QPainter class is not currently active and your program will not trigger its paint event. To solve this problem, set the main window as the parent of the QPainter class. Usually, if you're writing code in the mainwindow.cpp file, all you need to do is to put this in the bracket when initializing QPainter. For example, note the following:

```
QPainter linePainter(this);
```

QImage can load images from both the computer directories and from the program resources.

There's more...

Think of QPainter as a robot with a pen and an empty canvas. You just have to tell the robot what type of shape it should be drawing and its location on the canvas, then the robot will do its job based on your description. To make your life easier, the **QPainter** class also provides numerous functions, such as drawArc(), drawEllipse(), drawLine(), drawRect(), and drawPie(), that allow you to easily render a predefined shape. In Qt, all the widget classes (including the main window) have an event handler called QWidget::paintEvent(). This event handler will be triggered whenever the operating system thinks that the main window should re-draw its widgets. Many things can lead to that decision, such as the main window being scaled, a widget changing its state (that is, a button being pressed), or functions such as repaint() or update() being invoked manually in the code. Different operating systems may behave differently when it comes to deciding whether or not to trigger the update event on the same set of conditions. If you're making a program that requires continuous and consistent graphical updates, call repaint() or update() manually with a timer.

Exporting shapes to SVG files

SVG is an XML-based language for describing two-dimensional vector graphics. Qt provides classes for saving vector shapes as SVG file. This feature can be used to create a simple vector graphics editor similar to Adobe Illustrator and Inkscape. In the next example, we will continue using the same project file from the previous example.

How to do it...

Let's learn how to create a simple program that displays SVG graphics onscreen:

1. First of all, let's create a menu bar by right-clicking the main window widget on the hierarchy window and selecting the **Create Menu Bar** option from the pop-up menu. After that, add a **File** option to the menu bar and a **Save as SVG** action underneath it:

2. After that, you will see an item called **actionSave_as_SVG** in the **Action Editor** window at the bottom of the Qt Creator window. Right-click on the item and choose **Go to slot...** from the pop-up menu. A window will now appear, which carries a list of slots available for the particular action. Choose the default signal, called **triggered()**, and click the **OK** button:

3. Once you have clicked the **OK** button, Qt Creator will switch over to the script editor. You will realize that a slot called `on_actionSave_as_SVG_triggered()` has been automatically added to your main window class. At the bottom of your `mainwindow.h` file, you will see something like this:

```
void MainWindow::on_actionSave_as_SVG_triggered() {}
```

4. The preceding function will be called when you clicked on the **Save as SVG** option from the menu bar. We will write our code within this function to save all the vector graphics into an SVG file. To do that, we need to first of all include a class header called `QSvgGenerator` at the top of our source file. This header is very important as it's required for generating SVG files. Then, we also need to include another class header called `QFileDialog`, which will be used to open the save dialog:

```
#include <QtSvg/QSvgGenerator>
#include <QFileDialog>
```

5. We also need to add the `svg` module to our project file, like so:

```
QT += core gui svg
```

6. Then, create a new function called `paintAll()` within the `mainwindow.h` file, as shown in the following code:

```
public:
    explicit MainWindow(QWidget *parent = 0);
    ~MainWindow();
    virtual void paintEvent(QPaintEvent *event);
    void paintAll(QSvgGenerator *generator = 0);
```

7. After that, in the `mainwindow.cpp` file, move all the code from `paintEvent()` to the `paintAll()` function. Then, replace all the individual `QPainter` objects with a single, unified `QPainter` for drawing all the graphics. Also, call the `begin()` function before drawing anything and call the `end()` function after finishing drawing. The code should look like this:

```
void MainWindow::paintAll(QSvgGenerator *generator) {
    QPainter painter;
    if (engine)
        painter.begin(engine);
    else
        painter.begin(this);
    painter.setFont(QFont("Times", 14, QFont::Bold));
    painter.drawText(QPoint(20, 30), "Testing");
    painter.drawLine(QPoint(50, 60), QPoint(100, 100));
    painter.setBrush(Qt::BDiagPattern);
    painter.drawRect(QRect(40, 120, 80, 30));
```

8. We go on to create `ellipsePen` and `rectPath`:

```
QPen ellipsePen;
ellipsePen.setColor(Qt::red);
```

```
ellipsePen.setStyle(Qt::DashDotLine);
painter.setPen(ellipsePen);
painter.drawEllipse(QPoint(80, 200), 50, 20);

QPainterPath rectPath;
rectPath.addRect(QRect(150, 20, 100, 50));
painter.setPen(QPen(Qt::red, 1, Qt::DashDotLine, Qt::FlatCap,
Qt::MiterJoin));
painter.setBrush(Qt::yellow);
painter.drawPath(rectPath);
```

9. Then, we go on to create `ellipsePath` and `image`:

```
QPainterPath ellipsePath;
ellipsePath.addEllipse(QPoint(200, 120), 50, 20);
painter.setPen(QPen(QColor(79, 106, 25), 5, Qt::SolidLine,
Qt::FlatCap, Qt::MiterJoin));
painter.setBrush(QColor(122, 163, 39));
painter.drawPath(ellipsePath);

QImage image;
image.load("tux.png");
painter.drawImage(QPoint(100, 150), image);
painter.end();
}
```

10. Since we have moved all the code from `paintEvent()` to `paintAll()`, we shall now call the `paintAll()` function inside `paintEvent()`, like so:

```
void MainWindow::paintEvent(QPaintEvent *event) {
    paintAll();
}
```

11. Then, we will write the code for exporting the graphics as an SVG file. The code will be written inside the slot function called `on_actionSave_as_SVG_triggered()`, which was generated by Qt. We start by calling the save file dialog and obtain the directory path with the desired filename from the user:

```
void MainWindow::on_actionSave_as_SVG_triggered() {
    QString filePath = QFileDialog::getSaveFileName(this, "Save
SVG", "", "SVG files (*.svg)");
    if (filePath == "")
        return;
}
```

12. After that, create a `QSvgGenerator` object and save the graphics to an SVG file by passing the `QSvgGenerator` object to the `paintAll()` function:

```
void MainWindow::on_actionSave_as_SVG_triggered() {
    QString filePath = QFileDialog::getSaveFileName(this, "Save
SVG", "", "SVG files (*.svg)");
    if (filePath == "")
        return;
    QSvgGenerator generator;
    generator.setFileName(filePath);
    generator.setSize(QSize(this->width(), this->height()));
    generator.setViewBox(QRect(0, 0, this->width(),
this->height()));
    generator.setTitle("SVG Example");
    generator.setDescription("This SVG file is generated by
Qt.");
    paintAll(&generator);
}
```

13. Compile and run the program now and you should be able to export the graphics by going to **File** | **Save as SVG**:

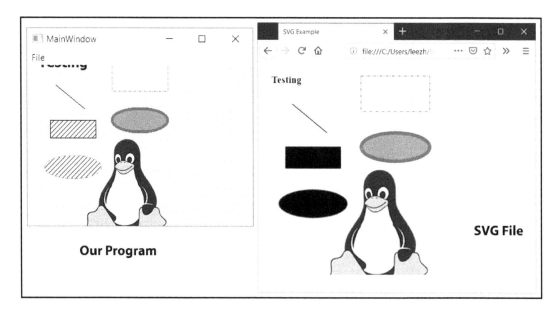

How it works...

By default, `QPainter` will use the paint engine from its parent object to draw the graphics assigned to it. If you don't assign any parent to `QPainter`, you can manually assign a paint engine to it, which is what we have done in this example.

The reason why we placed the code into `paintAll()` is because we want to reuse the same code for two different purposes: for displaying the graphics on the window and exporting the graphics to an SVG file. Notice the default value of the generator variable in the `paintAll()` function is set to 0, which means no `QSvgGenerator` object is required to run the function unless specified. Later on, in the `paintAll()` function, we check whether the generator object exists. If it does exist, use it as the paint engine for the painter, as shown in the following code:

```
if (engine)
    painter.begin(engine);
else
    painter.begin(this);
```

Otherwise, pass the main window to the `begin()` function (since we're writing the code in `mainwindow.cpp` file, we can directly use this to refer to the main window's pointer) so that it will use the paint engine of the main window itself, which means the graphics will be drawn onto the surface of the main window. In this example, it's required to use a single `QPainter` object to save the graphics into the SVG file. If you use multiple `QPainter` objects, the resulting SVG file will contain multiple XML header definitions and thus the file will be deemed to be invalid by any graphics editor software out there.

`QFileDialog::getSaveFileName()` will open up the native save file dialog for the user to choose the save directory and set a desired filename. Once the user is done with that, the full path will be returned as a string and we will be able to pass that information to the `QSvgGenerator` object to export the graphics.

Notice that in the previous screenshot, the penguin in the SVG file has been cropped. This is because the canvas size of the SVG was set to follow the size of the main window. To help the poor penguin getting its body back, scale the window bigger before exporting the SVG file.

There's more…

SVG defines the graphics in XML format. Since it is a form of vector graphics, SVG files do not lose any quality if they are zoomed in on or resized. The SVG format not only allows you to store vector graphics in the working file, but it also allows you to store raster graphics and text, which is more or less similar to Adobe Illustrator's format. The SVG also allows you to group, style, transform, and composite graphical objects into previously rendered objects.

> You can check out the full specification of SVG graphics at `https://www.w3.org/TR/SVG`.

Coordinate transformation

In this example, we will learn how to use coordinate transformation and a timer to create a real-time clock display.

How to do it…

To create our first graphical clock display, let's follow these steps:

1. First, create a new `Qt Widgets Application` project. Then, open up `mainwindow.ui` and remove the **menuBar**, **mainToolBar**, and **statusBar** as we did before.

2. After that, open up the `mainwindow.h` file and include the following headers:

```
#include <QTime>
#include <QTimer>
#include <QPainter>
```

3. Then, declare the `paintEvent()` function, like so:

```
public:
    explicit MainWindow(QWidget *parent = 0);
    ~MainWindow();
    virtual void paintEvent(QPaintEvent *event);
```

4. In the `mainwindow.cpp` file, create three arrays to store the shapes of the hour hand, minute hand, and second hand, where each of the arrays contains three sets of coordinates:

```cpp
void MainWindow::paintEvent(QPaintEvent *event) {
    static const QPoint hourHand[3] = {
        QPoint(4, 4),
        QPoint(-4, 4),
        QPoint(0, -40)
    };
    static const QPoint minuteHand[3] = {
        QPoint(4, 4),
        QPoint(-4, 4),
        QPoint(0, -70)
    };
    static const QPoint secondHand[3] = {
        QPoint(2, 2),
        QPoint(-2, 2),
        QPoint(0, -90)
    };
}
```

5. After that, add the following code below the arrays to create the painter and move it to the center of the main window. Also, we adjust the size of the painter so that it fits nicely in the main window, even when the window is being resized:

```cpp
int side = qMin(width(), height());
QPainter painter(this);
painter.setRenderHint(QPainter::Antialiasing);
painter.translate(width() / 2, height() / 2);
painter.scale(side / 250.0, side / 250.0);
```

6. Once you are done with that, we will start drawing the dials by using a `for` loop. Each dial is rotated by an increment of 6 degrees, so 60 dials would complete a full circle. Also, the dial at every 5 minutes will look slightly longer:

```cpp
for (int i = 0; i < 60; ++i) {
    if ((i % 5) != 0)
        painter.drawLine(92, 0, 96, 0);
    else
        painter.drawLine(86, 0, 96, 0);
    painter.rotate(6.0);
}
```

7. Then, we proceed with drawing the hands of the clock. Each hand's rotation is calculated according to the current time and its respective equivalent location over 360 degrees:

```
QTime time = QTime::currentTime();

// Draw hour hand
painter.save();
painter.rotate((time.hour() * 360) / 12);
painter.setPen(Qt::NoPen);
painter.setBrush(Qt::black);
painter.drawConvexPolygon(hourHand, 3);
painter.restore();
```

8. Let's go on to draw the minute hand of the clock:

```
// Draw minute hand
painter.save();
painter.rotate((time.minute() * 360) / 60);
painter.setPen(Qt::NoPen);
painter.setBrush(Qt::black);
painter.drawConvexPolygon(minuteHand, 3);
painter.restore();
```

9. Then, we also draw the hand for seconds:

```
// Draw second hand
painter.save();
painter.rotate((time.second() * 360) / 60);
painter.setPen(Qt::NoPen);
painter.setBrush(Qt::black);
painter.drawConvexPolygon(secondHand, 3);
painter.restore();
```

10. Last but not least, create a timer to refresh the graphics every second so that the program will work like a real clock:

```
MainWindow::MainWindow(QWidget *parent) : QMainWindow(parent),
ui(new Ui::MainWindow) {
    ui->setupUi(this);
    QTimer* timer = new QTimer(this);
    timer->start(1000);
    connect(timer, QTimer::timeout, this, MainWindow::update);
}
```

11. Compile and run the program now, and you should see something like this:

How it works...

Each of the arrays contain three QPoint data instances, which form the shape of an elongated triangle. The arrays are then passed to the painter and rendered as a convex polygon using the drawConvexPolygon() function. Before drawing each of the clock hands, we use painter.save() to save the state of the QPainter object and then proceed with drawing the hand using coordinate transformation.

Once we're done with the drawing, we restore the painter to its previous state by calling painter.restore(). This function will undo all the transformations before painter.restore() so that the next clock hand will not inherit the transformations of the previous one. Without using painter.save() and painter.restore(), we will have to manually change back the position, rotation, and scale before drawing the next hand.

A good example of not using painter.save() and painter.restore() is when drawing the dials. Since each dial's rotation is an increment of 6 degrees from the previous one, we don't need to save the painter's state at all. We just have to call painter.rotate(6.0) in a loop and each dial will inherit the previous dial's rotation. We also use a modulus operator (%) to check whether the unit represented by the dial can be divided by 5. If it can, then we draw it slightly longer.

Without using a timer to constantly call the `update()` slot, the clock will not function properly. This is because `paintEvent()` will not be called by Qt when there is no change to the state of the parent widget, which in this case is the main window. Therefore, we need to manually tell Qt that we need to refresh the graphics by calling `update()` every second. We used the `painter.setRenderHint(QPainter::Antialiasing)` function to enable anti-aliasing when rendering the clock. Without anti-aliasing, the graphics will look very jagged and pixelated:

There's more...

The `QPainter` class uses the coordinate system to determine the position and size of the graphics before rendering them onscreen. This information can be altered to make the graphics appear at a different position, rotation, and size. This process of altering the coordinate information of a graphic is what we called **coordinate transformation**. There are several types of transformation; among them are translation, rotation, scaling, and shearing:

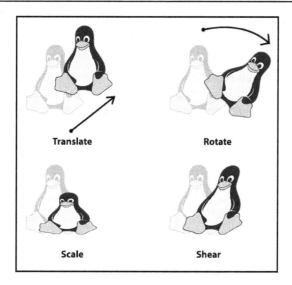

Qt uses a coordinate system that has its origin at the top-left corner, meaning the *x* values increase to the right and the *y* values increase downward. This coordinate system might be different from the coordinate system used by the physical device, such as a computer screen. Qt handles this automatically by using the QPaintDevice class, which maps Qt's logical coordinates to the physical coordinates.

QPainter provides four transform operations to perform different types of transformation:

- QPainter::translate(): Offsets the graphic's position by a given set of units
- QPainter::rotate(): Rotates the graphics around the origin in a clockwise direction
- QPainter::scale(): Offsets the graphic's size by a given factor
- QPainter::shear(): Twists the graphic's coordinate system around the origin

Displaying images onscreen

Qt not only allows us to draw shapes and images onscreen, but it also allows us to overlay multiple images on top of each other and combine the pixel information from all the layers using different types of algorithms to create very interesting results. In this example, we will learn how to overlay images on top of each other and apply different composition effects to them.

How to do it...

Let's create a simple demo that shows the effect of different image compositions by following these steps:

1. First, set up a new Qt Widgets Application project and remove the **menuBar**, **mainToolBar**, and **statusBar**, as we did in the first recipe.

2. Next, add the QPainter class header to the mainwindow.h file:

    ```
    #include <QPainter>
    ```

3. After that, declare the paintEvent() virtual function, like so:

    ```
    virtual void paintEvent(QPaintEvent* event);
    ```

4. In mainwindow.cpp, we will first load several image files using the QImage class:

    ```
    void MainWindow::paintEvent(QPaintEvent* event) {
        QImage image;
        image.load("checker.png");
        QImage image2;
        image2.load("tux.png");
        QImage image3;
        image3.load("butterfly.png");
    }
    ```

5. Then, create a QPainter object and use it to draw two pairs of images, where one image is on top of another:

    ```
    QPainter painter(this);
    painter.drawImage(QPoint(10, 10), image);
    painter.drawImage(QPoint(10, 10), image2);
    painter.drawImage(QPoint(300, 10), image);
    painter.drawImage(QPoint(300, 40), image3);
    ```

6. Compile and run the program now and you should see something like this:

7. Next, we will set the composition mode before drawing each image onscreen:

```
QPainter painter(this);
painter.setCompositionMode(QPainter::CompositionMode_Difference
);
painter.drawImage(QPoint(10, 10), image);
painter.setCompositionMode(QPainter::CompositionMode_Multiply);
painter.drawImage(QPoint(10, 10), image2);
painter.setCompositionMode(QPainter::CompositionMode_Xor);
painter.drawImage(QPoint(300, 10), image);
painter.setCompositionMode(QPainter::CompositionMode_SoftLight)
;
painter.drawImage(QPoint(300, 40), image3);
```

8. Compile and run the program again and you will now see something like this:

How it works...

When drawing images with Qt, the sequence of calling the `drawImage()` function will determine which image is being rendered first and which one is rendered later. This will affect the depth order of the images and yield different outcomes.
In the previous example, we called `drawImage()` function four times to draw four different images onscreen. The first `drawImage()` function renders `checker.png`, and the second `drawImage()` function renders `tux.png` (the penguin). The image that gets rendered later will always appear in front of the others, which is why the penguin is showing in front of the checker pattern. The same goes for the butterfly and the checker on the right. The reason why you can still see the checker even though the butterfly is rendered in front of it is because the butterfly image is not fully opaque.

Now, let's invert the render sequence and see what happens. We will try to render the penguin first, followed by the checker box. The same goes for the other pair of images on the right: the butterfly gets rendered first, followed by the checker box:

To apply a composition effect to the image, we'll have to set the painter's composition mode before drawing the image, by calling the `painter.setCompositionMode()` function. You can pick a desired composition mode from the auto-complete menu by typing `QPainter::CompositionMode`.

In the previous example, we applied `QPainter::CompositionMode_Difference` to the checker box on the left, which inverted its color. Next, we applied `QPainter::CompositionMode_Overlay` to the penguin, which makes it blend with the checker, and were able to see both images overlaying each other. On the right-hand side, we applied `QPainter::CompositionMode_Xor` to the checker, where if differences exist between the source and destination, colors are shown; otherwise, it will be rendered black. Since it's comparing differences with the white background, the non-transparent part of the checker becomes completely black. We also applied `QPainter::CompositionMode_SoftLight` to the butterfly image. This blends the pixels with the background with reduced contrast. If you want to disable the composition mode that you've just set for the previous rendering before proceeding to the next, simply set it back to the default mode, which is `QPainter::CompositionMode_SourceOver`.

There's more...

For example, we can overlay multiple images on top of each other and use Qt's Image Composition feature to merge them together and calculate the resulting pixels onscreen, based on the composition mode we used. This is often used in image editing software such as Photoshop and GIMP to composite image layers.

There are more than 30 types of composition mode available in Qt. Some of the most commonly used modes are as follows:

- `Clear`: The pixels in the destination are set to fully transparent, independent of the source.
- `Source`: The output is the source pixel. This mode is the inverse of `CompositionMode_Destination`.
- `Destination`: The output is the destination pixel. This means that the blending has no effect. This mode is the inverse of `CompositionMode_Source`.
- `Source Over`: This is often referred to as alpha blending. The alpha of the source is used to blend the pixel on top of the destination. This is the default mode used by `QPainter`.

- Destination Over: The output is the blend between the alpha of the destination on top of the source pixels. The opposite of this mode is CompositionMode_SourceOver.
- Source In: The output is the source, where the alpha is reduced by that of the destination.
- Destination In: The output is the destination, where the alpha is reduced by that of the source. This mode is the inverse of CompositionMode_SourceIn.
- Source Out: The output is the source, where the alpha is reduced by the inverse of the destination.
- Destination Out: The output is the destination, where the alpha is reduced by the inverse of the source. This mode is the inverse of CompositionMode_SourceOut.
- Source Atop: The source pixel is blended on top of the destination, with the alpha of the source pixel reduced by the alpha of the destination pixel.
- Destination Atop: The destination pixel is blended on top of the source, with the alpha of the source pixel reduced by the alpha of the destination pixel. This mode is the inverse of CompositionMode_SourceAtop.
- Xor: This is short for **Exclusive OR**, which is an advanced blending mode that is primarily used for image analysis. Using this is much more complicated with this composition mode. First, the alpha of the source is reduced by the inverse of the destination alpha. Then, the alpha of the destination is reduced by the inverse of the source alpha. Finally, both the source and destination are then merged to produce the output.

For more, you can visit this link: pyside.github.io.

The following image shows the outcome of overlaying two images with different composition modes:

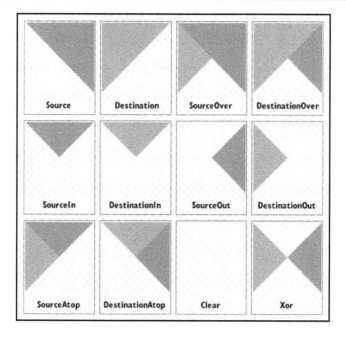

Applying image effects to graphics

Qt provides an easy way to add image effects to any graphics drawn using the `QPainter` class. In this example, we will learn how to apply different images effects such as drop shadow, blur, colorize, and opacity effects, to a graphic before displaying it onscreen.

How to do it...

Let's learn how to apply image effects to text and graphics by following these steps:

1. Create a new `Qt Widgets Application` project and remove the **menuBar**, **mainToolBar**, and **StatusBar**.

2. Create a new resource file by going to **File | New File or Project** and adding all the images required by the project:

3. Next, open up `mainwindow.ui` and add four labels to the window. Two of the labels will be text, and the two others we will load with the images we have just added to the resource file:

4. You may already notice that the font sizes are way bigger than the default size. That can be achieved by adding a style sheet to the label widget, for example, as follows:

```
font: 26pt "MS Shell Dlg 2";
```

5. After that, open up `mainwindow.cpp` and include the following headers at the top of the source code:

```
#include <QGraphicsBlurEffect>
#include <QGraphicsDropShadowEffect>
#include <QGraphicsColorizeEffect>
#include <QGraphicsOpacityEffect>
```

6. Then, within the constructor of the `MainWindow` class, add the following code to create a `DropShadowEffect`, and apply it to one of the labels:

```
MainWindow::MainWindow(QWidget *parent) : QMainWindow(parent),
ui(new Ui::MainWindow) {
    ui->setupUi(this);
    QGraphicsDropShadowEffect* shadow = new
    QGraphicsDropShadowEffect();
    shadow->setXOffset(4);
    shadow->setYOffset(4);
    ui->label->setGraphicsEffect(shadow);
}
```

7. Next, we will create a `ColorizedEffect` and apply it to one of the images, in this case the butterfly. We also set the effect color to red:

```
QGraphicsColorizeEffect* colorize = new
QGraphicsColorizeEffect();
colorize->setColor(QColor(255, 0, 0));
ui->butterfly->setGraphicsEffect(colorize);
```

8. Once we're done with that, create a `BlurEffect` and set its `radius` to 12. Then, apply the graphics effect to the other label:

```
QGraphicsBlurEffect* blur = new QGraphicsBlurEffect();
blur->setBlurRadius(12);
ui->label2->setGraphicsEffect(blur);
```

9. Lastly, create an `alpha` effect and apply it to the `penguin` image. We set the `opacity` value to `0.2`, which means 20% opacity:

```
QGraphicsOpacityEffect* alpha = new QGraphicsOpacityEffect();
alpha->setOpacity(0.2);
ui->penguin->setGraphicsEffect(alpha);
```

10. Compile and run the program now, and you should be able to see something like this:

How it works...

Each of the graphic effects is a class of its own that inherits the `QGraphicsEffect` parent class. You can create your own custom effect by creating a new class that inherits `QGraphicsEffect` and re-implementing some of the functions in it.

Each effect has its own set of variables that are specifically created for it. For example, you can set the color of the colorized effect, but there is no such variable in the blur effect. This is because each effect is vastly different from the others, which is also why it needs to be a class of its own rather than using the same class for all the different effects.

It's only possible to add a single graphics effect to a widget at a time. If you add more than one effect, only the last one will be applied to the widget, as it replaces the previous one. Other than that, be aware that if you create a graphics effect, say, the drop shadow effect, you can't assign it to two different widgets either, as it will only get assigned to the last widget you applied it to. If you need to apply the same type of effect to several different widgets, create a few graphics effects of the same type and apply each of them to their respective widgets.

There's more...

Currently, Qt supports blur, drop shadow, colorize, and opacity effects. These effects can be used by calling the following classes: `QGraphicsBlurEffect`, `QGraphicsDropShadowEffect`, `QGraphicsColorizeEffect`, and `QGraphicsOpacityEffect`. All these classes are inherited from the `QGraphicsEffect` class. You can also create your own custom image effect by creating a subclass of `QGrapicsEffect` (or any other existing effects) and re-implementing the `draw()` function.

The graphics effect changes only the bounding rectangle of the source. If you want to increase the margin of the bounding rectangle, re-implement the virtual `boundingRectFor()` function, and call `updateBoundingRect()` to notify the framework whenever this rectangle changes.

Creating a basic paint program

Since we have learned so much about the `QPainter` class and how to use it to display graphics onscreen, I guess it's time for us to do something fun with which we can put our knowledge into practice.

In this recipe, we will learn how to make a basic paint program that allows us to draw lines on a canvas with different brush sizes and colors. We will also learn how to use the `QImage` class and mouse events in order to construct the paint program.

How to do it...

Let's start our fun project through the following steps:

1. Again, we start by creating a new `Qt Widgets Application` project and removing the tool bar and status bar. We will keep the menu bar this time.

2. After that, set up the menu bar like so:

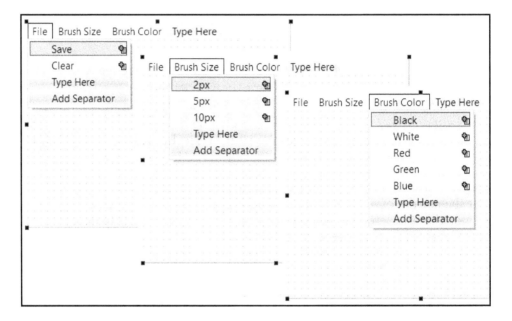

3. We will leave the menu bar as it is for the moment, so let's proceed to the `mainwindow.h` file. First, include the following header files, as they are required for the project:

```
#include <QPainter>
#include <QMouseEvent>
#include <QFileDialog>
```

4. Next, declare the variables that we'll be using for this project, like so:

```
private:
    Ui::MainWindow *ui;
    QImage image;
    bool drawing;
    QPoint lastPoint;
    int brushSize;
    QColor brushColor;
```

5. Then, declare the event callback functions, which are inherited from the `QWidget` class. These functions will be triggered by Qt when the respective event happens. We will override these functions and tell Qt what to do when these events get called:

```
public:
    explicit MainWindow(QWidget *parent = 0);
    ~MainWindow();
    virtual void mousePressEvent(QMouseEvent *event);
    virtual void mouseMoveEvent(QMouseEvent *event);
    virtual void mouseReleaseEvent(QMouseEvent *event);
    virtual void paintEvent(QPaintEvent *event);
    virtual void resizeEvent(QResizeEvent *event);
```

6. After that, go to the `mainwindow.cpp` file and add the following code to the class constructor to set up some of the variables:

```
MainWindow::MainWindow(QWidget *parent) : QMainWindow(parent),
ui(new Ui::MainWindow) {
    ui->setupUi(this);
    image = QImage(this->size(), QImage::Format_RGB32);
    image.fill(Qt::white);
    drawing = false;
    brushColor = Qt::black;
    brushSize = 2;
}
```

7. Next, we will construct the `mousePressEvent()` event and tell Qt what to do when the left mouse button is pressed:

```
void MainWindow::mousePressEvent(QMouseEvent *event) {
    if (event->button() == Qt::LeftButton) {
        drawing = true;
        lastPoint = event->pos();
    }
}
```

8. Then, we will construct the `mouseMoveEvent()` event and tell Qt what to do when the mouse is moving. In this case, we want to draw the lines on the canvas if the left mouse button is being held:

```
void MainWindow::mouseMoveEvent(QMouseEvent *event) {
    if ((event->buttons() & Qt::LeftButton) && drawing) {
        QPainter painter(&image);
        painter.setPen(QPen(brushColor, brushSize,
Qt::SolidLine, Qt::RoundCap, Qt::RoundJoin));
        painter.drawLine(lastPoint, event->pos());
```

```
                        lastPoint = event->pos();
                        this->update();
                }
        }
```

9. After that, we will also construct the `mouseReleaseEvent()` event, which will be triggered when the mouse button is released:

```
void MainWindow::mouseReleaseEvent(QMouseEvent *event) {
        if (event->button() == Qt::LeftButton) {
                drawing = false;
        }
}
```

10. Once you're done with that, we will proceed to the `paintEvent()` event, which is surprisingly simple compared to the other examples we have seen in previous sections:

```
void MainWindow::paintEvent(QPaintEvent *event) {
        QPainter canvasPainter(this);
        canvasPainter.drawImage(this->rect(), image, image.rect());
}
```

11. Remember how we have a menu bar sitting around doing nothing? Let's right-click on each of the actions below the GUI editor and select **Go to slot...** in the pop-up menu. We want to tell Qt what to do when each of these options on the menu bar is selected:

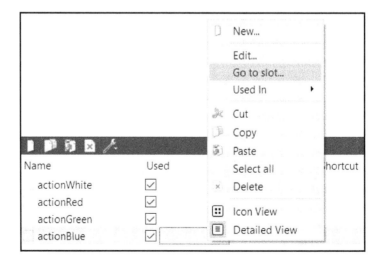

12. Then, select the default slot called **triggered()** and press the **OK** button. Qt will automatically generate a new slot function in both your `mainwindow.h` and `mainwindow.cpp` files. Once you are done with all the actions, you should see something like this in your `mainwindow.h` file:

```
private slots:
    void on_actionSave_triggered();
    void on_actionClear_triggered();
    void on_action2px_triggered();
    void on_action5px_triggered();
    void on_action10px_triggered();
    void on_actionBlack_triggered();
    void on_actionWhite_triggered();
    void on_actionRed_triggered();
    void on_actionGreen_triggered();
    void on_actionBlue_triggered();
```

13. Next, we will tell Qt what to do when each of these slots is triggered:

```
void MainWindow::on_actionSave_triggered() {
    QString filePath = QFileDialog::getSaveFileName(this, "Save
Image", "", "PNG (*.png);;JPEG (*.jpg *.jpeg);;All files
(*.*)");
    if (filePath == "")
        return;
    image.save(filePath);
}
void MainWindow::on_actionClear_triggered() {
    image.fill(Qt::white);
    this->update();
}
```

14. Then, we continue to implement the other slots:

```
void MainWindow::on_action2px_triggered() {
    brushSize = 2;
}
void MainWindow::on_action5px_triggered() {
    brushSize = 5;
}
void MainWindow::on_action10px_triggered() {
    brushSize = 10;
}
void MainWindow::on_actionBlack_triggered() {
    brushColor = Qt::black;
}
```

15. Finally, we implement the rest of the slot functions:

```
void MainWindow::on_actionWhite_triggered() {
    brushColor = Qt::white;
}
void MainWindow::on_actionRed_triggered() {
    brushColor = Qt::red;
}
void MainWindow::on_actionGreen_triggered() {
    brushColor = Qt::green;
}
void MainWindow::on_actionBlue_triggered() {
    brushColor = Qt::blue;
}
```

16. If we compile and run the program now, we will get a simple but usable paint program:

How it works...

In this example, we created a `QImage` widget when the program started. This widget acts as the canvas and will follow the size of the window whenever the window gets resized. In order to draw something on the canvas, we will need to use the mouse events provided by Qt. These events will tell us the position of the cursor, and we will be able to use this information to change the pixels on the canvas.

We use a Boolean variable called `drawing` to let the program know whether it should start drawing when a mouse button is pressed. In this case, when the left mouse button is pressed, the `drawing` variable will be set to `true`. We also save the current cursor position to the `lastPoint` variable when the left mouse button is pressed, so that Qt will know where it should start drawing. When the mouse moves, the `mouseMoveEvent()` event will be triggered by Qt. This is where we need to check whether the `drawing` variable is set to `true`. If it is, then `QPainter` can start drawing the lines onto the `QImage` widget based on the brush settings that we provide. The brush settings consist of `brushColor` and `brushSize`. These settings are being saved as variables and can be altered by selecting a different setting from the menu bar.

Please remember to call the `update()` function when the user is drawing on the canvas. Otherwise, the canvas will remain empty even though we have changed the pixel information of the canvas. We also have to call the `update()` function when we select **File | Clear** from the menu bar to reset our canvas.

In this example, we use `QImage::save()` to save the image file, which is very easy and straightforward. We use the file dialog to let the user decide where to save the image and its desired filename. Then, we pass the information to `QImage`, and it will do the rest by itself. If we don't specify the file format to the `QImage::save()` function, `QImage` will try to figure it out by looking at the extension of the desired filename.

Rendering a 2D canvas in QML

In all the previous examples of this chapter, we have discussed the methods and techniques used to render 2D graphics with Qt's C++ API. However, we have yet to learn how to achieve similar results using the powerful QML script.

How to do it...

In this project, we'll be doing something quite different:

1. As usual, the first step we should do is to create a new project by going to **File | New File or Project** and selecting **Qt Quick Application - Empty** as the project template:

2. Once you are done creating the new project, open up `main.qml`, which is listed under `qml.qrc` in the project pane. After that, set an ID for the window and adjust its `width` and `height` to larger values, like so:

```
import QtQuick 2.11
import QtQuick.Window 2.11

Window {
    id: myWindow
    visible: true
    width: 640
    height: 480
    title: qsTr("Hello World")
}
```

3. Then, add a `Canvas` object under `myWindow` and call it `myCanvas`. After that, we make its `width` and `height` the same as `myWindow`:

```
Window {
    id: myWindow
    visible: true
    width: 640
    height: 480
    Canvas {
        id: myCanvas
        width: myWindow.width
        height: myWindow.height
    }
}
```

5. Next, we define what will happen when the `onPaint` event is triggered; in this case, we will draw a cross on the window:

```
Canvas {
    id: myCanvas
    width: myWindow.width
    height: myWindow.height
    onPaint: {
        var context = getContext('2d')
        context.fillStyle = 'white'
        context.fillRect(0, 0, width, height)
        context.lineWidth = 2
        context.strokeStyle = 'black'
```

6. Let's continue to write the code, like so:

```
// Draw cross
context.beginPath()
context.moveTo(50, 50)
context.lineTo(100, 100)
context.closePath()
context.stroke()
context.beginPath()
context.moveTo(100, 50)
context.lineTo(50, 100)
context.closePath()
context.stroke()
    }
  }
```

7. After that, we add the following code to draw a tick beside the cross:

```
// Draw tick
context.beginPath()
context.moveTo(150, 90)
context.lineTo(158, 100)
context.closePath()
context.stroke()
context.beginPath()
context.moveTo(180, 100)
context.lineTo(210, 50)
context.closePath()
context.stroke()
```

8. Then, draw a triangle shape by adding the following code:

```
// Draw triangle
context.lineWidth = 4
context.strokeStyle = "red"
context.fillStyle = "salmon"
context.beginPath()
context.moveTo(50,150)
context.lineTo(150,150)
context.lineTo(50,250)
context.closePath()
context.fill()
context.stroke()
```

9. After that, draw a half circle and a full circle with the following code:

```
// Draw circle
context.lineWidth = 4
```

```
context.strokeStyle = "blue"
context.fillStyle = "steelblue"
var pi = 3.141592653589793
context.beginPath()
context.arc(220, 200, 60, 0, pi, true)
context.closePath()
context.fill()
context.stroke()
```

10. Then, we draw an arc:

```
context.beginPath()
context.arc(220, 280, 60, 0, 2 * pi, true)
context.closePath()
context.fill()
context.stroke()
```

11. Finally, we draw a 2D image from a file:

```
// Draw image
context.drawImage("tux.png", 280, 10, 150, 174)
```

12. However, the preceding code alone will not successfully render an image onscreen because you must also load the image file beforehand. Add the following code within the `Canvas` object to ask QML to load the image file when the program is started, then call the `requestPaint()` signal when the image is loaded so that the `onPaint()` event slot will be triggered:

```
onImageLoaded: requestPaint();
onPaint: {
    // The code we added previously
}
```

13. Then, open up `qml.qrc` by right-clicking it on the project panel, and select **Open in Editor**. After that, add the `tux.png` image file into our project resource:

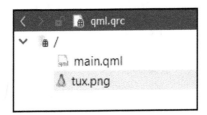

14. Build and run the program now, and you should get the following result:

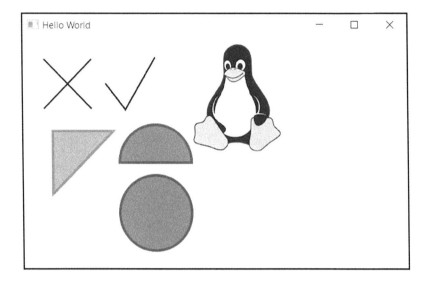

Isn't that wonderful?

5
OpenGL Implementation

n this chapter, we will cover the following recipes:

- Setting up **Open Graphics Library** (**OpenGL**) in Qt
- Hello World!
- Rendering 2D shapes
- Rendering 3D shapes
- Texturing in OpenGL
- Basic lighting in OpenGL
- Moving an object using keyboard controls
- 3D Canvas in QML

Introduction

In this chapter, we will learn how to use OpenGL, a powerful rendering **Application Program Interface** (**API**), and combine it with Qt. OpenGL is a cross-language, cross-platform API for drawing 2D and 3D graphics on screen through the **Graphics Processing Unit** (**GPU**) within our computer's graphics chip. In this chapter, we will be learning about OpenGL 3 instead of 2 because, even though the fixed-function pipeline is easier for beginners to grasp compared to the newer programmable pipeline, it is considered legacy code and has been deprecated by most modern 3D rendering software. Qt 5 supports both versions, so there should be no problem switching over to OpenGL 2 if you need backward compatibility for your software.

Technical requirements

The technical requirements for this chapter include Qt 5.11.2 MinGW 32-bit, Qt Creator 4.8.2, and Windows 10.

All of the code that's used in this chapter can be downloaded from the following GitHub link: `https://github.com/PacktPublishing/Qt5-CPP-GUI-Programming-Cookbook-Second-Edition/tree/master/Chapter05`.

Check out the following video to see the code in action: `http://bit.ly/2FrX4Ho`

Setting up OpenGL in Qt

In this recipe, we will learn how to set up OpenGL in Qt 5.

How to do it...

Follow these steps to learn how to set up OpenGL in Qt:

1. Create a new **Qt Widgets Application** by going to **File | New File or Project**.
2. We will remove the `mainwindow.ui` file because we are not going to use it in this example. Right-click on the `mainwindow.ui` file and select **Remove File** from the dropdown menu. Then, a message box will appear and ask for your confirmation. Tick **Delete file permanently** and press the **OK** button.
3. Repeat Step 2 for both `mainwindow.h` and `mainwindow.cpp` as well. We don't need these two files in this project either.
4. Open up your project file (`.pro`) and add the `OpenGL` module to your project by adding an `opengl` keyword behind `QT +=`, like so:

   ```
   QT += core gui opengl
   ```

5. You also need to add another line in your project file so that it will load both the `OpenGL` and `GLu` (OpenGL Utilities) libraries during startup. Without these two libraries, your program will not be able to run:

   ```
   LIBS += -lopengl32 -lglu32
   ```

6. Open up `main.cpp` and replace `mainwindow.h` with the `QtOpenGL` header:

```
#include <QtOpenGL>
```

7. Remove all of the code related to the `MainWindow` class from your `main.cpp` file and replace it with the code that's highlighted in the following snippet:

```
#include <QApplication>
#include <QtOpenGL>

int main(int argc, char *argv[]) {
    QApplication app(argc, argv);

    QOpenGLWindow window;
    window.setTitle("Hello World!");
    window.resize(640, 480);
    window.show();

    return app.exec();
}
```

8. If you compile and run the project now, you will see an empty window with a black background. Don't worry about it—your program is now running on OpenGL:

How it works...

The `OpenGL` module must be added to the project file (`.pro`) in order to access header files that are related to OpenGL, such as `QtOpenGL` and `QOpenGLFunctions`. We used the `QOpenGLWindow` class instead of `QMainWindow` for the main window because it is designed to easily create windows that perform OpenGL rendering, and it offers better performance compared to `QOpenGLWidget` due to the fact that it has no dependencies in its widget module.

We must call `setSurfaceType(QWindow::OpenGLSurface)` to tell Qt we prefer to use OpenGL to render the images to screen instead of `QPainter`. The `QOpenGLWindow` class provides several virtual functions (`initializeGL()`, `resizeGL()`, `paintGL()`, and so on) for us to conveniently set up OpenGL and perform graphics rendering. We will be learning how to use these functions in the following example.

There's more...

OpenGL is a cross-language, cross-platform API for drawing 2D and 3D graphics on screen through the GPU within our computer's graphics chip. Computer graphics technology has been evolving rapidly over the years—so rapidly that the software industry can hardly keep up with its pace.

In 2008, Khronos Group, the company that maintains and develops OpenGL, announced the release of the OpenGL 3.0 specification, which created a huge uproar and controversy throughout the industry. That was mainly because OpenGL 3.0 was supposed to deprecate the entire fixed-function pipeline from the OpenGL API, and it was simply an impossible task for the big players to make the sudden switch overnight from a fixed-function pipeline to a programmable pipeline. This resulted in two different major versions of OpenGL being maintained.

In this chapter, we will use the newer OpenGL 3 instead of the older, deprecated OpenGL 2. The coding style and syntax are very different between this two versions, which makes the switch over very troublesome. However, the performance improvement will make it worth the time switching over to OpenGL 3.

Hello World!

In this chapter, we will learn how to use OpenGL 3 with Qt 5. Common OpenGL functions such as `glBegin`, `glVertex2f`, `glColor3f`, `glMatrixMode`, and `glLoadIdentity` have all been removed from OpenGL 3. OpenGL 3 uses vertex buffer objects to send data to the GPU in batches instead of sending them one by one through functions such as `glVertex2f()`, which slows down the rendering while waiting for the CPU to submit the data one by one. Therefore, we will pack all of the data into vertex buffer objects and send it all in one huge package to the GPU and instruct the GPU to calculate the resulting pixels through shader programming. We will also be learning about how to create simple shader programs through a C-like programming language called **OpenGL Shading Language** (GLSL).

How to do it...

Let's get started by following these steps:

1. We will create a new class called `RenderWindow`, which inherits from the `QOpenGLWindow` class. Go to **File** | **New File or Project**, then select **C++ Class** under **Files and Classes** category. Name the class `RenderWindow` and set its base class as `QOpenGLWindow`. Then, proceed to create the C++ class:

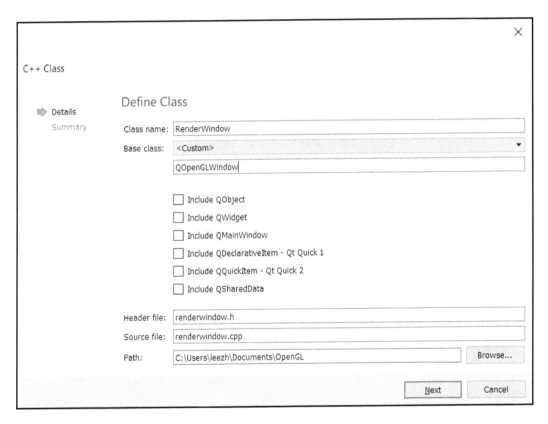

2. Go to the `renderwindow.h` file we just created and add the following headers at the top of the source code:

```
#include <GL/glu.h>
#include <QtOpenGL>
#include <QSurfaceFormat>
#include <QOpenGLFunctions>
#include <QOpenGLWindow>
#include <QOpenGLBuffer>
```

```
#include <QOpenGLVertexArrayObject>
#include <QOpenGLShader>
#include <QOpenGLShaderProgram>
```

3. We need to create several functions and variables that look like this:

```
class RenderWindow : public QOpenGLWindow {
public:
    RenderWindow();

protected:
    void initializeGL();
    void paintGL();
    void paintEvent(QPaintEvent *event);
    void resizeEvent(QResizeEvent *event);
```

4. We will continue and add some private variables:

```
private:
    QOpenGLContext* openGLContext;
    QOpenGLFunctions* openGLFunctions;
    QOpenGLShaderProgram* shaderProgram;
    QOpenGLVertexArrayObject* vao;
    QOpenGLBuffer* vbo_vertices;
};
```

5. Open up `renderwindow.cpp` and define the class constructor, as follows. We must tell the render window to use the OpenGL surface type; enable core profile (rather than compatibility profile) that runs version 3.2; create an OpenGL context; and, finally, apply the profile we just created into the context:

```
RenderWindow::RenderWindow() {
    setSurfaceType(QWindow::OpenGLSurface);

    QSurfaceFormat format;
    format.setProfile(QSurfaceFormat::CoreProfile);
    format.setVersion(3, 2);
    setFormat(format);

    openGLContext = new QOpenGLContext();
    openGLContext->setFormat(format);
    openGLContext->create();
    openGLContext->makeCurrent(this);
}
```

6. We need to define the `initializeGL()` function, as follows. This function will be called before the rendering starts. First, we define the vertex and fragment shaders:

```
void RenderWindow::initializeGL() {
    openGLFunctions = openGLContext->functions();

    static const char *vertexShaderSource =
    "#version 330 core\n"
    "layout(location = 0) in vec2 posAttr;\n"
    "void main() {\n"
    "gl_Position = vec4(posAttr, 0.0, 1.0); }";

    static const char *fragmentShaderSource =
    "#version 330 core\n"
    "out vec4 col;\n"
    "void main() {\n"
    "col = vec4(1.0, 0.0, 0.0, 1.0); }";
```

7. We initiate `shaderProgram` and declare a `vertices` array. Then, we also create a `QOpenGLVertexArrayObject` object:

```
shaderProgram = new QOpenGLShaderProgram(this);
shaderProgram->addShaderFromSourceCode(QOpenGLShader::Vertex,
vertexShaderSource);
shaderProgram->addShaderFromSourceCode(QOpenGLShader::Fragment,
fragmentShaderSource);
shaderProgram->link();

GLfloat vertices[] = {
-1.0f, -1.0f,
1.0f, -1.0f,
0.0f, 1.0f };

vao = new QOpenGLVertexArrayObject();
vao->create();
vao->bind();
```

8. Let's continue to write our code by defining `vbo_vertices`:

```
vbo_vertices = new QOpenGLBuffer(QOpenGLBuffer::VertexBuffer);
vbo_vertices->create();
vbo_vertices->setUsagePattern(QOpenGLBuffer::StaticDraw);
vbo_vertices->bind();
vbo_vertices->allocate(vertices, sizeof(vertices) *
sizeof(GLfloat));

    vao->release();
}
```

9. We will start by adding some code to the `paintEvent()` function:

```
void RenderWindow::paintEvent(QPaintEvent *event) {
    Q_UNUSED(event);
    glViewport(0, 0, width(), height());
    glClearColor(0.39f, 0.58f, 0.93f, 1.f);
    glClear(GL_COLOR_BUFFER_BIT);
```

10. We will then bind the VAO and shader program before calling `glDrawArrays()`:

```
vao->bind();
shaderProgram->bind();
shaderProgram->bindAttributeLocation("posAttr", 0);
shaderProgram->enableAttributeArray(0);
shaderProgram->setAttributeBuffer(0, GL_FLOAT, 0, 2);
glDrawArrays(GL_TRIANGLES, 0, 3);
shaderProgram->release();
vao->release();
}
```

11. You can refresh the viewport whenever the render window is being resized by adding the following code:

```
void RenderWindow::resizeEvent(QResizeEvent *event) {
    Q_UNUSED(event);
    glViewport(0, 0, this->width(), this->height());
    this->update();
}
```

12. If you compile and run the project now, you should be able to see a red rectangle being drawn in front of a blue background:

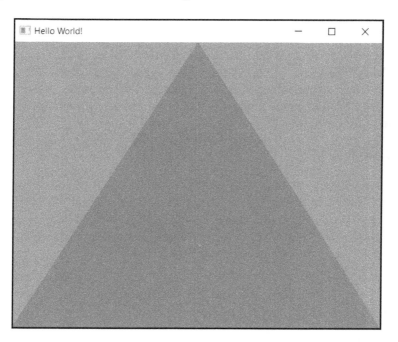

How it works...

We must set the OpenGL version to 3.x and the surface format to core profile so that we can access the newer shader pipeline, which is completely different from the older, deprecated compatibility profile. OpenGL 2.x still exists in the compatibility profile, solely for the sake of allowing OpenGL programs to run on old hardware. The profile that's created must be applied to the OpenGL context before it will work.

In OpenGL 3 and the later versions, most of the calculations are done in the GPU through shader programs, since all of the common fixed functions have now been completely deprecated. Therefore, we created a very simple vertex shader and fragment shader in the preceding example.

A shader program consists of three different parts: geometry shader (optional), vertex shader, and fragment shader. The geometry shader calculates the creation of geometry before passing the data to vertex shader; the vertex shader handles the position and motion of the vertices before passing the data to the fragment shader; and finally, the fragment shader calculates and displays the resulting pixels on screen.

In the preceding example, we only used vertex and fragment shaders, and excluded the geometry shader since it is optional. You can save the GLSL code in a text file and load it in to your Qt 5 program by calling `addShaderFromFile()`, but since our shaders are very simple and short, we just define it directly in our C++ source code.

After that, we use something called the **Vertex Buffer Object** (**VBO**) to store the vertex positions in bulk before sending it to the GPU. We can also use the VBO to store other information such as normals, texture coordinates, and vertex colors. You can send anything you want to the GPU as long as it matches the input inside your shader code. Then, we add the VBO into a **Vertex Array Object** (**VAO**) and send the whole VAO to the GPU for processing. You can add many different VBOs into the VAO, since the VAO is just like any ordinary C++ array.

Just like what we have learned in the previous chapters, all drawings happen within the `paintEvent()` function, and it will only be called by Qt when it thinks it is necessary to refresh the screen. To force Qt to update the screen, call `update()` manually. Also, we must update the viewport whenever the window screen has been resized, by calling `glViewport(x, y ,width, height)`.

Rendering 2D shapes

Since we have already learned how to draw our first rectangle on screen, we will further enhance it in this section. We will take the previous example and continue from there.

How to do it...

Let's get started by following this example:

1. Open up `renderwindow.h` and add two more VBOs, one called `vbo_vertices2` and another called `vbo_colors`, as highlighted in the following code:

```
private:
    QOpenGLContext* openGLContext;
    QOpenGLFunctions* openGLFunctions;
    QOpenGLShaderProgram* shaderProgram;
    QOpenGLVertexArrayObject* vao;
    QOpenGLBuffer* vbo_vertices;
    QOpenGLBuffer* vbo_vertices2;
    QOpenGLBuffer* vbo_colors;
```

2. Open up `renderwindow.cpp` and add the following code to the shader code, as highlighted in the following snippet:

```
static const char *vertexShaderSource =
    "#version 330 core\n"
    "layout(location = 0) in vec2 posAttr;\n"
    "layout(location = 1) in vec3 colAttr;\n"
    "out vec3 fragCol;\n"
    "void main() {\n"
    "fragCol = colAttr;\n"
    "gl_Position = vec4(posAttr, 1.0, 1.0); }";
```

3. Add the highlighted code to the fragment shader, which looks like this:

```
static const char *fragmentShaderSource =
    "#version 330 core\n"
    "in vec3 fragCol;\n"
    "out vec4 col;\n"
    "void main() {\n"
    "col = vec4(fragCol, 1.0); }";
```

4. Change the `vertices` array to something like this:

```
GLfloat vertices[] = {
    -0.3f, -0.5f,
    0.8f, -0.4f,
    0.2f, 0.6f };

GLfloat vertices2[] = {
    0.5f, 0.3f,
    0.4f, -0.8f,
    -0.6f, -0.2f };

GLfloat colors[] = {
    1.0f, 0.0f, 0.0f,
    0.0f, 1.0f, 0.0f,
    0.0f, 0.0f, 1.0f };
```

5. Since we already initialized `vbo_vertices` in the previous example, this time, we only need to initialize two other VBOs, namely `vbo_vertices` and `vbo_colors`:

```
vbo_vertices2 = new QOpenGLBuffer(QOpenGLBuffer::VertexBuffer);
vbo_vertices2->create();
vbo_vertices2->setUsagePattern(QOpenGLBuffer::StaticDraw);
vbo_vertices2->bind();
vbo_vertices2->allocate(vertices2, sizeof(vertices2) *
```

```
        sizeof(GLfloat));

        vbo_colors = new QOpenGLBuffer(QOpenGLBuffer::VertexBuffer);
        vbo_colors->create();
        vbo_colors->setUsagePattern(QOpenGLBuffer::StaticDraw);
        vbo_colors->bind();
        vbo_colors->allocate(colors, sizeof(colors) * sizeof(GLfloat));
```

6. Before we start drawing the triangle using glDrawArrays(), we must also add the data of vbo_colors into our shader's colAttr attribute. Make sure you call bind() to set the VBO as the current active VBO, before sending the data to the shader. The location ID (in this case, 0 and 1) must match the location ID that's used in your shader:

```
        vbo_vertices->bind();
        shaderProgram->bindAttributeLocation("posAttr", 0);
        shaderProgram->enableAttributeArray(0);
        shaderProgram->setAttributeBuffer(0, GL_FLOAT, 0, 2);

        vbo_colors->bind();
        shaderProgram->bindAttributeLocation("colAttr", 1);
        shaderProgram->enableAttributeArray(1);
        shaderProgram->setAttributeBuffer(1, GL_FLOAT, 0, 3);

        glDrawArrays(GL_TRIANGLES, 0, 3);
```

7. Right after the preceding code, we will send vbo_vertices2 and vbo_colors to the shader attribute and call glDrawArrays() again to draw the second triangle:

```
        vbo_vertices2->bind();
        shaderProgram->bindAttributeLocation("posAttr", 0);
        shaderProgram->enableAttributeArray(0);
        shaderProgram->setAttributeBuffer(0, GL_FLOAT, 0, 2);

        vbo_colors->bind();
        shaderProgram->bindAttributeLocation("colAttr", 1);
        shaderProgram->enableAttributeArray(1);
        shaderProgram->setAttributeBuffer(1, GL_FLOAT, 0, 3);

        glDrawArrays(GL_TRIANGLES, 0, 3);
```

8. If you build the program now, you should be able to see two triangles on screen, and one of the triangles sitting on top of the other:

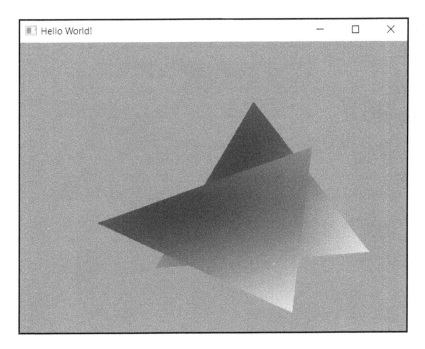

How it works...

The geometric primitive types supported by OpenGL are points, lines, linestrips, line loops, polygons, quads, quad strips, triangles, triangle strips, and triangle fans. In this example, we drew two triangles, where each of the shapes is provided with a set of vertices and colors so that OpenGL knows how the shapes should be rendered.

The rainbow color effect is created by giving a different color to each of the vertices. OpenGL will automatically interpolate the colors between each vertex and display it on screen. Currently, the shape that gets rendered first will appear at the back of other shapes that get rendered later. This is because we are rendering the shapes in a 2D space and no depth information is involved to check which shape is located at the front and so on. We will learn how to do depth checking in the following example.

Rendering 3D shapes

We learned how to draw simple 2D shapes onscreen in the previous section. However, to fully utilize the OpenGL API, we also need to learn how to use it to render 3D images. In a nutshell, 3D images are simply illusions that are created using 2D shapes, stacked in such a way that it makes them look like they're 3D.

How to do it...

The main ingredient here is the depth value, which determines which shapes should appear in front of or behind the other shapes. The primitive shape that is positioned behind another surface (with a shallower depth than another shape) will not be rendered (or will be partially rendered). OpenGL provides a simple way to achieve this:

1. Let's continue our project from the previous 2D example. Enable depth testing by adding glEnable(GL_DEPTH_TEST) to the initializeGL() function in renderwindow.cpp:

```
void RenderWindow::initializeGL()
{
    openGLFunctions = openGLContext->functions();
    glEnable(GL_DEPTH_TEST);
```

2. We will change our vertices array into something longer, which is the vertex information of a 3D cube shape. We can remove the colors array for now since you are not supplying the color information to the shader this time. We can also remove the vbo_colors VBO for the same reason:

```
GLfloat vertices[] = {
    -1.0f,-1.0f,-1.0f,1.0f,-1.0f,-1.0f,-1.0f,-1.0f, 1.0f,
    1.0f,-1.0f,-1.0f,1.0f,-1.0f, 1.0f,-1.0f,-1.0f, 1.0f,
    -1.0f, 1.0f,-1.0f,-1.0f, 1.0f, 1.0f,1.0f, 1.0f,-1.0f,
    1.0f, 1.0f,-1.0f,-1.0f, 1.0f, 1.0f,1.0f, 1.0f, 1.0f,
    -1.0f,-1.0f, 1.0f,1.0f,-1.0f, 1.0f,-1.0f, 1.0f, 1.0f,
    1.0f,-1.0f, 1.0f,1.0f, 1.0f, 1.0f,-1.0f, 1.0f, 1.0f,
    -1.0f,-1.0f,-1.0f,-1.0f, 1.0f,-1.0f,1.0f,-1.0f,-1.0f,
    1.0f,-1.0f,-1.0f,-1.0f, 1.0f,-1.0f,1.0f, 1.0f,-1.0f,
    -1.0f,-1.0f, 1.0f,-1.0f, 1.0f,-1.0f,-1.0f,-1.0f,-1.0f,
    -1.0f,-1.0f, 1.0f,-1.0f, 1.0f, 1.0f,-1.0f, 1.0f,-1.0f,
    1.0f,-1.0f, 1.0f,1.0f,-1.0f,-1.0f,1.0f, 1.0f,-1.0f,
    1.0f,-1.0f, 1.0f,1.0f, 1.0f,-1.0f,1.0f, 1.0f, 1.0f
};
```

3. In the `paintEvent()` function, we must add `GL_DEPTH_BUFFER_BIT` to the `glClear()` function since we enabled depth checking in `initializeGL()` in the previous step:

```
glClear(GL_COLOR_BUFFER_BIT | GL_DEPTH_BUFFER_BIT);
```

4. After that, we need to send a matrix information to the shader called **Model-View-Projection** (**MVP**) so that the GPU knows how render the 3D shapes on a 2D screen. The MVP matrix is the result of multiplication between the projection matrix, view matrix, and model matrix. The multiplication order is very important so that you get the correct result:

```
QMatrix4x4 matrixMVP;
QMatrix4x4 model, view, projection;
model.translate(0, 1, 0);
model.rotate(45, 0, 1, 0);
view.lookAt(QVector3D(5, 5, 5), QVector3D(0, 0, 0),
QVector3D(0, 1, 0));
projection.perspective(60.0f,
((float)this->width()/(float)this->height()), 0.1f, 100.0f);
matrixMVP = projection * view * model;
shaderProgram->setUniformValue("matrix", matrixMVP);
```

5. Change the last value in `glDrawArrays()` to 36 since we now have 36 triangles in the cube shape:

```
glDrawArrays(GL_TRIANGLES, 0, 36);
```

6. We have to go back to our shader code and change some parts of it, as highlighted in the following code:

```
static const char *vertexShaderSource =
    "#version 330 core\n"
    "layout(location = 0) in vec3 posAttr;\n"
    "uniform mat4 matrix;\n"
    "out vec3 fragPos;\n"
    "void main() {\n"
    "fragPos = posAttr;\n"
    "gl_Position = matrix * vec4(posAttr, 1.0); }";

static const char *fragmentShaderSource =
    "#version 330 core\n"
    "in vec3 fragPos;\n"
    "out vec4 col;\n"
    "void main() {\n"
    "col = vec4(fragPos, 1.0); }";
```

7. If you build and run the project now, you should see a colorful cube appear on the screen. We use the same `vertices` array for the color, which gives this colorful result:

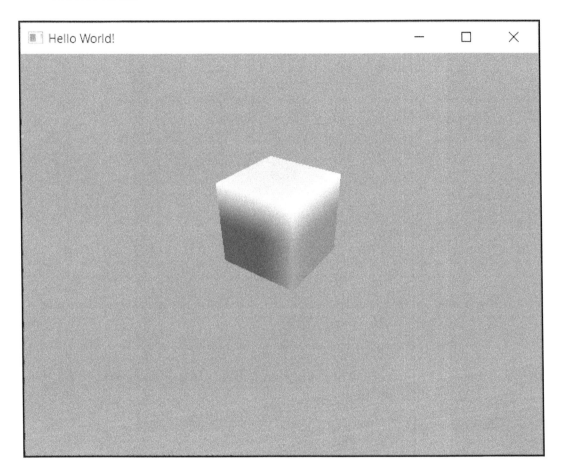

8. Even though the result looks pretty good, if we want to really show off the 3D effect, it would be by animating the cube. To do that, first, we need to open up `renderwindow.h` and add the following variables to it. Note that you are allowed to initialize variables in the header file in modern C++ standard, which was not the case back in the older C++ standard:

```
QTime* time;
int currentTime = 0;
int oldTime = 0;
float deltaTime = 0;
float rotation = 0;
```

9. Open up `renderwindow.cpp` and add the following highlighted code to the class constructor:

```
openGLContext = new QOpenGLContext();
openGLContext->setFormat(format);
openGLContext->create();
openGLContext->makeCurrent(this);

time = new QTime();
time->start();
```

10. After that, add the following highlighted code to the top of your `paintEvent()` function. `deltaTime` is the value of the elapsed time of each frame, which is used to make animation speed consistent, regardless of frame rate performance:

```
void RenderWindow::paintEvent(QPaintEvent *event) {
    Q_UNUSED(event);
    // Delta time for each frame
    currentTime = time->elapsed();
    deltaTime = (float)(currentTime - oldTime) / 1000.0f;
    oldTime = currentTime;
```

11. Add the following highlighted code on top of your MVP matrix code and apply the `rotation` variable to the `rotate()` function, like so:

```
rotation += deltaTime * 50;

QMatrix4x4 matrixMVP;
QMatrix4x4 model, view, projection;
model.translate(0, 1, 0);
model.rotate(rotation, 0, 1, 0);
```

12. Call the `update()` function at the end of the `paintEvent()` function so that `paintEvent()` will be called again and again at the end of each draw call. Since we are changing the `rotation` value in the `paintEvent()` function, we can give the viewer the illusion of a rotating cube:

```
glDrawArrays(GL_TRIANGLES, 0, 36);

shaderProgram->release();
vao->release();

this->update();
}
```

13. If you compile and run the program now, you should see a spinning cube in your render window!

How it works...

In any 3D rendering, depth is very important and hence we need to enable the depth testing feature in OpenGL by calling `glEnable(GL_DEPTH_TEST)`. When we clear the buffer, we must also specify `GL_DEPH_BUFFER_BIT` so that the depth information is also being cleared, in order for the next image to be rendered correctly.

We use the MVP matrix in OpenGL so that the GPU knows how to render the 3D graphics correctly. In OpenGL 3 and later versions, OpenGL no longer handles this automatically through fixed functions. Programmers are given the freedom and flexibility to define their own matrices based on their use cases, then simply supply it to the GPU through a shader for rendering the final image. The model matrix contains the transformation data of the 3D object, namely the position, rotation, and scale of the object. The view matrix, on the other hand, is the camera or view information. Lastly, the projection matrix tells the GPU which projection method to use when projecting the 3D world onto the 2D screen.

In our example, we used the **perspective** projection method, which gives better perception of distance and depth. The opposite of perspective projection is **orthographic** projection, which makes everything look flat and parallel:

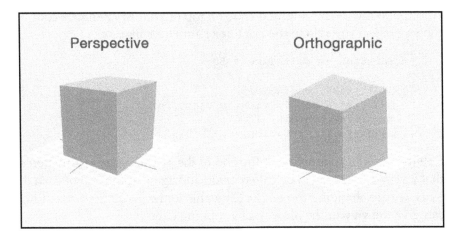

In this example, we used a timer to increase the rotation value by 50. Multiplying it with the `deltaTime` value. The `deltaTime` value varies, depending on your rendering frame rate. However, it makes the resulting animation speed consistent across different hardware that renders at a different frame rate.

Remember to call `update()` manually so that the screen gets refreshed, otherwise the cube will not be animated.

Texturing in OpenGL

OpenGL allows us to map an image (also referred to as a texture) to a 3D shape or polygon. This process is also called texture mapping. Qt 5 appears to be the best combination with OpenGL in this case because it provides an easy way to load images that belong to one of the common formats (BMP, JPEG, PNG, TARGA, TIFF, and so on), and you do not have to implement it by yourself. We will use the previous example with a spinning cube and try to map it with a texture!

How to do it...

Let's follow these steps to learn how to use textures in OpenGL:

1. Open up `renderwindow.h` and add the variables, that are highlighted in the following code block:

```
QOpenGLContext* openGLContext;
QOpenGLFunctions* openGLFunctions;
QOpenGLShaderProgram* shaderProgram;
QOpenGLVertexArrayObject* vao;
QOpenGLBuffer* vbo_vertices;
QOpenGLBuffer* vbo_uvs;
QOpenGLTexture* texture;
```

2. We must call `glEnable(GL_TEXTURE_2D)` in the `initializeGL()` function to enable the texture mapping feature:

```
void RenderWindow::initializeGL()
{
    openGLFunctions = openGLContext->functions();
    glEnable(GL_DEPTH_TEST);
    glEnable(GL_TEXTURE_2D);
```

3. We need to initialize our `texture` variable under the `QOpenGLTexture` class. We will load a texture image called `brick.jpg` from our application folder and flip the image by calling `mirrored()`. OpenGL uses a different coordinate system, which is why we need to flip our texture before passing it to the shader. We will also set the `min` and `max` filters to `Nearest` and `Linear` accordingly, like so:

```
texture = new QOpenGLTexture(QImage(qApp->applicationDirPath()
+ "/brick.jpg").mirrored());
texture->setMinificationFilter(QOpenGLTexture::Nearest);
texture->setMagnificationFilter(QOpenGLTexture::Linear);
```

4. Add another array called `uvs`. This is where we save the texture coordinates for our cube object:

```
GLfloat uvs[] = {
    0.0f, 0.0f, 1.0f, 0.0f, 0.0f, 1.0f,
    1.0f, 0.0f, 1.0f, 1.0f, 0.0f, 1.0f,
    0.0f, 0.0f, 0.0f, 1.0f, 1.0f, 0.0f,
    1.0f, 0.0f, 0.0f, 1.0f, 1.0f, 1.0f,
    1.0f, 0.0f, 0.0f, 0.0f, 1.0f, 1.0f,
    0.0f, 0.0f, 0.0f, 1.0f, 1.0f, 1.0f,
    0.0f, 0.0f, 0.0f, 1.0f, 1.0f, 0.0f,
    1.0f, 0.0f, 0.0f, 1.0f, 1.0f, 1.0f,
    0.0f, 1.0f, 1.0f, 0.0f, 0.0f, 0.0f,
    0.0f, 1.0f, 1.0f, 1.0f, 1.0f, 0.0f,
    1.0f, 1.0f, 1.0f, 0.0f, 0.0f, 0.0f,
    1.0f, 1.0f, 0.0f, 0.0f, 0.0f, 1.0f
};
```

5. We have to amend our vertex shader so that it takes in the texture coordinates for calculating where the texture will be applied to the object surface. Here, we simply pass the texture coordinate to the fragment shader without modifying:

```
static const char *vertexShaderSource =
    "#version 330 core\n"
    "layout(location = 0) in vec3 posAttr;\n"
    "layout(location = 1) in vec2 uvAttr;\n"
    "uniform mat4 matrix;\n"
    "out vec3 fragPos;\n"
    "out vec2 fragUV;\n"
    "void main() {\n"
    "fragPos = posAttr;\n"
    "fragUV = uvAttr;\n"
    "gl_Position = matrix * vec4(posAttr, 1.0); }";
```

6. In the fragment shader, we create a texture by calling the `texture()` function, which receives the texture coordinate information from `fragUV` and the image sampler from `tex`:

```
static const char *fragmentShaderSource =
    "#version 330 core\n"
    "in vec3 fragPos;\n"
    "in vec2 fragUV;\n"
    "uniform sampler2D tex;\n"
    "out vec4 col;\n"
    "void main() {\n"
    "vec4 texCol = texture(tex, fragUV);\n"
    "col = texCol; }";
```

7. We have to initialize the VBO for texture coordinate as well:

```
vbo_uvs = new QOpenGLBuffer(QOpenGLBuffer::VertexBuffer);
vbo_uvs->create();
vbo_uvs->setUsagePattern(QOpenGLBuffer::StaticDraw);
vbo_uvs->bind();
vbo_uvs->allocate(uvs, sizeof(uvs) * sizeof(GLfloat));
```

8. In the `paintEvent()` function, we must send the texture coordinate information to the shader and then bind the texture before calling `glDrawArrays()`:

```
vbo_uvs->bind();
shaderProgram->bindAttributeLocation("uvAttr", 1);
shaderProgram->enableAttributeArray(1);
shaderProgram->setAttributeBuffer(1, GL_FLOAT, 0, 2);

texture->bind();
glDrawArrays(GL_TRIANGLES, 0, 36);
```

9. If you compile and run the program now, you should see a brick cube rotating on the screen:

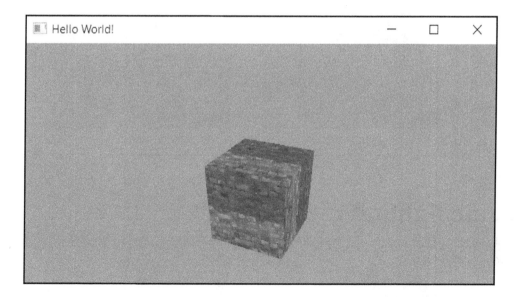

How it works...

Qt 5 makes loading textures a really easy job. All it takes is just a single line of code to load an image file, flip it, and convert it into an OpenGL-compatible texture. The texture coordinates are pieces information that let OpenGL know how to stick the texture onto the object's surface before displaying it on screen.

The `min` and `max` filters are filters that make the texture look better when it is applied on a surface that is bigger than what its resolution can cover. The default setting for this is **GL_NEAREST**, which stands for **nearest neighbor filtering**. This filter tends to make texture look pixelated when viewed close up. Another common setting is **GL_LINEAR**, which stands for **bilinear filtering**. This filter takes two neighboring fragments and interpolates them to create an approximated color, which looks a lot better than **GL_NEAREST**:

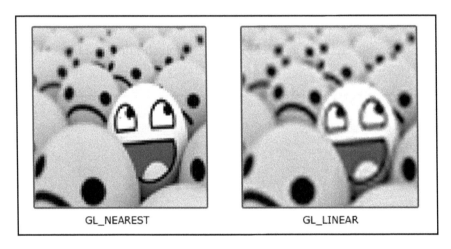

Basic lighting in OpenGL

In this example, we will learn how to add a simple point light to our 3D scene by using OpenGL and Qt 5.

How to do it...

Let's get started by following these steps:

1. Again, we will use the previous example and add a point light near the spinning cube. Open up `renderwindow.h` and add another variable called `vbo_normals` to the file:

```
QOpenGLBuffer* vbo_uvs;
QOpenGLBuffer* vbo_normals;
QOpenGLTexture* texture;
```

2. Open `renderwindow.cpp` and add another array called `normals` to the `initializeGL()` function:

```
GLfloat normals[] = {
    0.0f, -1.0f, 0.0f, 0.0f, -1.0f, 0.0f, 0.0f, -1.0f, 0.0f,
    0.0f, -1.0f, 0.0f, 0.0f, -1.0f, 0.0f, 0.0f, -1.0f, 0.0f,
    0.0f, 1.0f, 0.0f, 0.0f, 1.0f, 0.0f, 0.0f, 1.0f, 0.0f,
    0.0f, 1.0f, 0.0f, 0.0f, 1.0f, 0.0f, 0.0f, 1.0f, 0.0f,
    1.0f, 0.0f, 0.0f, 1.0f, 0.0f, 0.0f, 1.0f, 0.0f, 0.0f,
    1.0f, 0.0f, 0.0f, 1.0f, 0.0f, 0.0f, 1.0f, 0.0f, 0.0f,
    0.0f, 0.0f, 1.0f, 0.0f, 0.0f, 1.0f, 0.0f, 0.0f, 1.0f,
    0.0f, 0.0f, 1.0f, 0.0f, 0.0f, 1.0f, 0.0f, 0.0f, 1.0f,
    -1.0f, 0.0f, 0.0f, -1.0f, 0.0f, 0.0f, -1.0f, 0.0f, 0.0f,
    -1.0f, 0.0f, 0.0f, -1.0f, 0.0f, 0.0f, -1.0f, 0.0f, 0.0f,
    0.0f, 0.0f, -1.0f, 0.0f, 0.0f, -1.0f, 0.0f, 0.0f, -1.0f,
    0.0f, 0.0f, -1.0f, 0.0f, 0.0f, -1.0f, 0.0f, 0.0f, -1.0f
};
```

3. Initialize the `vbo_normals` VBO in `initializeGL()` by adding the following code:

```
vbo_normals = new QOpenGLBuffer(QOpenGLBuffer::VertexBuffer);
vbo_normals->create();
vbo_normals->setUsagePattern(QOpenGLBuffer::StaticDraw);
vbo_normals->bind();
vbo_normals->allocate(normals, sizeof(normals) *
sizeof(GLfloat));
```

4. Since the shader we will be writing this time will be much longer than what we used in the previous examples, let's move the shader code over to text files and load them into the program by calling `addShaderFromSourceFile()`:

```
shaderProgram = new QOpenGLShaderProgram(this);
shaderProgram->addShaderFromSourceFile(QOpenGLShader::Vertex,
qApp->applicationDirPath() + "/vertex.txt");
shaderProgram->addShaderFromSourceFile(QOpenGLShader::Fragment,
qApp->applicationDirPath() + "/fragment.txt");
shaderProgram->link();
```

5. Once you are done with that, add the following code to the `paintEvent()` function to pass the normals VBO over to the shader:

```
vbo_normals->bind();
shaderProgram->bindAttributeLocation("normalAttr", 2);
shaderProgram->enableAttributeArray(2);
shaderProgram->setAttributeBuffer(2, GL_FLOAT, 0, 3);
```

6. Let's open up the two text files we just created that contain the shader code. First, we need to make some changes to the vertex shader, like so:

```
#version 330 core
layout(location = 0) in vec3 posAttr;
layout(location = 1) in vec2 uvAttr;
layout(location = 2) in vec3 normalAttr;
uniform mat4 matrix;
out vec3 fragPos;
out vec2 fragUV;
out vec3 fragNormal;

void main() {
    fragPos = posAttr;
    fragUV = uvAttr;
    fragNormal = normalAttr;
    gl_Position = matrix * vec4(posAttr, 1.0);
}
```

7. We will also make some changes to the fragment shader. We will create a function called `calcPointLight()` in the shader code:

```
#version 330 core
in vec3 fragPos;
in vec2 fragUV;
in vec3 fragNormal;
uniform sampler2D tex;
out vec4 col;
```

```
vec3 calcPointLight() {
    vec4 texCol = texture(tex, fragUV);
    vec3 lightPos = vec3(1.0, 2.0, 1.5);
    vec3 lightDir = normalize(lightPos - fragPos);
    vec4 lightColor = vec4(1.0, 1.0, 1.0, 1.0);
    float lightIntensity = 1.0;
```

8. Continuing from the preceding code, we calculated the lighting using `calcPointLight()` and output the resulting fragment to the `col` variable, as follows:

```
    // Diffuse
    float diffuseStrength = 1.0;
    float diff = clamp(dot(fragNormal, lightDir), 0.0, 1.0);
    vec4 diffuse = diffuseStrength * diff * texCol * lightColor
* lightIntensity;
    return diffuse;
}

void main() {
    vec3 finalColor = calcPointLight();
    col = vec4(finalColor, 1.0);
}
```

9. If you compile and run the program now, you should see the lighting in action:

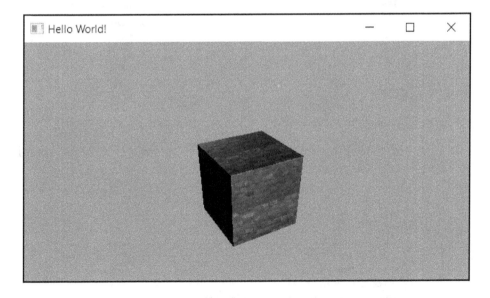

How it works...

In OpenGL 3 and later versions, fixed function lighting no longer exists. You can no longer call `glEnable(GL_LIGHT1)` to add light to your 3D scene. The new method for adding light is to calculate your own lighting in the shader. This gives you the flexibility of creating all types of lights, depending on your needs. The old method has a limitation of up to 16 lights in most hardware but, with the new programmable pipeline, you can have any number of lights in the scene; however, the lighting model will need to be coded entirely by you in the shaders, which is not an easy task.

Other than that, we also need to add a surface normal value to every surface of the cube. Surface normal indicates where the surface is facing and is used for lighting calculations.

The preceding example is very simplified to let you understand how lighting works in OpenGL. In actual use cases, you may need to pass some variables such as light intensity, light color, and light position from C++ or load it from a material file instead of hardcoding it in the shader code.

Moving an object using keyboard controls

In this section, we will be looking at how to move an object in OpenGL using keyboard controls. Qt provides an easy way to detect keyboard events using virtual functions, namely `keyPressEvent()` and `keyReleaseEvent()`. We will be using the previous example and adding to it.

How to do it...

To move an object using keyboard controls, follow these steps:

1. Open up `renderwindow.h` and declare two floating-point numbers called `moveX` and `moveZ`. Then, declare a `QVector3D` variable called `movement`:

```
QTime* time;
int currentTime = 0;
int oldTime = 0;
float deltaTime = 0;
float rotation = 0;
float moveX = 0;
float moveZ = 0;
QVector3D movement = QVector3D(0, 0, 0);
```

2. We will also declare two functions called `keyPressEvent()` and `keyReleaseEvent()`:

```
protected:
    void initializeGL();
    void paintEvent(QPaintEvent *event);
    void resizeEvent(QResizeEvent *event);
    void keyPressEvent(QKeyEvent *event);
    void keyReleaseEvent(QKeyEvent *event);
```

3. We will implement the `keyPressEvent()` function in `renderwindow.cpp`:

```
void RenderWindow::keyPressEvent(QKeyEvent *event) {
    if (event->key() == Qt::Key_W) { moveZ = -10; }
    if (event->key() == Qt::Key_S) { moveZ = 10; }
    if (event->key() == Qt::Key_A) { moveX = -10; }
    if (event->key() == Qt::Key_D) { moveX = 10; }
}
```

4. We will also implement the `keyReleaseEvent()` function:

```
void RenderWindow::keyReleaseEvent(QKeyEvent *event) {
    if (event->key() == Qt::Key_W) { moveZ = 0; }
    if (event->key() == Qt::Key_S) { moveZ = 0; }
    if (event->key() == Qt::Key_A) { moveX = 0; }
    if (event->key() == Qt::Key_D) { moveX = 0; }
}
```

5. After that, we will comment out the rotation code in `paintEvent()` and add the movement code, as highlighted in the following snippet. We do not want to get distracted by the rotation and just want to focus on the movement:

```
//rotation += deltaTime * 50;
movement.setX(movement.x() + moveX * deltaTime);
movement.setZ(movement.z() + moveZ * deltaTime);

QMatrix4x4 matrixMVP;
QMatrix4x4 model, view, projection;
model.translate(movement.x(), 1, movement.z());
```

6. If you compile and run the program now, you should be able to move the cube around by pressing *W*, *A*, *S*, and *D*.

How it works...

What we did here was constantly add the `moveX` and `moveZ` value's `movement` vector's x and z values. When a key is pressed, `moveX` and `moveZ` will become a positive or negative number, depending on which button is pressed; otherwise, it will be zero. In the `keyPressEvent()` function, we checked whether the keyboard button that was pressed was *W*, *A*, *S*, or *D*; we then set the variables accordingly. To get the full list of key names that are used by Qt, visit `http://doc.qt.io/qt-5/qt.html#Key-enum`.

One way we can do the movement input is by holding down the same key and not releasing it. Qt 5 will repeat the key press event after an interval, but it is not very fluid as modern operating systems limit the key press event to prevent double typing. The keyboard input interval varies between different operating systems. You can set the interval by calling `QApplication::setKeyboardInterval()`, but this may not work on every operating system. Therefore, we did not go for this method.

Instead, we only set `moveX` and `moveZ` once when the key was pressed or released, and then we constantly apply the value to the `movement` vector in our game loop so that it is moving continuously without being affected by the input interval.

3D canvas in QML

In this recipe, we will learn how to render 3D images using Qt 5.

How to do it...

Let's learn how to use a 3D canvas in QML by following this example:

1. Let's start this example by creating a new project in Qt Creator. This time around, we will go for **Qt Quick Application—Canvas 3D** and not the other options that we chose in the previous examples:

2. After that, Qt Creator will ask you whether to create a project that is based on the `three.js` JavaScript library. Check the **Create a three.js based application** option and press the **Next** button to proceed:

3. Once the project is created, you will notice that there are some JavaScript (.js) files already in to your project's resources. This is normal as the Qt Canvas 3D application uses JavaScript and WebGL technology to render 3D images on screen. In this case, it is running a WebGL-based rendering library called three.js, which makes our programming job simpler and easier compared to writing pure WebGL code:

4. Add an image file to our project resources—we will be using it in this example. Open up qml.qrc with Qt Creator by right-clicking on it in the **Projects** pane and selecting **Open in Editor**. Once the resources file is opened by Qt Creator, click the **Add** button, followed by the **Add File** button, and then select the image file you want from your computer. In my case, I've added a brick.jpg image, which will be used as the surface texture for our 3D object:

5. After that, open up `glcode.js` using Qt Creator. You will see that there is already plenty of code written in the file. What it does is basically render a simple 3D cube on screen using the `three.js` library. You can build the project right away and run it to see what it looks like. However, we will change the code a little bit to customize its output.

6. In the `initializeGL()` function, we will add a directional light to the scene, load the texture file we just added to our project resources, and then apply the texture to the material that defines the surface properties of the 3D cube:

```
function initializeGL(canvas) {
    scene = new THREE.Scene();
    camera = new THREE.PerspectiveCamera(75, canvas.width /
canvas.height, 0.1, 1000);
    camera.position.z = 5;
    var directionalLight = new
THREE.DirectionalLight(0xffffff);
    directionalLight.position.set(1, 1, 1).normalize();
    scene.add(directionalLight);
    var texture = THREE.ImageUtils.loadTexture('brick.jpg');
    var material = new THREE.MeshLambertMaterial({ map: texture
});
```

7. We will also make the scale of the cube slightly bigger by setting its scale to 3 in all dimensions. We also set the background color to a light gray color:

```
    var cubeGeometry = new THREE.BoxGeometry(3, 3, 3);
    cube = new THREE.Mesh(cubeGeometry, material);
    cube.rotation.set(0.785, 0.785, 0.0);
    scene.add(cube);
    renderer = new THREE.Canvas3DRenderer({ canvas: canvas,
antialias: true, devicePixelRatio: canvas.devicePixelRatio });
    renderer.setSize(canvas.width, canvas.height);
    renderer.setClearColor(0xa9a9a9, 1);
}
```

8. In the `paintGL()` function, add an extra line of code to rotate the 3D cube before rendering the scene:

```
function paintGL(canvas) {
    cube.rotation.y -= 0.005;
    renderer.render(scene, camera);
}
```

9. I personally find the window size to be a little bit too small, so I also changed the `width` and `height` of the window in the `main.qml` file, as highlighted in the following code:

```
import QtQuick 2.4
import QtCanvas3D 1.0
import QtQuick.Window 2.2
import "glcode.js" as GLCode
Window {
    title: qsTr("Qt_Canvas_3D")
    width: 800
    height: 600
    visible: true
```

10. Once you are done, build and run the project. You should be able to see a 3D cube with a brick texture, spinning slowly on the screen:

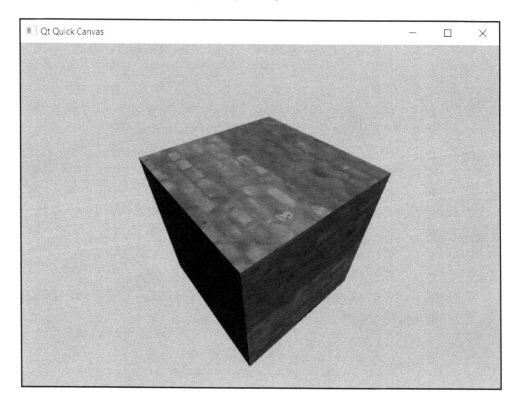

How it works...

Originally, three.js was a cross-browser JavaScript library/API that used WebGL technology to display animated 3D computer graphics in a web browser. Qt Canvas 3D, however, also uses web technology, specifically the WebGL technology, to render 3D images like it would on a web browser. This means that not only is three.js supported on Qt Canvas 3D, but all of the different types of library that are based on the WebGL technology will work flawlessly on Qt Canvas 3D. However, Qt Canvas 3D only works on QML-based projects and does not work in C++.

 If you are interested to learn more about three.js, check out their website at http://threejs.org.

6
Using Network and Managing Large Documents

In this chapter, we will cover the following recipes:

- Creating a TCP server
- Creating a TCP client
- Uploading and downloading files using FTP

Introduction

In this chapter, we will learn how to use create a networking server program and a client program using Qt 5's networking module. We will also learn how to create a program that uses **File Transfer Protocol** (**FTP**) to upload and download files from the server. Lastly, we will learn how to send HTTP requests to a specific web service using Qt 5 and C++ language.

Technical requirements

The technical requirements for this chapter include Qt 5.11.2 MinGW 32 bit, Qt Creator 4.8.2, Windows 10, FileZilla Server 0.9.60.

All the code used in this chapter can be downloaded from the following GitHub link: `https://github.com/PacktPublishing/Qt5-CPP-GUI-Programming-Cookbook-Second-Edition/tree/master/Chapter06`.

Check out the following video to see the code in action: `http://bit.ly/2TqR9XQ`

Creating a TCP server

In this recipe, we will learn how to create a **Transmission Control Protocol** (**TCP**) server in Qt 5. Before we're able to create a server that lets you upload and download files, let's scale it down a bit and learn how to create a networking server that receives and delivers texts.

How to do it...

Follow these steps to create a TCP server:

1. First, let's create a **Qt Console Application** project from **File** | **New File or Project**, as shown in the following screenshot:

2. After that, go to **File** | **New File or Project** again. But this time, select **C++ Class** under the **C++** category, as shown in the following screenshot:

3. Then, name your class as `server`. Set its base class to `QObject` and make sure the **Include QObject** option is checked before clicking the **Next** button. Once the class has been created, two files will be created for you—`server.h` and `server.cpp`, as shown in the following screenshot:

4. After that, open up your project file (`.pro`) and add in the `network` module, as shown in the following code:

```
QT += core network
```

5. Once you're done, open up `server.h` and add the following headers to it:

```
#include <QTcpServer>
#include <QTcpSocket>
#include <QVector>
#include <QDebug>
```

6. Right after that, declare `startServer()` and `sendMessageToClients()` functions, as shown in the following code:

```
public:
    server(QObject *parent = nullptr);
    void startServer();
    void sendMessageToClients(QString message);
```

7. Then declare the following slot functions for the `server` class:

```
public slots:
    void newClientConnection();
    void socketDisconnected();
    void socketReadReady();
    void socketStateChanged(QAbstractSocket::SocketState
state);
```

8. Finally, declare two private variables, as shown in the following code:

```
private:
    QTcpServer* chatServer;
    QVector<QTcpSocket*>* allClients;
```

9. Once you're done with the preceding step, open up `server.cpp` and define the `startServer()` function. Here, we create a `QVector` container to store all the clients that are connected to the server and use it to send out messages in later steps. This is shown in the following example:

```
void server::startServer() {
    allClients = new QVector<QTcpSocket*>;
    chatServer = new QTcpServer();
    chatServer->setMaxPendingConnections(10);
    connect(chatServer, &QTcpServer::newConnection, this,
&server::newClientConnection);
    if (chatServer->listen(QHostAddress::Any, 8001))
        qDebug() << "Server has started. Listening to port
8001.";
    else
        qDebug() << "Server failed to start. Error: " +
chatServer->errorString();
}
```

10. Next, we implement the `sendMessageToClients()` function, where we iterate through the `allClients` container we just created in the previous step, and send the message to each of them, as shown in the following example:

```
void server::sendMessageToClients(QString message) {
    if (allClients->size() > 0) {
        for (int i = 0; i < allClients->size(); i++) {
            if (allClients->at(i)->isOpen() &&
allClients->at(i)->isWritable()) {
                allClients->at(i)->write(message.toUtf8());
            }
        }
    }
}
```

11. After that, we will start implementing the slot functions. Let's start off with the following code:

```
void server::newClientConnection() {
    QTcpSocket* client = chatServer->nextPendingConnection();
    QString ipAddress = client->peerAddress().toString();
    int port = client->peerPort();
    connect(client, &QTcpSocket::disconnected, this,
&server::socketDisconnected);
    connect(client, &QTcpSocket::readyRead,this,
&server::socketReadReady);
    connect(client, &QTcpSocket::stateChanged, this,
&server::socketStateChanged);
    allClients->push_back(client);
    qDebug() << "Socket connected from " + ipAddress + ":" +
QString::number(port);
}
```

12. Then, we'll proceed with the `socketDisconnected()` function. This slot function will be called when a client has been disconnected from the server, as shown in the following example:

```
void server::socketDisconnected() {
    QTcpSocket* client =
qobject_cast<QTcpSocket*>(QObject::sender());
    QString socketIpAddress = client->peerAddress().toString();
    int port = client->peerPort();
    qDebug() << "Socket disconnected from " + socketIpAddress +
":" + QString::number(port);
}
```

13. Next, we'll define the `socketReadReady()` function, which will be triggered when a client is sending in a text message to the server, as shown in the following example:

```
void server::socketReadReady() {
    QTcpSocket* client =
qobject_cast<QTcpSocket*>(QObject::sender());
    QString socketIpAddress = client->peerAddress().toString();
    int port = client->peerPort();
    QString data = QString(client->readAll());
    qDebug() << "Message: " + data + " (" + socketIpAddress +
":" + QString::number(port) + ")";
    sendMessageToClients(data);
}
```

14. After that, let's implement the `socketStateChanged()` function, which will be called when the networking state of a client has changed, as shown in the following example:

```
void server::socketStateChanged(QAbstractSocket::SocketState
state) {
    QTcpSocket* client =
qobject_cast<QTcpSocket*>(QObject::sender());
    QString socketIpAddress = client->peerAddress().toString();
    int port = client->peerPort();

    qDebug() << "Socket state changed (" + socketIpAddress +
":" + QString::number(port) + "): " + desc;
}
```

15. We also need to add the following code into `socketStateChanged()` to print out the status of the client:

```
QString desc;
if (state == QAbstractSocket::UnconnectedState)
    desc = "The socket is not connected.";
else if (state == QAbstractSocket::HostLookupState)
    desc = "The socket is performing a host name lookup.";
else if (state == QAbstractSocket::ConnectingState)
    desc = "The socket has started establishing a connection.";
else if (state == QAbstractSocket::ConnectedState)
    desc = "A connection is established.";
else if (state == QAbstractSocket::BoundState)
    desc = "The socket is bound to an address and port.";
else if (state == QAbstractSocket::ClosingState)
    desc = "The socket is about to close (data may still be
waiting to be written).";
```

```
        else if (state == QAbstractSocket::ListeningState)
            desc = "For internal use only.";
```

16. Lastly, let's open up `main.cpp`, and add the highlighted code in the following example in order to initiate the server:

```
#include <QCoreApplication>
#include "server.h"

int main(int argc, char *argv[]) {
    QCoreApplication a(argc, argv);
    server* myServer = new server();
    myServer->startServer();
    return a.exec();
}
```

17. You can try and run the server program now, but you won't be able to test it as we have not created the client program yet, as the following screenshot shows:

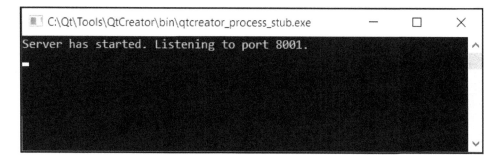

18. Let's proceed to the next example project and learn how to create the client program. We will come back to test this program again later on.

How it works...

There are mainly two types of network connections— the **Transmission Control Protocol (TCP)** connection and the **User Datagram Protocol (UDP)** connection. TCP is a reliable networking connection, while UDP is unreliable.

These two connections are designed for very different purposes:

- **TCP networking** is usually for programs that require every single piece of data to be sent and received in order. It also makes sure that the client receives the data and that the server gets notified for that. Programs like messaging software, web servers and databases use TCP networking.
- **UDP networking**, on the other hand, does not require constant handholding between the server and client. Since the connection is unreliable, there is also no feedback on whether the data has been successfully received. Dropping of packet is tolerated, and data may not even come in the same order as it was sent. UDP connections are usually used by applications that stream huge amounts of data to their clients without strict requirements on its packet delivery, such as video games, video conferencing software, and domain name systems.

Creating networking software using Qt 5 is a lot easier through its signals and slots mechanism. All we need to do is to connect the signals emitted by the QTcpServer class and QTcpSocket class to our slot functions. We will then implement these slot functions and define what to do within those functions.

 We used a **QVector** container to store the pointers to all the clients that have connected to the server so that we can use it to deliver the messages later on.

To keep this example project simple, we simply send text messages to all the clients, sort of like a group chat. You are free to explore other possibilities and make your own changes to improve the program.

Creating a TCP client

Since we have created a TCP server in the previous recipe, we now need a client program to complete the project. Therefore, in this recipe, we will learn how to create a TCP client program using Qt 5 and its networking module.

How to do it...

To create a TCP client in Qt 5, let's do the following:

1. First off, let's create a new **Qt Widgets Application** project from **Files | New File or Project**.

2. Once the project has been created, let's open up `mainwindow.ui` and set up the GUI as shown in the following diagram. Please note that the layout direction of the central widget has to be vertical:

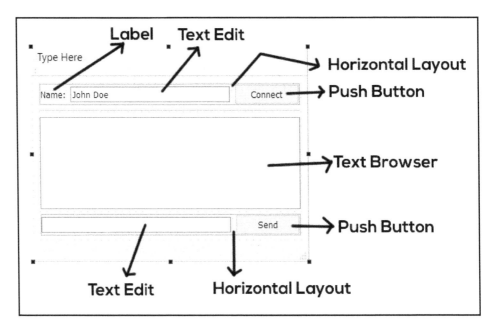

3. Then, right-click on the push button that says **Connect** and create a `clicked()` slot function from the menu. Then, repeat the same step on the **Send** button as well. As a result, two slot functions will be created for you in the source code, which may or may not look like what we see in the following code, depending on your widget's name:

```
void on_connectButton_clicked();
void on_sendButton_clicked();
```

4. Next, open up `mainwindow.h` and add the following headers:

```
#include <QDebug>
#include <QTcpSocket>
```

5. Then, declare the `printMessage()` function and three slot functions: `socketConnected()`, `socketDisconnected()`, and `socketReadyRead()`, as shown in the following code:

```
public:
    explicit MainWindow(QWidget *parent = 0);
    ~MainWindow();
    void printMessage(QString message);

private slots:
    void on_connectButton_clicked();
    void on_sendButton_clicked();
    void socketConnected();
    void socketDisconnected();
    void socketReadyRead();
```

6. After that, declare the following variables as well:

```
private:
    Ui::MainWindow *ui;
    bool connectedToHost;
    QTcpSocket* socket;
```

7. Once you're done with that, you can proceed to `mainwindow.cpp` and define the `printMessage()` function, as shown in the following example:

```
void MainWindow::printMessage(QString message) {
    ui->chatDisplay->append(message);
}
```

8. Then, we'll implement the `on_connectButton_clicked()` function, which will be triggered when the **Connect** button has been clicked, as shown in the following code:

```
void MainWindow::on_connectButton_clicked() {
    if (!connectedToHost) {
        socket = new QTcpSocket();
        connect(socket, &QTcpSocket::connected, this,
&MainWindow::socketConnected);
        connect(socket, &QTcpSocket::disconnected, this,
&MainWindow::socketDisconnected);
        connect(socket, &QTcpSocket::readyRead, this,
&MainWindow::socketReadyRead);
        socket->connectToHost("127.0.0.1", 8001);
    } else {
        QString name = ui->nameInput->text();
        socket->write("<font color=\"Orange\">" + name.toUtf8()
```

```
          + " has left the chat room.</font>");
               socket->disconnectFromHost();
          }
     }
```

9. We also define the `on_sendButton_clicked()` function, which will be called when the **Send** button has been clicked, as shown in the following example:

```
void MainWindow::on_sendButton_clicked() {
     QString name = ui->nameInput->text();
     QString message = ui->messageInput->text();
     socket->write("<font color=\"Blue\">" + name.toUtf8() +
"</font>: " + message.toUtf8());
     ui->messageInput->clear();
}
```

10. Right after that, we implement the `socketConnected()` function, which will be called when the client program has been successfully connected to the server, as shown in the following code:

```
void MainWindow::socketConnected() {
     qDebug() << "Connected to server.";
     printMessage("<font color=\"Green\">Connected to
server.</font>");
     QString name = ui->nameInput->text();
     socket->write("<font color=\"Purple\">" + name.toUtf8() + "
has joined the chat room.</font>");
     ui->connectButton->setText("Disconnect");
     connectedToHost = true;
}
```

11. We are not yet done at this point. We also need to implement the `socketDisconnected()` function, which will be triggered whenever the client has been disconnected from the server, as shown in the following code:

```
void MainWindow::socketDisconnected() {
     qDebug() << "Disconnected from server.";
     printMessage("<font color=\"Red\">Disconnected from
server.</font>");
     ui->connectButton->setText("Connect");
     connectedToHost = false;
}
```

12. Lastly, we also need to define the `socketReadyRead()` function, which prints out the message sent from the server, as shown in the following example:

```
void MainWindow::socketReadyRead() {
    printMessage(socket->readAll());
}
```

13. Before we run the client program, we must first turn on the server program which we have created in the previous recipe. Then, build and run the client program. Once the program has been opened, go and click the **Connect** button. After you have successfully connected to the server, type something in the line edit widget located at the bottom and press the **Send** button. You should see something similar to the following screenshot:

14. Let's go to the server program, shown in the following screenshot, and see whether there is anything printed on the terminal window:

```
C:\Qt\Tools\QtCreator\bin\qtcreator_process_stub.exe                              —    □    ×
Server has started. Listening to port 8001.
"Socket connected from ::ffff:127.0.0.1:54597"
"Message: <font color=\"Purple\">John Doe has joined the chat room.</font> (::ffff:127.0.0.1:54597)"
"Message: <font color=\"Blue\">John Doe</font>: Hello everyone! (::ffff:127.0.0.1:54597)"
"Socket state changed (::ffff:127.0.0.1:54597): The socket is about to close (data may still be waiting to be written)."

"Socket state changed (::ffff:127.0.0.1:54597): The socket is not connected."
"Socket disconnected from ::ffff:127.0.0.1:54597"
```

15. Congratulations, you have successfully created a program that looks a bit like an **Internet Relay Chat (IRC)** chat room!

How it works...

In order for this to work, we need two programs: a server program that connects all the clients and delivers their messages, and a client program used by the users to send and receive messages from other users.

Since the server program just sits behind the scenes and works out everything in silence, it doesn't need any user interface, and thus we only need it as a Qt Console Application.

The client program, however, requires a visually pleasant yet easy-to-use GUI for the users to read and write their messages. Therefore, we created the client program as a Qt Widgets Application instead.

The client program is relatively simple when compared to the server program. All it does is to connect to the server, send out the message input by the user, and print out everything the server sent to it.

Uploading and downloading files using FTP

We have learned how to create simple chat software which distributes text messages among the users. Next, we will learn how to create a program that uploads and downloads files using FTP.

How to do it...

Let's get started by observing the following steps:

1. For this project, we need to install software called **FileZilla Server**, which we will use as the FTP server. FileZilla server can be downloaded from `https://filezilla-project.org` by clicking on the **Download FileZilla Server** button, as shown in the following screenshot:

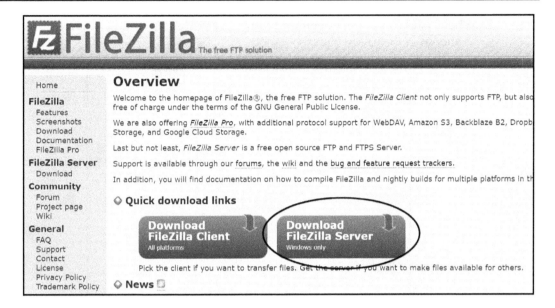

2. Once you have downloaded the installer, run it and install **FileZilla Server** by agreeing to all the default options, as shown in the following screenshot:

3. When it has completed, open up FileZilla Server and press the **Connect** button, as shown in the following screenshot:

4. After the server has been started, click on the user icon located at the top of the FileZilla Server control panel, as highlighted in the following screenshot:

5. Once the **Users** window has been opened, click on the **Add** button located under the **Users** list to add a new user. Then, add a shared folder under the **Shared folders** list, where your users will be uploading and downloading files from, as shown in the following screenshot:

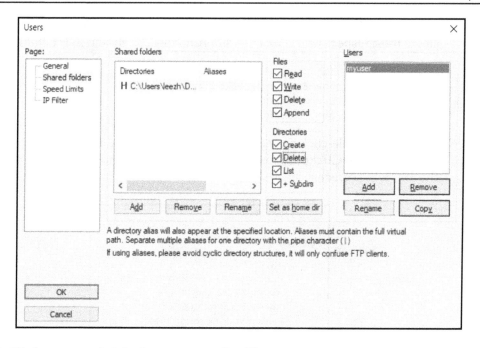

6. We have now finished setting up **FileZilla Server**. Let's move on to Qt Creator and create a new **Qt Widgets Application** project. Then, open up `mainwindow.ui` and set up the GUI, as shown in the following diagram:

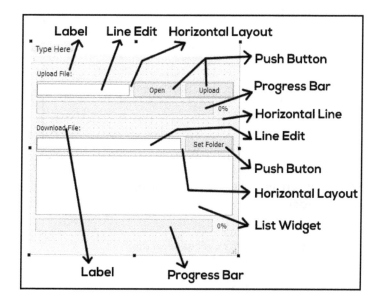

7. Then, right-click on the **Open** button, **Upload** button, and **Set Folder** button and create their respective `clicked()` slot functions, as shown in the following code:

```
private slots:
    void on_openButton_clicked();
    void on_uploadButton_clicked();
    void on_setFolderButton_clicked();
```

8. After that, double-click on the list widget and select **Go to slot....** Then, select the **itemDoubleClicked(QListWidgetItem*)** option and click **OK**, as shown in the following screenshot:

9. Once you have created the slot function, open up `mainwindow.h` and add the following headers:

```
#include <QDebug>
#include <QNetworkAccessManager>
#include <QNetworkRequest>
#include <QNetworkReply>
#include <QFile>
#include <QFileInfo>
```

```
#include <QFileDialog>
#include <QListWidgetItem>
#include <QMessageBox>
```

10. Then, declare the `getFileList()` function, as follows:

```
public:
    explicit MainWindow(QWidget *parent = 0);
    ~MainWindow();
    void getFileList();
```

11. Then declare the following slot functions:

```
void downloadFileListFinished();
void uploadFileListFinished();
void uploadFileProgress(qint64 bytesSent, qint64 bytesTotal);
void uploadFileFinished();
void downloadFileProgress(qint64 byteReceived,qint64
bytesTotal);
void downloadFileFinished();
```

12. Right after that, declare the following variables:

```
private:
    Ui::MainWindow *ui;
    QNetworkAccessManager* manager;
    QString ftpAddress;
    int ftpPort;
    QString username;
    QString password;
    QNetworkReply* downloadFileListReply;
    QNetworkReply* uploadFileListReply;
    QNetworkReply* uploadFileReply;
    QNetworkReply* downloadFileReply;
    QStringList fileList;
    QString uploadFileName;
    QString downloadFileName;
```

13. Then, open up `mainwindow.cpp` and add the following code to the class constructor:

```
MainWindow::MainWindow(QWidget *parent) : QMainWindow(parent),
ui(new Ui::MainWindow) {
    ui->setupUi(this);
    manager = new QNetworkAccessManager(this);
    ftpAddress = "ftp://127.0.0.1/";
    ftpPort = 21;
    username = "myuser";
```

```
        password = "123456";
        getFileList();
}
```

14. After that, implement the `getFileList()` function, as shown in the following code:

```
void MainWindow::getFileList() {
    QUrl ftpPath;
    ftpPath.setUrl(ftpAddress + "files.txt");
    ftpPath.setUserName(username);
    ftpPath.setPassword(password);
    ftpPath.setPort(ftpPort);
    QNetworkRequest request;
    request.setUrl(ftpPath);
    downloadFileListReply = manager->get(request);
    connect(downloadFileListReply, SIGNAL(finished()), this,
SLOT(downloadFileListFinished()));
}
```

15. Then, define the `on_openButton_clicked()` slot function, which gets triggered when the **Open** button has been clicked, as shown in the following code:

```
void MainWindow::on_openButton_clicked() {
    QString fileName = QFileDialog::getOpenFileName(this,
"Select File", qApp->applicationDirPath());
    ui->uploadFileInput->setText(fileName);
}
```

16. Once you're done with that, implement the slot function that gets called when the **Upload** button has been clicked, as shown in the following example:

```
void MainWindow::on_uploadButton_clicked() {
    QFile* file = new QFile(ui->uploadFileInput->text());
    QFileInfo fileInfo(*file);
    uploadFileName = fileInfo.fileName();

    QUrl ftpPath;
    ftpPath.setUrl(ftpAddress + uploadFileName);
    ftpPath.setUserName(username);
    ftpPath.setPassword(password);
    ftpPath.setPort(ftpPort);

    if (file->open(QIODevice::ReadOnly)) {
        ui->uploadProgress->setEnabled(true);
        ui->uploadProgress->setValue(0);
```

17. Then, continue to implement the previous function, as shown in the following code:

```
QNetworkRequest request;
request.setUrl(ftpPath);

uploadFileReply = manager->put(request, file);
connect(uploadFileReply, QNetworkReply::uploadProgress,
this, &MainWindow::uploadFileProgress);
connect(uploadFileReply, QNetworkReply::finished, this,
&MainWindow::uploadFileFinished);
    } else {
        QMessageBox::warning(this, "Invalid File", "Failed to
open file for upload.");
    }
}
```

18. The following code shows what the on_setFolderButton_clicked() slot function looks like:

```
void MainWindow::on_setFolderButton_clicked() {
    QString folder = QFileDialog::getExistingDirectory(this,
tr("Open Directory"), qApp->applicationDirPath(),
QFileDialog::ShowDirsOnly);
    ui->downloadPath->setText(folder);
}
```

19. Next, define the slot function which will be triggered when one of the list widget's items gets double-clicked, as shown in the following code:

```
void MainWindow::on_fileList_itemDoubleClicked(QListWidgetItem
*item) {
    downloadFileName = item->text();

    QString folder = ui->downloadPath->text();
    if (folder != "" && QDir(folder).exists()) {
        QUrl ftpPath;
        ftpPath.setUrl(ftpAddress + downloadFileName);
        ftpPath.setUserName(username);
        ftpPath.setPassword(password);
        ftpPath.setPort(ftpPort);
```

20. Then, continue to implement the previous function by using the following code:

```
QNetworkRequest request;
request.setUrl(ftpPath);

downloadFileReply = manager->get(request);
connect(downloadFileReply, QNetworkReply::downloadProgress,
this, MainWindow::downloadFileProgress);
connect(downloadFileReply, &QNetworkReply::finished, this,
&MainWindow::downloadFileFinished);
    } else {
        QMessageBox::warning(this, "Invalid Path", "Please set
the download path before download.");
    }
}
```

21. We're not quite done yet. Next, we will implement the `downloadFileListFinished()` function, which will be called automatically when the file list has been downloaded from the server, as shown in the following code:

```
void MainWindow::downloadFileListFinished() {
    if(downloadFileListReply->error() !=
QNetworkReply::NoError)
        QMessageBox::warning(this, "Failed", "Failed to load
file list: " + downloadFileListReply->errorString());
    else {
        QByteArray responseData;
        if (downloadFileListReply->isReadable())
            responseData = downloadFileListReply->readAll();
        ui->fileList->clear();
        fileList = QString(responseData).split(",");
        if (fileList.size() > 0) {
            for (int i = 0; i < fileList.size(); i++) {
                if (fileList.at(i) != "") {
                    ui->fileList->addItem(fileList.at(i));
                }
            }
        }
    }
}
```

22. We also need to implement the function that will be called when we finish updating the file list to the server, as shown in the following example:

```
void MainWindow::uploadFileListFinished() {
    if(uploadFileListReply->error() != QNetworkReply::NoError)
        QMessageBox::warning(this, "Failed", "Failed to update
file list: " + uploadFileListReply->errorString());
    else
        getFileList();
}
```

23. The `uploadFileProgress()` function is used to display the progress bar when uploading a file to server, and it looks something like the following code:

```
void MainWindow::uploadFileProgress(qint64 bytesSent, qint64
bytesTotal) {
    qint64 percentage = 100 * bytesSent / bytesTotal;
    ui->uploadProgress->setValue((int) percentage);
}
```

24. Next, we will define what happens after a file has been uploaded to the server. This function is slightly longer than the others, so we will split it into a few sections so that you don't get confused by it. First, we will loop through the file list and see if it already exists, as shown in the following example:

```
void MainWindow::uploadFileFinished() {
    if(uploadFileReply->error() != QNetworkReply::NoError)
        QMessageBox::warning(this, "Failed", "Failed to upload
file: " + uploadFileReply->errorString());
    else {
        bool exists = false;
        if (fileList.size() > 0) {
            for (int i = 0; i < fileList.size(); i++) {
                if (fileList.at(i) == uploadFileName)
                    exists = true;
            }
        }
        if (!exists)
            fileList.append(uploadFileName);
```

25. Then, we will create a text file called `files.txt` and save the latest file list in it, as shown in the following code:

```
QString fileName = "files.txt";
QFile* file = new QFile(qApp->applicationDirPath() + "/" +
fileName);
file->open(QIODevice::ReadWrite);
if (fileList.size() > 0) {
    for (int j = 0; j < fileList.size(); j++) {
        if (fileList.at(j) != "")
            file->write(QString(fileList.at(j) +
",").toUtf8());
    }
}
file->close();
```

26. After that, open up `files.txt` and send it to the FTP server to update the file list, as shown in the following code:

```
QFile* newFile = new QFile(qApp->applicationDirPath() + "/" +
fileName);
if (newFile->open(QIODevice::ReadOnly)) {
    QUrl ftpPath;
    ftpPath.setUrl(ftpAddress + fileName);
    ftpPath.setUserName(username);
    ftpPath.setPassword(password);
    ftpPath.setPort(ftpPort);
```

27. Then, continue to write the code that sends the file list to the FTP server, as shown in the following example:

```
            QNetworkRequest request;
            request.setUrl(ftpPath);
            uploadFileListReply = manager->put(request,
newFile);
            connect(uploadFileListReply,
&QNetworkReply::finished, this,
&MainWindow::uploadFileListFinished);
            file->close();
        }
        QMessageBox::information(this, "Success", "File
successfully uploaded.");
    }
}
```

28. We also need to define the function which updates the progress bar for downloading a file from the FTP server, as shown in the following code:

```
void MainWindow::downloadFileProgress(qint64
byteReceived,qint64 bytesTotal) {
    qint64 percentage = 100 * byteReceived / bytesTotal;
    ui->downloadProgress->setValue((int) percentage);
}
```

29. Right after that, we can start implementing the downloadFileFinished() function, which gets called when a file has been downloaded from the server. First, we need to check whether the file has successfully downloaded, as shown in the following example:

```
void MainWindow::downloadFileFinished() {
    if(downloadFileReply->error() != QNetworkReply::NoError)
        QMessageBox::warning(this, "Failed", "Failed to
download file: " + downloadFileReply->errorString());
    else {
        QByteArray responseData;
        if (downloadFileReply->isReadable())
            responseData = downloadFileReply->readAll();
```

30. If it has, we'll save the file into the download directory which the user has set, as shown in the following code:

```
        if (!responseData.isEmpty()) {
            QString folder = ui->downloadPath->text();
            QFile file(folder + "/" + downloadFileName);
            file.open(QIODevice::WriteOnly);
            file.write((responseData));
            file.close();
            QMessageBox::information(this, "Success", "File
successfully downloaded.");
        }
    }
}
```

31. Before we start testing the program, let's create an empty text file called files.txt and place it in the folder which you have linked to the FTP user you set in FileZilla Server.

32. Lastly, build and run the program. Try and upload some files to the FTP server. If it works, the file list should be updated and be displayed on the **List Widget**. Then, try and double-click on the filename on the list widget and download the file to your computer, as shown in the following screenshot:

33. Congratulations, you have now successfully created a working FTP program!

How it works...

Although this project is much larger and with longer code, it is actually pretty similar to the TCP networking projects we have done in the previous recipes. We have also made use of the signals and slots mechanism provided by Qt 5 to make our life easier.

In the past, Qt used to support FTP directly through the `QFtp` class. However, the `QFtp` class has since been deprecated in the newer versions and so we have to implement our own by using networking classes such as `QNetworkRequest`, `QNetworkReply`, and so on.

Since we no longer have the `QFtp` class, there is no way to acquire the file list directly from **FileZilla Server**. Therefore, we develop a workaround to solve this problem, which is to use a text file for storing the file list.

The progress bar is very important for this project to show the upload and download progresses. This is especially useful for uploading or downloading large files.

7
Threading Basics - Asynchronous Programming

This chapter will cover the following recipes:

- Using threads
- QObject and QThread
- Data protection and sharing data between threads
- Working with QRunnable processes

Introduction

Most modern software runs its processes in parallel and offloads tasks to different threads to take advantage of modern CPU multicore architecture. In this way, software can be more efficient by running multiple processes simultaneously without affecting performance. In this chapter, we will learn how to make use of threads to boost our Qt 5 application's performance and efficiency.

Technical requirements

The technical requirements for this chapter include having Qt 5.11.2 MinGW 32-bit, Qt Creator 4.8.2, and Windows 10 installed.

All of the code that's used in this chapter can be downloaded from the following GitHub link: `https://github.com/PacktPublishing/Qt5-CPP-GUI-Programming-Cookbook-Second-Edition/tree/master/Chapter07`.

Check out the following video to see the code in action: `http://bit.ly/2TnFJUU`

Using threads

Qt 5 provides multiple methods for creating and using threads. You can choose between high-level methods and low-level ones. High-level methods are much easier to get started, but are limited in what you can do with them. Low-level methods, on the other hand, are more flexible, but not beginner-friendly. In this recipe, we will learn how to use one of the high-level methods to easily create a multithreading Qt 5 application.

How to do it…

Let's learn how to create multithreading applications by following these steps:

1. Create a **Qt Widgets Application** and open up `main.cpp`. Then, add the following headers at the top of the file:

```
#include <QFuture>
#include <QtConcurrent/QtConcurrent>
#include <QFutureWatcher>
#include <QThread>
#include <QDebug>
```

2. Then, create a function called `printText()` before the `main()` function:

```
void printText(QString text, int count) {
    for (int i = 0; i < count; ++i)
        qDebug() << text << QThread::currentThreadId();
    qDebug() << text << "Done";
}
```

3. After that, add the following code to the `main()` function:

```
int main(int argc, char *argv[]) {
    QApplication a(argc, argv);
    MainWindow w;
    w.show();
    printText("A", 100);
    printText("B", 100);
    return a.exec();
}
```

4. If you build and run the program now, you should see that A gets printed first before printing B. Note that their thread IDs are all the same. This is because we are running the `printText()` functions in the main thread:

```
. . .
"A"  0x2b82c
"A"  0x2b82c
"A"  0x2b82c
"A"  Done
. . .
"B"  0x2b82c
"B"  0x2b82c
"B"  0x2b82c
"B"  Done
```

5. To separate them into different threads, let's use a high-level class provided by Qt 5 called QFuture. Let's comment out the two `printText()` functions in `main()` and use the following code instead:

```
QFuture<void> f1 = QtConcurrent::run(printText, QString("A"),
100);
QFuture<void> f2 = QtConcurrent::run(printText, QString("B"),
100);
QFuture<void> f3 = QtConcurrent::run(printText, QString("C"),
100);
f1.waitForFinished();
f2.waitForFinished();
f3.waitForFinished();
```

6. If you build and run the program again, you should see something like this being printed out on the debug window, which means that the three `printText()` functions are now running in parallel:

```
. . .
"A"  0x271ec
"C"  0x26808
"B"  0x27a40
"A"  0x271ec
"C"  Done
"B"  0x27a40
"A"  Done
"B"  Done
```

7. We can also use `QFutureWatcher` to notify a `QObject` class through a signals and slots mechanism:

```
QFuture<void> f1 = QtConcurrent::run(printText, QString("A"),
100);
QFuture<void> f2 = QtConcurrent::run(printText, QString("B"),
100);
QFuture<void> f3 = QtConcurrent::run(printText, QString("C"),
100);

QFutureWatcher<void> futureWatcher;
QObject::connect(&futureWatcher,
QFutureWatcher<void>::finished, &w, MainWindow::mySlot);
futureWatcher.setFuture(f1);

f1.waitForFinished();
f2.waitForFinished();
f3.waitForFinished();
```

8. After that, open up `mainwindow.h` and declare the slot function:

```
public slots:
    void mySlot();
```

9. The `mySlot()` function looks like this in `mainwindow.cpp`:

```
void MainWindow::mySlot() {
    qDebug() << "Done!" << QThread::currentThreadId();
}
```

10. If you build and run the program again, this time, you will see results like this:

```
...
"A" 0x271ec
"C" 0x26808
"B" 0x27a40
"A" 0x271ec
"C" Done
"B" 0x27a40
"A" Done
"B" Done
Done! 0x27ac0
```

11. Even though QFutureWatcher is linked to f1, the Done! message only gets printed after all of the threads have finished executing. This is because mySlot() is running in the main thread, proven by the thread ID shown in the debug window alongside the Done! message.

How it works...

By default, there is a main thread (also known as a GUI thread) in any Qt 5 applications. Other threads that you create are called the **worker threads**.

GUI-related classes, such as QWidgets and QPixmap, can only exist in the main thread, so you must be extra careful when dealing with these classes.

QFuture is a high-level class that deals with asynchronous computation.

We use the QFutureWatcher class to let QFuture interact with signals and slots. You can even use this for displaying the progress of the operation on a progress bar.

QObject and QThread

Next, we want to explore some other methods so that we can use threads in Qt 5 applications. Qt 5 provides a class called QThread, which gives you more control of how you create and execute a thread. A QThread object begins to execute its event loops in a thread by calling the run() function. In this example, we will learn how to make QObject work together asynchronously through QThread.

How to do it...

Let's get started by preforming the following steps:

1. Create a new **Qt Widgets Application** project. Then, go to **File** | **New File or Project...** and create a **C++ Class**:

2. After that, name the new class MyWorker and make it inherit from the QObject class. Don't forget to include the QObject class by default as well:

3. Once you have created the `MyWorker` class, open up `myworker.h` and add the following headers at the top:

```
#include <QObject>
#include <QDebug>
```

4. After that, add the following signals and slot functions to the file as well:

```
signals:
    void showResults(int res);
    void doneProcess();

public slots:
    void process();
```

5. Next, open up `myworker.cpp` and implement the `process()` function:

```
void MyWorker::process() {
    int result = 0;
    for (int i = 0; i < 2000000000; ++i) {
        result += 1;
    }
    emit showResults(result);
    emit doneProcess();
}
```

6. After that, open up `mainwindow.h` and add the following headers at the top:

```
#include <QDebug>
#include <QThread>
#include "myworker.h"
```

7. Then, declare a slot function, as shown in the following code:

```
public slots:
    void handleResults(int res);
```

8. Once you're done, open up `mainwindow.cpp` and implement the `handResults()` function:

```
void MainWindow::handleResults(int res) {
    qDebug() << "Handle results" << res;
}
```

9. Lastly, we will add the following code to the class constructor of the `MainWindow` class:

```
MainWindow::MainWindow(QWidget *parent) : QMainWindow(parent),
ui(new Ui::MainWindow){
    ui->setupUi(this);
    QThread* workerThread = new QThread;
    MyWorker *workerObject = new MyWorker;
    workerObject->moveToThread(workerThread);
    connect(workerThread, &QThread::started, workerObject,
```

```
&MyWorker::process);
    connect(workerObject, &MyWorker::doneProcess, workerThread,
&QThread::quit);
    connect(workerObject, &MyWorker::doneProcess, workerObject,
&MyWorker::deleteLater);
    connect(workerObject, &MyWorker::showResults, this,
&MainWindow::handleResults);
    connect(workerThread, &QThread::finished, workerObject,
&MyWorker::deleteLater);
    workerThread->start();
}
```

10. Build and run the program now. You should see that the main window pops out and does nothing for a couple of seconds before a line of message is printed on the debug window:

```
Final result: 2000000000
```

11. The result was calculated in a separate thread, which is why the main window can display smoothly, and can even be moved around by a mouse during the calculation. To see the difference when running the calculation on the main thread, let's comment out some of the code and call the process() function directly:

```
//QThread* workerThread = new QThread;
MyWorker *workerObject = new MyWorker;
//workerObject->moveToThread(workerThread);
//connect(workerThread, &QThread::started, workerObject,
&MyWorker::process);
//connect(workerObject, &MyWorker::doneProcess, workerThread,
&QThread::quit);
connect(workerObject, &MyWorker::doneProcess, workerObject,
&MyWorker::deleteLater);
connect(workerObject, &MyWorker::showResults, this,
&MainWindow::handleResults);
//connect(workerThread, &QThread::finished, workerObject,
&MyWorker::deleteLater);
//workerThread->start();
workerObject->process();
```

12. Build and run the project now. This time, the main window will only appear on the screen once the calculation has been done. This is because the calculation was blocking the main thread (or GUI thread) and prevented the main window from being displayed.

How it works...

`QThread` is an alternative method for running a process asynchronously, besides using the `QFuture` class. It gives us more control compared with `QFuture`, which we will demonstrate in the following recipe.

Do note that the `QObject` class that gets moved to the working thread cannot have any parent, as Qt is designed in such a way that an entire object tree must exist in the same thread. Therefore, all of the children of a `QObject` class will also be moved to the working thread when you call `moveToThread()`.

Use a signals and slots mechanism if you want your working thread to communicate with the main thread.

We used the `started` signal that's provided by the `QThread` class to inform our working object to start the calculation since the working thread has already been created.

Then, when the calculation has been completed, we emit the `showResult` and `doneProcess` signals to inform the thread to quit, while passing the final result to the main thread for it to be printed.

Lastly, we also use the signals and slots mechanism to safely delete both the working thread and working object when everything is done.

Data protection and sharing data between threads

Even though multithreading makes processes run asynchronously, there will be times where threads must be stopped and wait for other threads. This usually happens when both threads are modifying the same variable simultaneously. It is common to force threads to wait for one another to protect shared resources, such as data. Qt 5 also provides both low-level methods and high-level mechanisms to synchronize threads.

How to do it...

We will continue to use the code from the previous example project since we have already established a working program with multithreading:

1. Open up `myworker.h` and add the following header:

   ```
   #include <QObject>
   #include <QDebug>
   #include <QMutex>
   ```

2. Then, we will add two new variables and make some changes to the class constructor:

   ```
   public:
       explicit MyWorker(QMutex *mutex);
       int* myInputNumber;
       QMutex* myMutex;

   signals:
       void showResults(int res);
       void doneProcess();
   ```

3. After that, open up `myworker.cpp` and change the class constructor to look like the following code. We no longer require the parent input since the object will not have a parent:

   ```
   MyWorker::MyWorker(QMutex *mutex) {
       myMutex = mutex;
   }
   ```

4. We will also change the `process()` function to look like this:

   ```
   void MyWorker::process() {
       myMutex->lock();
       for (int i = 1; i < 100000; ++i){
           *myInputNumber += i * i + 2 * i + 3 * i;
       }
       myMutex->unlock();
       emit showResults(*myInputNumber);
       emit doneProcess();
   }
   ```

5. Once you're done, open up `mainwindow.cpp` and make some changes to the code:

```
MainWindow::MainWindow(QWidget *parent) : QMainWindow(parent),
ui(new Ui::MainWindow) {
    ui->setupUi(this);

    int myNumber = 5;
    QMutex* newMutex = new QMutex;

    QThread* workerThread = new QThread;
    QThread* workerThread2 = new QThread;
    QThread* workerThread3 = new QThread;
    MyWorker *workerObject = new MyWorker(newMutex);
    MyWorker *workerObject2 = new MyWorker(newMutex);
    MyWorker *workerObject3 = new MyWorker(newMutex);
```

6. After that, we will set the `myInputNumber` variable of the worker object to `myNumber`. Note that we are referencing its pointer instead of the value:

```
workerObject->myInputNumber = &myNumber;
workerObject->moveToThread(workerThread);
connect(workerThread, &QThread::started, workerObject,
&MyWorker::process);
connect(workerObject, &MyWorker::doneProcess, workerThread,
&QThread::quit);
connect(workerObject, &MyWorker::doneProcess, workerObject,
&MyWorker::deleteLater);
connect(workerObject, &MyWorker::showResults, this,
&MainWindow::handleResults);
connect(workerThread, &QThread::finished, workerObject,
&MyWorker::deleteLater);
```

7. Repeat the previous step two more times for setting `workerObject2`, `workerThread2`, `workerObject3`, and `workerThread3`:

```
workerObject2->myInputNumber = &myNumber;
workerObject2->moveToThread(workerThread2);
connect(workerThread2, &QThread::started, workerObject2,
&MyWorker::process);
connect(workerObject2, &MyWorker::doneProcess, workerThread2,
&QThread::quit);
connect(workerObject2, &MyWorker::doneProcess, workerObject2,
&MyWorker::deleteLater);
connect(workerObject2, &MyWorker::showResults, this,
&MainWindow::handleResults);
connect(workerThread2, &QThread::finished, workerObject2,
```

```
&MyWorker::deleteLater);

workerObject3->myInputNumber = &myNumber;
workerObject3->moveToThread(workerThread3);
connect(workerThread3, &QThread::started, workerObject3,
&MyWorker::process);
connect(workerObject3, &MyWorker::doneProcess, workerThread3,
&QThread::quit);
connect(workerObject3, &MyWorker::doneProcess, workerObject3,
&MyWorker::deleteLater);
connect(workerObject3, &MyWorker::showResults, this,
&MainWindow::handleResults);
connect(workerThread3, &QThread::finished, workerObject3,
&MyWorker::deleteLater);
```

8. Finally, we will start running those threads by calling `start()`:

```
workerThread->start();
workerThread2->start();
workerThread3->start();
```

9. If you build and run the program now, you should see a consistent result, no matter how many times you run it:

```
Final result: -553579035
Final result: -1107158075
Final result: -1660737115
```

10. We are getting results every time we run the program because the mutex lock ensures that only one of the threads is able to modify the data while other threads await their completion. To see the difference without mutex locking, let's comment out the code:

```
void MyWorker::process() {
    //myMutex->lock();

    for (int i = 1; i < 100000; ++i) {
        *myInputNumber += i * i + 2 * i + 3 * i;
    }

    //myMutex->unlock();

    emit showResults(*myInputNumber);
    emit doneProcess();
}
```

11. Build and run the program again. This time, you will get a very different result when you run the program. For example, I've obtained the following results when running it on three occasions:

```
1st time:
Final result: -589341102
Final result: 403417142
Final result: -978935318

2nd time:
Final result: 699389030
Final result: -175723048
Final result: 1293365532

3rd time:
Final result: 1072831160
Final result: 472989964
Final result: -534842088
```

12. This happens because the `myNumber` data is being manipulated by all the threads simultaneously in a random order, due to the nature of parallel computation. By locking the mutex, we make sure that the data can only be modified by a single thread and, hence, eliminated this issue.

How it works...

Qt 5 provides two classes, namely `QMutex` and `QReadWriteLock`, for data protection when multiple threads are accessing and modifying the same data. We only used `QMutex` in the previous example, but both classes are very similar in nature. The only difference is that `QReadWriteLock` allows data to be read simultaneously by other threads while the data is being written. Unlike `QMutex`, it separates the read and write states, but only one can occur at a time (either lock for read, or lock for write), and not both. For complex functions and statements, use the high-level `QMutexLocker` class instead of `QMutex` for simplifying the code and easier debugging.

The downside of this method is that all of the other threads will be idling around while the data is being modified by a single thread. It is best not to share data with multiple threads unless there is no other way to do so, as it will halt the other threads and defeat the object of parallel computation.

Working with QRunnable processes

In this recipe, we will learn how to use another type of high-level method to easily create a multithreading Qt 5 application. We will be using the QRunnable and QThreadPool classes in this recipe.

How to do it...

Let's get started by performing the following steps:

1. Create a new **Qt Widgets Application** project and create a new **C++ Class** called MyProcess, which inherits the QRunnable class.

2. Next, open up myprocess.h and add the following headers:

```
#include <QRunnable>
#include <QDebug>
```

3. Then, declare the run() function, as follows:

```
class MyProcess : public QRunnable {
public:
    MyProcess();
    void run();
};
```

4. After that, open up myprocess.cpp and define the run() function:

```
void MyProcess::run() {
    int myNumber = 0;
    for (int i = 0; i < 100000000; ++i) {
        myNumber += i;
    }
    qDebug() << myNumber;
}
```

5. Once you're done, add the following headers to mainwindow.h:

```
#include <QMainWindow>
#include <QThreadPool>
#include "myprocess.h"
```

6. After that, we will implement the class constructor by adding the following code:

```
MainWindow::MainWindow(QWidget *parent) : QMainWindow(parent),
ui(new Ui::MainWindow) {
  ui->setupUi(this);

  MyProcess* process = new MyProcess;
  MyProcess* process2 = new MyProcess;
  MyProcess* process3 = new MyProcess;
  MyProcess* process4 = new MyProcess;

  QThreadPool::globalInstance()->start(process);
  QThreadPool::globalInstance()->start(process2);
  QThreadPool::globalInstance()->start(process3);
  QThreadPool::globalInstance()->start(process4);

  qDebug() <<
QThreadPool::globalInstance()->activeThreadCount();
}
```

7. Now, build and run the project. You should see that the processes are successfully being run in different threads where the active thread count is four.

8. The QThreadPool class automatically deactivates threads when its last process has been executed. Let's try and prove that by pausing the program for three seconds and printing out the active thread count again:

```
qDebug() << QThreadPool::globalInstance()->activeThreadCount();
this->thread()->sleep(3);
qDebug() << QThreadPool::globalInstance()->activeThreadCount();
```

9. Build and run the program again. This time, you should see that the active thread count is four, and then, after three seconds, the active thread count becomes zero. This is because all of the processes have been executed.

How it works...

The QRunnable class works hand-in-hand with the QThreadPool class, which manages a collection of threads. The QThreadPool class automatically manages and recycles individual QThreads objects to avoid creating and destroying threads too frequently, which helps in reducing computing costs.

To use QThreadPool, you must sub-class the QRunnable object and implement the virtual function called run(). By default, QThreadPool will automatically delete the QRunnable object when the last thread exits the run function. You can change this behavior by calling setAutoDelete() to change the autoDelete variable to false.

By default, threads that are unused for more than 30 seconds will expire. You can change this duration by calling setExpiryTimeout() before the thread is running. Otherwise, it will not have any effect on the timeout setting.

You can also set the maximum number of threads that can be used by calling setMaxThreadCount(). To get the total number of current active threads, simply call activeThreadCount().

8
Building a Touch Screen Application with Qt5

This chapter will cover the following recipes:

- Setting up Qt for mobile applications
- Designing a basic user interface with QML
- Touch events
- Animation in QML
- Displaying information using model/view
- Integrating QML and C++

Introduction

Qt is not only a cross-platform software development kit for PC platforms; it also supports mobile platforms, such as iOS and Android. The developers of Qt introduced **Qt Quick** back in 2010, which provides an easy way to build custom user interfaces that are highly dynamic, where users can easily create fluid transitions and effects with only minimal coding. Qt Quick uses a declarative scripting language called **QML** that is similar to the **JavaScript** language used in web development. Advanced users can also create custom functions in C++ and port them over to Qt Quick to enhance its functionality. At the moment, Qt Quick supports multiple platforms, such as Windows, Linux, Mac, iOS, and Android.

Technical requirements

The technical requirements for this chapter include Qt 5.11.2 MinGW 32 bit/Android for armeabi-v7a, Qt Creator 4.8.2, and Windows 10.

All the code used in this chapter can be downloaded from the following GitHub link: `https://github.com/PacktPublishing/Qt5-CPP-GUI-Programming-Cookbook-Second-Edition/tree/master/Chapter08`.

Check out the following video to see the code in action: `http://bit.ly/2FlnIS0`

Setting up Qt for mobile applications

In this example, we will learn how to set up our Qt project in Qt Quick and enable it to be built and exported to mobile devices.

How to do it...

Let's get started and learn how to create our first mobile application using Qt 5:

1. First of all, let's create a new project by going to **File** | **New File or Project**. Then, a window will pop up for you to choose a project template. Select **Qt Quick Application - Empty** and click the **Choose...** button as shown in the following screenshot:

2. After that, insert the project name and select the project location. Click the **Next** button and it will ask you to select the minimum Qt version required for your project.

Please make sure that you select a version that exists on your computer, otherwise you won't be able to run it properly.

3. Once you have done that, proceed by clicking the **Next** button.

4. Then, Qt Creator will ask you which kit you want to use for your project. These **kits** are basically different compilers that you can use to compile your project for different platforms. Since we're doing an application for a mobile platform, we will enable the Android kit (or the iOS kit if you're running a Mac) in order to build and export your app to your mobile device, as shown in the following screenshot. You can also enable one of the desktop kits in order for you to test your program on the desktop beforehand. Do note that you need to configure the Android kit if you're using it for the first time, so that Qt can find the directory of the Android SDK. Click **Next** once you're done with it:

5. Once the project has been created, Qt Creator will automatically open up a file from your project, called `main.qml`. You will see a different type of script, as shown in the following code, that is very different from your usual C/C++ projects:

```
import QtQuick 2.11
import QtQuick.Window 2.11

Window {
    visible: true
    width: 640
    height: 480
    title: qsTr("Hello World")
}
```

6. Build and run the project now by clicking on the green arrow button located at the bottom-left corner of your Qt Creator, as shown in the following screenshot. If you set the default kit to one of the desktop kits, an empty window will pop up once the project has been compiled:

7. We can switch between different kits by going to the **Projects** interface and selecting the kit you want your project to be built with, as shown in the following screenshot. You can also manage all the kits available on your computer, or add a new kit to your project from the **Projects** interface:

8. If this is your first time building and running your project, you need to create a template for the Android kit under the **Build** settings. Once you have clicked the **Create Templates** button under the **Build Android APK** tab, as shown in the following screenshot, Qt will generate all the files required to run your app on an Android device. If you don't plan to use Gradle in your project, disable the **Copy the Gradles files to Android directory** option. Otherwise, you may encounter problems when trying to compile and deploy your app to your mobile device:

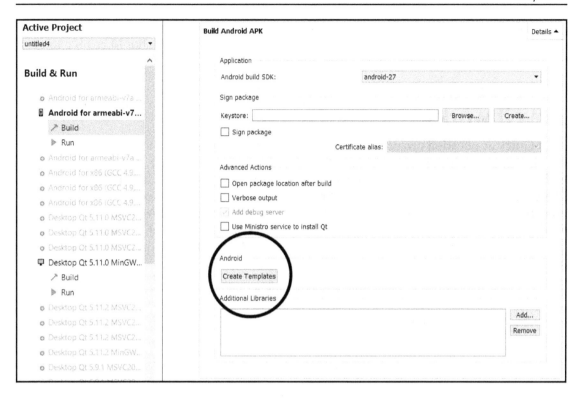

9. Once you have created the template, click on the **Run** button. You should now see the following window pop up, asking which device it should export to:

10. Select the device that is currently connected to your computer and press the **OK** button. Wait for a while for it to build the project, and you should be able to get a blank app running on your mobile device.

How it works...

A Qt Quick application project is quite different from a form application project. You will be writing QML script most of the time instead of writing C/C++ code. The **Android Software Development Kit** (**SDK**), **Android Native Development Kit** (**NDK**), **Java Development Kit** (**JDK**), and **Apache Ant** are required to build and export your app to the Android platform. Alternatively, you can also use Gradle instead of Apache Ant for your Android kit. All you need to do is to enable the **Use Gradle** instead of Ant option and provide Qt with Gradle's installation path. Note that Android Studio is currently not supported by Qt Creator:

If you're running the app on an Android device, make sure that you have enabled **USB debugging mode**. To enable USB debugging mode, you need to first enable the developer options on your Android device by going to **Settings | About Phone** and tapping **Build Number** seven times. After that, go to **Settings | Developer Options** and you will see the **USB debugging** option in the menu. Enable that option and you can now export your app to your device for testing.

To build for the iOS platform, you need to run Qt Creator on a Mac and make sure the latest Xcode is installed on your Mac as well. To test your app on an iOS device, you need to register a developer account with Apple, register your device at the developer portal, and install the provisioning to your Xcode, which is a lot trickier than Android. You will be given access to the developer portal once you have obtained a developer account from Apple.

Designing a basic user interface with QML

In this example, we will learn how to use Qt Quick Designer to design our program's user interface.

How to do it...

Let's follow these steps to get started:

1. First of all, create a new Qt Quick application project, just like we did in the previous recipe.

    You can also use the previous project files if you wish to.

2. You will see a QML file in your project resources—`main.qml`. This is where we implement the logic for our application, but we will also need another QML file where we define our user interface.

3. Let's create the QML UI file by going to **File | New File or Project**, then select **QtQuick UI File** under **Qt** category as shown in the following screenshot:

4. Let's call the **Component name** Main and **Component form name** MainForm as follows:

5. Once the `MainForm.ui.qml` file has been created, it will be opened by Qt Creator. You will see an entirely different user interface editor compared to the one we used in previous chapters. This editor is called the **Qt Quick Designer**, which is used specifically to design user interface for Qt Quick projects. The components of this editor are described as follows:

- **Library**: The **Library** window displays all the predefined QML types that you can add to your user interface canvas. You can also import custom Qt Quick components from the **Import** tab and display them here.
- **Navigator**: The **Navigator** window displays the items in the current QML file in a tree structure.
- **Connections**: You can use the tools provided in the **Connections** window to connect objects to signals, specify dynamic properties for objects, and create bindings between the properties of two objects.
- **State**: The **State** window displays the different states of an item. You can add a new state for an item by clicking on the **+** button on the right of the **State** window.
- **Canvas**: The canvas is where you design your program's user interface. You can drag and drop a Qt Quick component from the **Library** window onto the canvas and instantly see what it will look like in the program.
- **Properties**: This is where you change the properties of a selected item.

6. We're about to make a simple login screen. From the **Library** window, drag two text widgets onto the canvas.

7. Set the **Text** properties of both the text widgets to `Username:` and `Password::`

8. Drag two rectangles from the **Library** window to the canvas, then drag two text input widgets onto the canvas and parent each of them to the rectangles you just added to the canvas. Set the **Border** property of the rectangles to `1` and the **Radius** to `5`. Then, set the echo mode of one of the text fields to **Password**.

9. Now, we're going to manually create a button widget by combining a mouse area widget with a rectangle and a text widget. Drag a mouse area widget onto the canvas, then drag a rectangle and a text widget onto the canvas and parent them both to the mouse area. Set the color of the rectangle to `#bdbdbd`, then set its **Border** property to `1` and its **Radius** to `5`. Then, set the **text** to `Login` and make sure the size of the mouse area is the same as the rectangle.

10. After that, drag another rectangle onto the canvas to act as the container for the login form so that it will look neat. Set its **Border Color** to `#5e5858` and its **Border** property to `2`. Then, set its **Radius** property to `5` to make its corners look a little rounded.

11. Make sure the rectangle that we added in the previous step is positioned at the top of the hierarchy in the **Navigator** window so that it appears behind all the other widgets. You can arrange the widget positions within the hierarchy by pressing the arrow buttons located at the top of the **Navigator** window as follows:

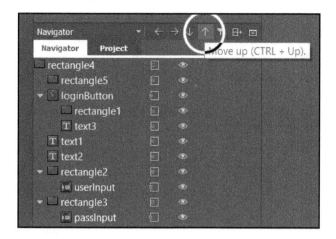

12. Next, we will export three widgets – mouse area and the two text input widgets – as alias properties of the root item so that later on we can access these widgets from the `main.qml` file. The widgets can be exported by clicking on the small icon behind the widget name and making sure the icon changes to the **On** status.

13. By now, your user interface should look something like this:

14. Now let's open up `main.qml`. Qt Creator will not open this file in Qt Quick Designer by default – instead, it will be opened with the script editor. This is because all the user interface design-related tasks were done in `MainForm.ui.qml`, and `main.qml` is only for defining the logic and functions that will be applied to the UI. You can, however, open it with Qt Quick Designer to preview the user interface by clicking on the **Design** button located in the side bar on the left of the editor.

15. At the top of the script, add the third line to import the dialog module to `main.qml`, as shown in the following code:

```
import QtQuick 2.9
import QtQuick.Window 2.3
import QtQuick.Dialogs 1.2
```

16. After that, replace the following code with this:

```
Window {
    visible: true
    width: 360
    height: 360
    MainForm {
        anchors.fill: parent
        loginButton.onClicked: {
            messageDialog.text = "Username is " +
userInput.text + " and password is " + passInput.text
            messageDialog.visible = true
        }
    }
```

17. We continue to define `messageDialog` as follows:

```
MessageDialog {
    id: messageDialog
    title: "Fake login"
    text: ""
    onAccepted: {
        console.log("You have clicked the login button")
        Qt.quit()
    }
}
}
```

18. Build and run this program on your PC and you should get a simple program that shows a message box when you click on the **Login** button:

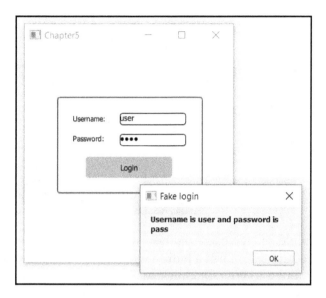

How it works...

Since Qt 5.4, a new file extension called .ui.qml has been introduced. The QML engine handles it like the normal .qml files, but forbids any logic implementation to be written in it. It serves as the user interface definition template that can be reused in different .qml files. The separation of UI definition and logic implementation improves the maintainability of QML code and creates a better workflow.

All the widgets under **Qt Quick – Basic** are the most basic widgets that we can use to mix and match and create a new type of widget as follows:

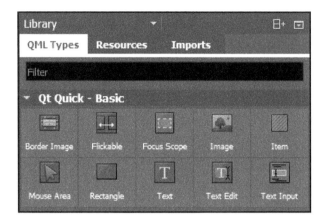

In the previous example, we have learned how to put three widgets together—a text, a mouse area, and a rectangle, to form a button widget. If you're lazy, however, you can import pre-made modules to your Qt Quick project by going to the **Imports** tab in the **Library** window and clicking the **<Add Import>** button. Then, select the module you want to add to your project from the drop-down list as follows. You can also create your own Qt Quick module once you have advanced in both QML scripting and C++ programming:

We imported the `QtQuick.Dialogs.qml 1.0` module in `main.qml` and created a message box that displays the user name and password filled in by the user when the **Login** button is pressed, so that we can prove that the user interface function is working. If the widgets are not exported from `MainForm.ui.qml`, we will not be able to access its properties in `main.qml`.

At this point, we can export the program to iOS and Android, but the user interface may not look accurate on some of the devices that have higher resolution or a higher **density-per-pixel** (**DPI**) unit. We will cover this issue later on in this chapter.

Touch events

In this section, we will learn how to develop a touch-driven application that runs on mobile devices using Qt Quick.

How to do it...

Let's get started by following this step-by-step guide:

1. Create a new **Qt Quick application – Empty** project.
2. In Qt Creator, right-click on `qml.qrc` and select **Open in Editor**. Then, click **Add | Add Files** and add `tux.png` to the project as follows:

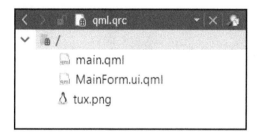

3. Next, open up `MainForm.ui.qml`. Drag an image widget from the **Library** window to the canvas. Then, set the source of the image to `tux.png` and set its `fillMode` to `PreserveAspectFit`. After that, set its width to `200` and its height to `220`.
4. Make sure that both the mouse area widget and the image widget are exported as alias properties of the root item by clicking on the small icon besides their respective widget name.
5. After that, switch over to the script editor by clicking on the **Edit** button on the side bar located at the left side of the editor. We need to change the mouse area widget to a multi-point touch area widget, as in the following code:

```
MultiPointTouchArea {
    id: touchArea
```

```
                  anchors.fill: parent
                  touchPoints: [
                      TouchPoint { id: point1 },
                      TouchPoint { id: point2 }
                  ]
          }
```

6. We also set the `Image` widget to be automatically placed at the center of the window by default as follows:

```
Image {
    id: tux
    x: (window.width / 2) - (tux.width / 2)
    y: (window.height / 2) - (tux.height / 2)
    width: 200
    height: 220
    fillMode: Image.PreserveAspectFit
    source: "tux.png"
}
```

7. The final user interface should look something like this:

8. Once you're done with that, let's open up `main.qml`. First, clear everything within the `MainForm` object except `anchors.fill: parent`, as shown in the following code:

```
import QtQuick 2.9
import QtQuick.Window 2.3
Window {
    visible: true
    MainForm {
        anchors.fill: parent
    }
}
```

9. After that, declare several variables within the `MainForm` object that will be used to rescale the image widget. If you want to know more about the property keyword used in the following code, check out the *There's more...* section at the end of this example:

```
property int prevPointX: 0
property int prevPointY: 0
property int curPointX: 0
property int curPointY: 0
property int prevDistX: 0
property int prevDistY: 0
property int curDistX: 0
property int curDistY: 0
property int tuxWidth: tux.width
property int tuxHeight: tux.height
```

10. Using the following code, we will define what will happen when our finger touches the multi-point area widget. In this case, we will save the positions of the first and second touch points if more than one finger touches the multi-point touch area. We also save the width and height of the image widget so that, later on, we can use these variables to calculate the scale of the image when the fingers start to move:

```
touchArea.onPressed: {
    if (touchArea.touchPoints[1].pressed) {
        if (touchArea.touchPoints[1].x < touchArea.touchPoints[0].x)
            prevDistX = touchArea.touchPoints[1].x -
touchArea.touchPoints[0].x
        else
            prevDistX = touchArea.touchPoints[0].x -
touchArea.touchPoints[1].x
        if (touchArea.touchPoints[1].y < touchArea.touchPoints[0].y)
            prevDistY = touchArea.touchPoints[1].y -
```

```
touchArea.touchPoints[0].y
        else
            prevDistY = touchArea.touchPoints[0].y -
touchArea.touchPoints[1].y
        tuxWidth = tux.width
        tuxHeight = tux.height
    }
}
```

11. The following diagram shows the example of touch points being registered when two fingers are touching the screen within the **touchArea** boundary. The **touchArea.touchPoints[0]** is the first registered touch point and **touchArea.touchPoints[1]** is the second. We then calculate the *X* and *Y* distance between the two touch points and save them as **prevDistX** and **prevDistY** as follows:

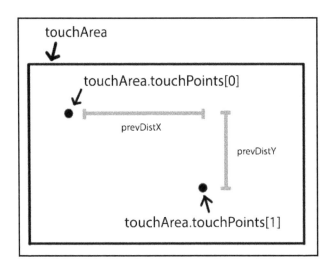

12. After that, we will define what will happen when our fingers move while remaining in contact with the screen and still within the boundary of the touch area using the following code. At this point, we will calculate the scale of the image by using the variables we saved in the previous step. At the same time, if we detect that only a single touch is found, then we will move the image instead of altering its scale:

```
touchArea.onUpdated: {
    if (!touchArea.touchPoints[1].pressed) {
        tux.x += touchArea.touchPoints[0].x -
touchArea.touchPoints[0].previousX
        tux.y += touchArea.touchPoints[0].y -
```

```
touchArea.touchPoints[0].previousY
    }
    else {
        if (touchArea.touchPoints[1].x <
touchArea.touchPoints[0].x)
            curDistX = touchArea.touchPoints[1].x -
touchArea.touchPoints[0].x
        else
            curDistX = touchArea.touchPoints[0].x -
touchArea.touchPoints[1].x
        if (touchArea.touchPoints[1].y <
touchArea.touchPoints[0].y)
            curDistY = touchArea.touchPoints[1].y -
touchArea.touchPoints[0].y
        else
            curDistY = touchArea.touchPoints[0].y -
touchArea.touchPoints[1].y
        tux.width = tuxWidth + prevDistX - curDistX
        tux.height = tuxHeight + prevDistY - curDistY
    }
}
```

13. The following diagram shows the example of moving touch points
    – **touchArea.touchPoints[0]** moved from point **A** to point **B** while
    touchArea.touchPoints[1] moved from point **C** to point **D**. We can then
    determine how many units have the touch points moved by looking at the
    differences between the previous **X**, **Y** variables with the current ones:

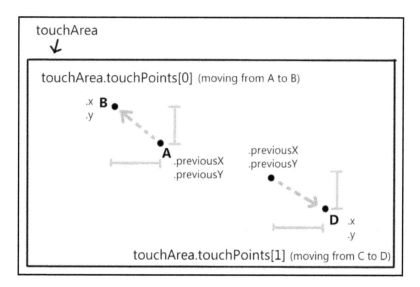

14. You can now build and export the program to your mobile device. You will not be able to test this program on a platform that does not support multi-touch. Once the program is running on the mobile device (or a desktop/laptop that supports multi-touch), try two things—put only one finger on the screen and move it around, and put two fingers on the screen and move them in opposite directions. What you should see is that the penguin will be moved to another place if you use only one finger, and it will be scaled up or down if you use two fingers, as shown in the following screenshot:

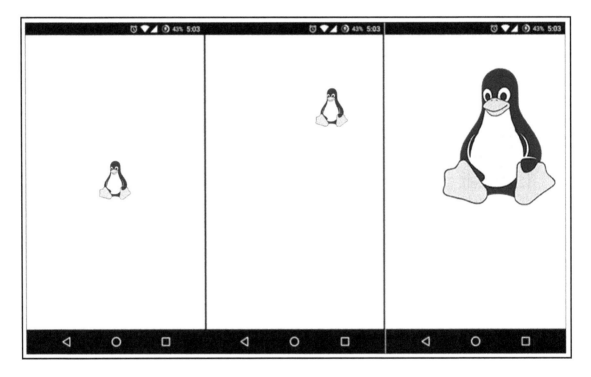

How it works...

When a finger touches the screen of the device, the multi-point touch area widget triggers the **onPressed** event and registers the position of each of the touch points in an internal array. We can get this data by telling Qt which touch point you want to get access to. The first touch will bear the index number of 0, the second touch will be 1, and so on. We will then save this data into variables so that we can retrieve it later to calculate the scaling of the penguin image.

When one or more fingers remain in contact with the screen while moving, a multi-point touch area will trigger the **onUpdated** event. We will then check how many touches there are—if only one touch is found, we will just move the penguin image based on how much our finger has moved. If there is more than one touch, we will compare the distance between the two touches and compare this with the previous variables we have saved to determine how much we should rescale the image.

The diagram shows tapping your finger on the screen will trigger the **onPressed** event, while swiping your finger on screen will trigger the **onUpdated** event:

We must also check whether the first touch is on the left side of the second touch or the right side. This way we can prevent the image from being scaled in the inverse direction of the finger movement and producing an inaccurate result. As for the movement of the penguin, we will just get the difference between the current touch position and the previous one, add that to the coordinate of the penguin, and it's done. A single touch event is usually a lot simpler and more straightforward than a multi-touch event.

There's more...

In Qt Quick, all its components have built-in properties such as `width`, `height`, and `color` that are attached to the components by default. However, Qt Quick also allows you to create your own custom properties and attach them to the components you declared in your QML script. A custom property of an object type may be defined in an object declaration in a QML document by adding the `property` keyword before the type (`int`, `float`, and so on) keyword, for example:

```
property int myValue;
```

You can also bind the custom `property` to a value by using a colon (`:`) before the value, as shown in the following code:

```
property int myValue: 100;
```

To learn more about the property types supported by Qt Quick, check out this link:
http://doc.qt.io/qt-5/qtqml-typesystem-basictypes.html

Animation in QML

Qt allows us to easily animate a user interface component without writing a bunch of code. In this example, we will learn how to make our program's user interface more interesting by applying animations to it.

How to do it...

Let's learn how to add animation to your Qt Quick application by following these steps:

1. Once again, we will start everything from scratch. Therefore, create a new **Qt Quick application – Empty** project in Qt Creator and create the `MainForm.ui.qml` file.
2. Open up `MainForm.ui.qml` and go to the **Imports** tab in the **Library** window and add a Qt Quick module called `QtQuick.Controls` to your project.
3. After that, you will see a new category appear in the **QML Types** tab called **Qt Quick – Controls**, which contains many new widgets that can be placed on the canvas.
4. Next, drag three button widgets to the canvas and set their height to `45`. Then, go to the **Layout** tab on the **Properties** window and enable both the left and right anchors for all the three button widgets. Make sure the target for the anchors are set to **Parent** and the margins remain as `0`. This will make the buttons resize horizontally according to the width of the main window. After that, set the y value of the first button to `0`, the second to `45`, and the third to `90`. The user interface should now look like this:

5. Now, open up `qml.qrc` with the editor and add `fan.png` to the project as follows:

6. Then, add two mouse area widgets to the canvas. After that, drag a **Rectangle** widget and an **Image** widget on the canvas. Parent the rectangle and image to the mouse areas we have just added before this.

7. Set the color of the rectangle to `#0000ff` and apply `fan.png` to the image widget. Your user interface should now look like this:

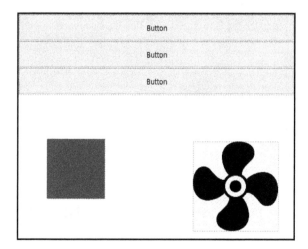

8. After that, export all the widgets in your `MainForm.ui.qml` as alias properties of the root item by clicking on the icons located to the right of the widget name as follows:

9. Next, we will apply animation and logic to the user interface, but we won't be doing it in `MainForm.ui.qml`. Instead, we will do it all in `main.qml`.

10. In `main.qml`, remove the default code for the mouse area and add in a width and height for the window so that we get more space to preview, as follows:

```
import QtQuick 2.5
import QtQuick.Window 2.2
Window {
    visible: true
    width: 480
    height: 550
    MainForm {
        anchors.fill: parent
    }
}
```

11. After that, add the following code that defines the behavior of the buttons in the `MainForm` widget:

```
button1 {
    Behavior on y { SpringAnimation { spring: 2; damping: 0.2 }
}
    onClicked: {
        button1.y = button1.y + (45 * 3)
    }
}
button2 {
    Behavior on y { SpringAnimation { spring: 2; damping: 0.2 }
```

```
    }
    onClicked: {
        button2.y = button2.y + (45 * 3)
    }
}
```

12. In the following code, we continue to define `button3`:

```
button3 {
    Behavior on y { SpringAnimation { spring: 2; damping: 0.2 }
}
    onClicked: {
        button3.y = button3.y + (45 * 3)
    }
}
```

13. Then, follow this with the behavior of the fan image and the mouse area widget it is attached to as follows:

```
fan {
    RotationAnimation on rotation {
        id: anim01
        loops: Animation.Infinite
        from: 0
        to: -360
        duration: 1000
    }
}
```

14. In the following code, we then define `mouseArea1`:

```
mouseArea1 {
    onPressed: {
        if (anim01.paused)
            anim01.resume()
        else
            anim01.pause()
    }
}
```

15. Last but not least, add the behavior of the rectangle and the mouse area widget it's attached to as follows:

```
rectangle2 {
    id: rect2
    state: "BLUE"
    states: [
        State {
```

```
                    name: "BLUE"
                    PropertyChanges {
                        target: rect2
                        color: "blue"
                    }
            },
```

16. In the following code, we continue to add the RED state:

```
            State {
                name: "RED"
                PropertyChanges {
                    target: rect2
                    color: "red"
                }
            }
        ]
    }
```

17. We then finish the code by defining `mouseArea2` as follows:

```
    mouseArea2 {
        SequentialAnimation on x {
            loops: Animation.Infinite
            PropertyAnimation { to: 150; duration: 1500 }
            PropertyAnimation { to: 50; duration: 500 }
        }
        onClicked: {
            if (rect2.state == "BLUE")
                rect2.state = "RED"
            else
                rect2.state = "BLUE"
        }
    }
```

18. If you compile and run the program now, you should see three buttons at the top of the window and a moving rectangle at the bottom left, followed by a spinning fan at the bottom right, as demonstrated in the following screenshot. If you click any of the buttons, they will move slightly downward with a nice, smooth animation. If you click on the rectangle, it will change color from **blue** to **red**. Meanwhile, the fan image will pause its animation if you click on it while it's animating, and it will resume the animation if you click on it again:

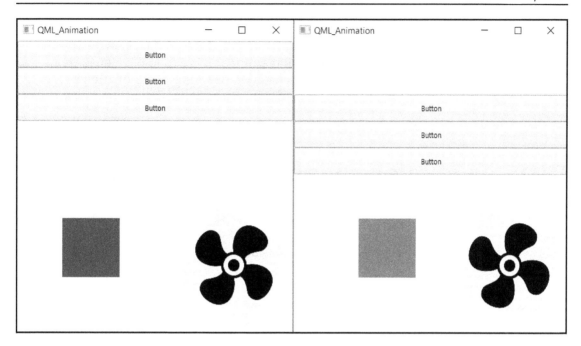

How it works...

Most of the animation elements supported by the C++ version of Qt, such as transition, sequential animation, and parallel animation, are also available in Qt Quick. If you are familiar with the Qt animation framework in C++, you should be able to grasp this pretty easily.

In this example, we added a spring animation element to all three buttons that specifically tracked their respective y-axes. If Qt detects that the y value has changed, the widget will not instantly pop to the new position—instead it will be interpolated, move across the canvas, and perform a little shaking animation when reaching its destination that simulates the spring effect. We just have to write one line of code and leave the rest to Qt.

As for the fan image, we added a rotation animation element to it and set the duration to `1000 milliseconds`, which means it will complete a full rotation in one second. We also set it to loop its animation infinitely. When we clicked on the mouse area widget it's attached to, we just called `pause()` or `resume()` to enable or disable the animation.

Next, for the rectangle widget, we added two states to it, one called **BLUE** and one called **RED**, each of which carries a **color** property that will be applied to the rectangle upon state change. At the same time, we added a **sequential animation group** to the mouse area widget that the rectangle is attached to, and then added two **property animation** elements to the group. You can also mix different types of group animation; Qt can handle this very well.

Displaying information using model/view

Qt includes a **model/view framework** that maintains separation between the way data is organized and managed and the way that it is presented to the user. In this section, we will learn how to make use of the model/view, in particular by using the list view to display information and, at the same time, apply our own customization to make it look slick.

How to do it...

Let's get started by following these steps:

1. Create a new **Qt Quick application – Empty** project and open up `qml.qrc` with Qt Creator. Add six images, `home.png`, `map.png`, `profile.png`, `search.png`, `settings.png`, and `arrow.png` to the project as follows:

2. After that, create and open `MainForm.ui.qml` as we did in all previous examples. Drag a **List View** widget from under the **Qt Quick – Views** category in the **Library** window onto the canvas. Then, set its **Anchors** setting to fill the parent size by clicking on the button located in the middle of the **Layout** window as shown in the following screenshot:

3. Next, switch over to the script editor, as we will define what the list view will look like as follows:

```
import QtQuick 2.9

Rectangle {
    id: rectangle1

    property alias listView1: listView1
    property double sizeMultiplier: width / 480
```

4. We will continue to write the code by adding the list view as follows:

```
ListView {
    id: listView1
    y: 0
    height: 160
    orientation: ListView.Vertical
    boundsBehavior: Flickable.StopAtBounds
    anchors.fill: parent
    delegate: Item {
        width: 80 * sizeMultiplier
        height: 55 * sizeMultiplier
```

5. We will continue to add rows to the list view as follows:

```
Row {
    id: row1
    Rectangle {
        width: listView1.width
        height: 55 * sizeMultiplier
        gradient: Gradient {
            GradientStop { position: 0.0; color: "#ffffff" }
            GradientStop { position: 1.0; color: "#f0f0f0" }
        }
        opacity: 1.0
```

6. We then add a mouse area and an image as shown in the following code snippet:

```
MouseArea {
    id: mouseArea
    anchors.fill: parent
}
Image {
    anchors.verticalCenter: parent.verticalCenter
    x: 15 * sizeMultiplier
    width: 30 * sizeMultiplier
    height: 30 * sizeMultiplier
    source: icon
}
```

7. Then, continue to add two text objects as follows:

```
Text {
    text: title
    font.family: "Courier"
    font.pixelSize: 17 * sizeMultiplier
    x: 55 * sizeMultiplier
    y: 10 * sizeMultiplier
}
Text {
    text: subtitle
    font.family: "Verdana"
    font.pixelSize: 9 * sizeMultiplier
    x: 55 * sizeMultiplier
    y: 30 * sizeMultiplier
}
```

8. After that, add an image object as follows:

```
Image {
    anchors.verticalCenter: parent.verticalCenter
    x: parent.width - 35 * sizeMultiplier
    width: 30 * sizeMultiplier
    height: 30 * sizeMultiplier
    source: "arrow.png"
                }
            }
        }
    }
```

9. Using the following code, we will then define the list model:

```
model: ListModel {
    ListElement {
        title: "Home"
        subtitle: "Go back to dashboard"
        icon: "home.png"
    }

    ListElement {
        title: "Map"
        subtitle: "Help navigate to your destination"
        icon: "map.png"
    }
```

10. We will continue to write the code:

```
    ListElement {
        title: "Profile"
        subtitle: "Customize your profile picture"
        icon: "profile.png"
    }

    ListElement {
        title: "Search"
        subtitle: "Search for nearby places"
        icon: "search.png"
    }
```

11. We will now add the final list element, as shown in the following code:

```
ListElement {
    title: "Settings"
    subtitle: "Customize your app settings"
    icon: "settings.png"
}
        }
    }
}
```

12. After that, open up `main.qml` and replace the code with the following:

```
import QtQuick 2.9
import QtQuick.Window 2.3
Window {
    visible: true
    width: 480
    height: 480
    MainForm {
        anchors.fill: parent
        MouseArea {
            onPressed: row1.opacity = 0.5
            onReleased: row1.opacity = 1.0
        }
    }
}
```

13. Build and run the program, and now your program should look like this:

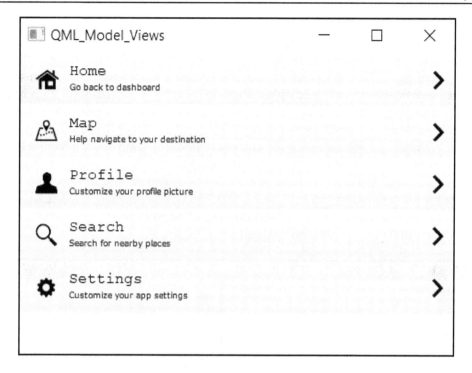

How it works...

Qt Quick allows us to customize the look of each row of the list view with ease. The delegate defines what each row will look like and the model is where you store the data that will be displayed on the list view.

In this example, we added a background with a gradient on each row, then we also added an icon on each side of the item, a title, a description, and a mouse area widget that makes each row of the list view clickable. The delegate is not static, as we allow the model to change the title, description, and the icon to make each row look unique.

In `main.qml`, we defined the behavior of the mouse area widget that will halve its own opacity value when pressed and return to fully opaque when released. Since all other elements, such as title and icon, are all the children of the mouse area widget, they all will also automatically follow their parent widget's behavior and become semi-transparent. Also, we have finally solved the display problem on mobile devices with high resolution and DPI. It's a very simple trick – first, we defined a variable called `sizeMultiplier`. The value of `sizeMultiplier` is the result of dividing the width of the window by a predefined value, say 480, which is the current window width we used for the PC. Then, multiply `sizeMultiplier` by all the widget variables that have to do with size and position, including font size. Do note that, in this case, you should use the `pixelSize` property for text instead of `pointSize`, so that you will get the correct display when multiplying by `sizeMultiplier`. The following screenshot shows you what the app looks like on the mobile device with and without `sizeMultiplier`:

Notice that you may get a messed up user interface in the editor once you multiply everything by the `sizeMultiplier` variable. This is because the width variable may return as 0 in the editor. Hence, by multiplying 0 by 480, you may get the result 0, which makes the entire user interface look funny. However, it will look fine when running the actual program. If you want to preview the
user interface on the editor, temporarily set `sizeMultiplier` to 1.

Integrating QML and C++

Qt supports bridging between C++ classes with the QML engine. This combination allows developers to take advantage of both the simplicity of QML and the flexibility of C++. You can even integrate features that are not supported by Qt from an external library, then pass the resulting data to Qt Quick to be displayed in the UI. In this example, we will learn how to export our user interface components from QML to the C++ framework and manipulate their properties before displaying them on screen.

How to do it...

Let's go through the following steps:

1. Once again, we will start everything from scratch. Therefore, create a new **Qt Quick application – Empty** project in Qt Creator and create `MainForm.ui.qml`. Then, open up `MainForm.ui.qml`.

2. We can keep the mouse area and text widget, but place the text widget at the bottom of the window. Change the **Text** property of the text widget to **Change this text** using C++ and set its **font size** to **18**. After that, go to the **Layout** tab and enable both **Vertical center anchor** and **Horizontal center anchor** to ensure it's always somewhere in the middle of the window, regardless of how you rescale the window.

Set the **Margin** for the **Vertical center anchor** to **120** as shown in the following screenshot:

3. Next, drag a rectangle widget from the **Library** window to the canvas and set its color to #ff0d0d. Set its **Width** and **Height** to **200** and enable both the vertical and horizontal center anchor. After that, set the **Margin** of the horizontal center anchor to **-14**. Your UI should now look something like this:

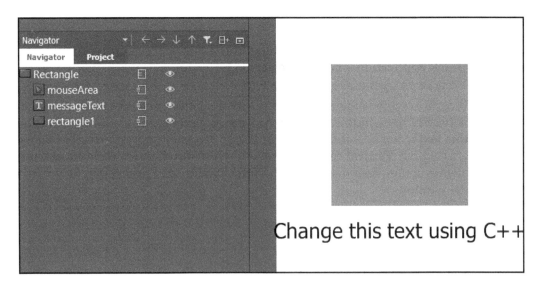

4. Once you are done with that, right-click on your project directory in Qt Creator and choose **Add New...**, as shown in the following screenshot. Then, a window will pop up and let you pick a file template. Select **C++ Class** and press **Choose...**. After that, it will ask you to define the C++ class by filling in the information for the class. In this case, insert `MyClass` in the **Class Name** field and select `QObject` as the **Base class**. Then, make sure the **Include QObject** option is ticked, and you can now click the **Next** button, followed by the **Finish** button. Two files—`myclass.h` and `myclass.cpp`, will now be created and added to your project:

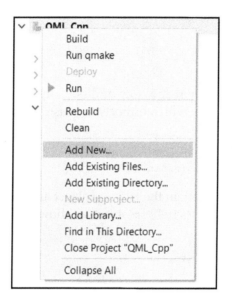

5. Now, open up `myclass.h` and add a variable and function under the class constructor, as shown in the following code:

```
#ifndef MYCLASS_H
#define MYCLASS_H
#include <QObject>
class MyClass : public QObject
{
    Q_OBJECT
    public:
    explicit MyClass(QObject *parent = 0);
    // Object pointer
    QObject* myObject;
    // Must call Q_INVOKABLE so that this function can be used
in QML
```

```
        Q_INVOKABLE void setMyObject(QObject* obj);
};
#endif // MYCLASS_H
```

6. After that, open up `myclass.cpp` and define the `setMyObject()` function as follows:

```
#include "myclass.h"
MyClass::MyClass(QObject *parent) : QObject(parent)
{
}
void MyClass::setMyObject(QObject* obj)
{
    // Set the object pointer
    myObject = obj;
}
```

7. We can now close `myclass.cpp` and open up `main.qml`. At the top of the file, add in the third line, which imports the custom library we just created in C++:

```
import QtQuick 2.9
import QtQuick.Window 2.3
import MyClassLib 1.0
```

8. Then, define `MyClass` in the `Window` object and call its `setMyObject()` function within the `MainForm` object, as shown in the following code:

```
Window {
    visible: true
    width: 480
    height: 320
    MyClass {
        id: myclass
    }
    MainForm {
        anchors.fill: parent
        mouseArea.onClicked: {
            Qt.quit();
        }
        Component.onCompleted:
        myclass.setMyObject(messageText);
    }
}
```

9. Lastly, open up `main.cpp` and register the custom class to the QML engine. We will also change the properties of the text widget and the rectangle here using C++ code as follows:

```
#include <QGuiApplication>
#include <QQmlApplicationEngine>
#include <QtQml>
#include <QQuickView>
#include <QQuickItem>
#include <QQuickView>
#include "myclass.h"
int main(int argc, char *argv[])
{
    // Register your class to QML
    qmlRegisterType<MyClass>("MyClassLib", 1, 0, "MyClass");
```

10. Then, proceed to create the objects, just like the highlighted section in the following code:

```
QGuiApplication app(argc, argv);
QQmlApplicationEngine engine;
engine.load(QUrl(QStringLiteral("qrc:/main.qml")));

QObject* root = engine.rootObjects().value(0);
QObject* messageText =
root->findChild<QObject*>("messageText");
    messageText->setProperty("text", QVariant("C++ is now in
control!"));
    messageText->setProperty("color", QVariant("green"));
    QObject* square = root->findChild<QObject*>("square");
    square->setProperty("color", QVariant("blue"));

    return app.exec();
}
```

11. Now build and run the program, and you should see the colors of the rectangle and the text are completely different from what you defined earlier in Qt Quick, as shown in the following screenshot. This is because their properties have been changed by the C++ code:

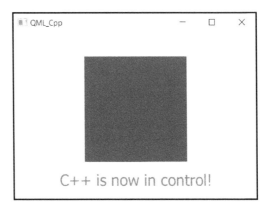

How it works...

QML is designed to be easily extensible through C++ code. The classes in the Qt QML module enable QML objects to be loaded and manipulated from C++.

Only classes that are inherited from the QObject base class can be integrated with QML, as it is part of the Qt ecosystem. Once the class has been registered with the QML engine, we get the root item from the QML engine and use it to find the objects we want to manipulate. After that, use the setProperty() function to change any of the properties belong to the widget.

Notice that the Q_INVOKABLE macro is required in front of the function that you intend to call in QML. Without it, Qt will not expose the function to Qt Quick and you will not be able to call it.

9
XML Parsing Made Easy

XML is the file extension of a file format called **Extensible Markup Language**, which is used to store information in a structured format. The XML format is used extensively for the web. HTML, for instance, is the file format used to create web pages and is based upon the XML format. Starting with Microsoft Office 2007, Microsoft Office has used XML-based file formats, such as `.docx`, `.xlsx`, and `.pptx`.

This chapter will cover the following recipes:

- Processing XML data using the stream reader
- Writing XML data using the Stream Writer
- Processing XML data using the QDomDocument class
- Writing XML data using the QDomDocument class
- Using Google's Geocoding API

Technical requirements

The technical requirements for this chapter include Qt 5.11.2 MinGW 32 bit, Qt Creator 4.8.2, and Windows 10.

All the code used in this chapter can be downloaded from the following GitHub link: `https://github.com/PacktPublishing/Qt5-CPP-GUI-Programming-Cookbook-Second-Edition/tree/master/Chapter09`.

Check out the following video to see the code in action: `http://bit.ly/2ToL7XU`

Processing XML data using the stream reader

In this recipe, we will learn how to process data taken from an XML file and extract it using the stream reader.

How to do it...

Let's create a simple program that reads and processes XML files by following these steps:

1. Create a new **Qt Widgets Application** project at your desired location.
2. Open any text editor and create an XML file that looks like the following, then save it as `scene.xml`:

```
<?xml version="1.0" encoding="UTF-8"?>
<scene>
    <object tag="building">
        <name>Library</name>
        <position>120.0,0.0,50.68</position>
        <rotation>0.0,0.0,0.0</rotation>
        <scale>1.0,1.0,1.0</scale>
    </object>
```

3. Continue to write the XML code, as shown in the following code:

```
    <object tag="building">
        <name>Town Hall</name>
        <position>80.2,0.0,20.5</position>
        <rotation>0.0,0.0,0.0</rotation>
        <scale>1.0,1.0,1.0</scale>
    </object>
    <object tag="prop">
        <name>Tree</name>
        <position>10.46,-0.2,80.2</position>
        <rotation>0.0,0.0,0.0</rotation>
        <scale>1.0,1.0,1.0</scale>
    </object>
</scene>
```

4. Go back to Qt Creator and open `mainwindow.h`. Add the following headers at the top of the script, right after `#include <QMainWindow>`:

```
#include <QXmlStreamReader>
#include <QDebug>
#include <QFile>
#include <QFileDialog>
```

5. Open `mainwindow.ui` and drag a **Push Button** from the widget box on the left side to the UI editor. Change the object name of the button to `loadXmlButton` and its display text to `Load XML`:

6. Right-click on the button and select **Go to slot....** A window will pop up with a list of signals available for selection.

7. Choose the default **clicked()** option and press the **OK** button. Qt will now insert a slot function in your header and source files, called `on_loadXmlButton_clicked()`.

8. Add the following code to the `on_loadXmlButton_clicked()` function:

```
void MainWindow::on_loadXmlButton_clicked() {
    QXmlStreamReader xml;

    QString filename = QFileDialog::getOpenFileName(this, "Open
Xml", ".", "Xml files (*.xml)");
    QFile file(filename);
    if (!file.open(QFile::ReadOnly | QFile::Text))
        qDebug() << "Error loading XML file.";
    xml.setDevice(&file);
```

9. We continue to write the code. The following code loops through the XML file and prints out each attribute's name and value:

```
while (!xml.atEnd()) {
    if (xml.isStartElement()) {
        QString name = xml.name().toString();

        if (name == "object") {
            qDebug() <<
"[Object]=================================";

            for (int i = 0; i < xml.attributes().size();
i++) {
                qDebug() << xml.attributes().at(i).name()
<< xml.attributes().at(i).value();
            }
        }
```

10. Read the element text from the XML file, as shown in the following code:

```
        if (name == "name" || name == "position" || name ==
"rotation" || name == "scale") {
            QString text = xml.readElementText();
            qDebug() << name << text;
        }
    }

    if (xml.isEndElement()) {
        QString name = xml.name().toString();

        if (name == "object") {
            qDebug() <<
"===========================================";
        }
    }
```

11. Check for error messages before finishing the code:

```
    xml.readNext();
}

if (xml.hasError()) {
    qDebug() << "Error loading XML:" << xml.errorString();
}
}
```

12. Build and run the project and you will see a window pop up that looks like the one you made in *step 4*:

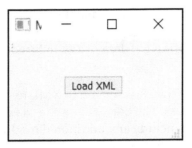

13. Click on the `Load XML` button and you should see the file selector window pop up on the screen. Select the XML file you created in *step 2* and press the **Select** button. You should see the following debug text appear on the application output window in Qt Creator, which indicates that the program has successfully loaded the data from the XML file you just selected:

```
[Object]==================================
"tag" "building"
"name" "Library"
"position" "120.0,0.0,50.68"
"rotation" "0.0,0.0,0.0"
"scale" "1.0,1.0,1.0"
==================================
[Object]==================================
"tag" "building"
"name" "Town Hall"
"position" "80.2,0.0,20.5"
"rotation" "0.0,0.0,0.0"
"scale" "1.0,1.0,1.0"
==================================
[Object]==================================
"tag" "prop"
"name" "Tree"
"position" "10.46,-0.2,80.2"
"rotation" "0.0,0.0,0.0"
"scale" "1.0,1.0,1.0"
==================================
```

How it works...

In this example, we're trying to extract and process data from an XML file using the `QXmlStreamReader` class. Imagine you're making a computer game and you're using XML files to store the attributes of all the objects in your game scene. In this case, the XML format plays an important role in storing the data in a structured way, which allows for easy extraction.

We need to add the header of the class related to XML to our source file, which in this case is the `QXmlStreamReader` class. The `QXmlStreamReader` class is built into Qt's core library, so there is no need to include any additional modules with it, which also means that it's the recommended class to use to process XML data in Qt. Once we click on the `Load XML` button, the `on_loadXmlButton_clicked()` slot will be called; this is where we write the code to process the XML data.

We use a file dialog to select the XML file we want to process. Then we send the selected file's filename, together with its path, to the `QFile` class to open and read the text data of the XML file. After that, the file's data is sent to the `QXmlStreamReader` class for processing.

We use a `while` loop to read through the entire XML file and check every element processed by the stream reader. We determine whether the element is a start element or an end element. If it's a start element, we check the name of the element to determine whether the element should contain any data that we need.

Then, we extract the data, either in the form of an attribute or text. An element may have more than one attribute, which is why we must loop through all the attributes and extract them one by one.

There's more...

Besides the web browser, many commercial game engines and interactive applications use the XML format to store information for in-game scenes, meshes, and other forms of assets used in their products. This is because the XML format provides many benefits over other file formats, such as a compact file size, high flexibility and extendibility, easy file recovery, and a relational tree structure that allows it to be used for highly efficient and performance-critical applications, such as search engines, intelligent data mining servers, and scientific simulations.

Let's learn a little bit about the format of an XML file. We will use `scene.xml`, which we used in the previous example in the *Processing XML data using the stream reader* recipe, and looks as follows:

```
<?xml version="1.0" encoding="UTF-8"?>
<scene>
    <object tag="building">
        <name>Library</name>
        <position>120.0,0.0,50.68</position>
        <rotation>0.0,0.0,0.0</rotation>
        <scale>1.0,1.0,1.0</scale>
    </object>
```

There can be more than one object tag:

```
    <object tag="building">
        <name>Town Hall</name>
        <position>80.2,0.0,20.5</position>
        <rotation>0.0,0.0,0.0</rotation>
        <scale>1.0,1.0,1.0</scale>
    </object>
    <object tag="prop">
        <name>Tree</name>
        <position>10.46,-0.2,80.2</position>
        <rotation>0.0,0.0,0.0</rotation>
        <scale>1.0,1.0,1.0</scale>
    </object>
</scene>
```

In XML, a tag is a line of markup text that starts with a < symbol and ends with a > symbol; `<scene>` is a tag called scene, `<object>` is a tag called object, and so on. Tags come in three flavors:

- The start tag, for example `<scene>`
- The end tag, for example `</scene>`
- An empty-element tag, for example `<scene />`

Whenever you write a start tag, it must end with an end tag, otherwise your XML data will be invalid. An empty-element tag, however, is a standalone tag and does not need an end tag behind it.

At the top of the `scene.xml` file, you will see a tag called `xml`, which stores the version of the XML format and the encoding type, which in this case is XML version 1.0 and UTF-8 (8-bit Unicode) encoding. This line is called the XML declaration and it must exist in one of your XML files to validate its format.

After that, you will see tags that have attributes stored in them, for example `<object tag="building">`. This means that the object tag contains an attribute called tag, which contains a value, building. You can put as many attributes as you like in a tag, for example `<object tag="building" color="red" name="LA Community Hospital" coordinate="34.0191757,-118.2567239">`. Each of these attributes stores distinct data that can be retrieved easily using Qt.

You can also store data between the start tag and the end tag; for example, `<name>Town Hall</name>`. This method, however, is not relevant to the empty-element tag, since it is a standalone tag and isn't followed by an end tag. Therefore, you can only store attributes in an empty-element tag.

 To learn more about the XML format, visit `http://www.w3schools.com/xml`.

Writing XML data using the Stream Writer

Since we have learned how to process data obtained from an XML file in the previous recipe, we will move on to learning how to save data to an XML file. We will continue with the previous example and add to it.

How to do it…

We will learn how to save data into an XML file through the following steps:

1. Add another button to `mainwindow.ui`, then set its object name as `saveXmlButton` and its label as `Save XML`:

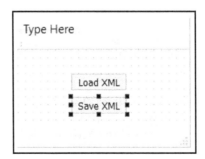

2. Right-click on the button and select **Go to slot...**. A window will pop up with a list of signals available for selection. Select the **clicked()** option and click **OK**. A signal function called `on_saveXmlButton_clicked()` will now be automatically added to both your `mainwindow.h` and `mainwindow.cpp` files by Qt:

3. Add the following code to the `on_saveXmlButton_clicked()` function:

```
QXmlStreamWriter xml;
QString filename = QFileDialog::getSaveFileName(this, "Save
Xml", ".", "Xml files (*.xml)");
QFile file(filename);
if (!file.open(QFile::WriteOnly | QFile::Text))
    qDebug() << "Error saving XML file.";
xml.setDevice(&file);
xml.setAutoFormatting(true);
xml.writeStartDocument();
```

4. Let's also write the first contact element:

```
xml.writeStartElement("contact");
xml.writeAttribute("category", "Friend");
xml.writeTextElement("name", "John Doe");
xml.writeTextElement("age", "32");
xml.writeTextElement("address", "114B, 2nd Floor, Sterling
Apartment, Morrison Town");
xml.writeTextElement("phone", "0221743566");
xml.writeEndElement();
```

5. Write the second contact element as follows:

```
xml.writeStartElement("contact");
xml.writeAttribute("category", "Family");
xml.writeTextElement("name", "Jane Smith");
xml.writeTextElement("age", "24");
xml.writeTextElement("address", "13, Ave Park, Alexandria");
xml.writeTextElement("phone", "0025728396");
xml.writeEndElement();
xml.writeEndDocument();
```

6. Build and run the program and you should see an additional button on the program UI:

7. Click on the Save XML button and a save file dialog will appear on the screen. Type the filename you desire and click the **Save** button.

8. Open up the XML file you just saved with any text editor. The first part of the file should look like this:

```
<?xml version="1.0" encoding="UTF-8"?>
<contact category="Friend">
    <name>John Doe</name>
    <age>32</age>
    <address>114B, 2nd Floor, Sterling Apartment, Morrison
Town</address>
```

```
        <phone>0221743566</phone>
    </contact>
```

9. The second part of the file should look something like this:

```
<contact category="Family">
    <name>Jane Smith</name>
    <age>24</age>
    <address>13, Ave Park, Alexandria</address>
    <phone>0025728396</phone>
</contact>
```

How it works...

The saving process is similar to loading an XML file in the previous example. The only difference is instead of using the QXmlStreamReader class, we switched to using the QXmlStreamWriter class. We are still using the file dialog and the QFile class to save the XML file. This time, we have to change the open mode from QFile::ReadOnly to QFile::WriteOnly before passing the QFile class to the Stream Writer.

Before we start writing any data to the new XML file, we must set auto-formatting to true, otherwise there will be no spacing; it also adds new lines and indentation to the XML file to make it tidy and easier to read. However, if your intention is to make it harder to read and edit by the user, you can just ignore the setAutoFormatting() function.

Next, start writing the XML file by calling writeStartDocument(), followed by all the elements you want to save to the file, and at the end we call the writeEndDocument() function to stop writing. Each element must have start and end tags in order for the reading process to work properly. The attributes of an element will be stored in the start tag, while the text data will be stored between the start and end tags.

If we're writing an element that contains a group of child elements, we must call writeStartElement() before writing the child elements. Call writeEndElement() after saving all its child elements to close the group with an end tag. The writetextElement() function, however, will automatically add the end tag for you, so you don't have to worry about that one. You can call the writeAttribute() function to add an attribute to an element. There is no limit on how many attributes you can add to a particular element.

Processing XML data using the QDomDocument class

Qt allows multiple ways to parse XML data, including the common method that we covered in the previous examples. This time around, we're going to learn how to read data from an XML file using another class, called QDomDocument.

How to do it...

Processing XML data using the QDomDocument class is really simple:

1. Add the XML module to the project by opening the project (.pro) file and adding the xml text after core and gui, as shown in the following code:

   ```
   QT += core gui xml
   ```

2. Create a user interface that carries a button that says Load XML:

3. Right-click on the button, choose **Go to slot...**, and select the **clicked()** option. Press the **OK** button and Qt will add a slot function to your source code.

4. Go to mainwindow.h and add the following headers so that we can make use of these classes:

   ```
   #include <QDomDocument>
   #include <QDebug>
   #include <QFile>
   #include <QFileDialog>
   ```

5. Go to mainwindow.cpp and insert the following code to the button's clicked() slot function:

   ```
   void MainWindow::on_loadXmlButton_clicked() {
       QDomDocument xml;
   ```

```
    QString filename = QFileDialog::getOpenFileName(this, "Open
Xml", ".", "Xml files (*.xml)");
    QFile file(filename);
    if (!file.open(QFile::ReadOnly | QFile::Text))
        qDebug() << "Error loading XML file.";
    if (!xml.setContent(&file)) {
        qDebug() << "Error setting content.";
        file.close();
        return;
    }
    file.close();
```

6. We continue to write the code to load XML:

```
QDomElement element = xml.documentElement();
    QDomNode node = element.firstChild();
    while(!node.isNull()) {
        QDomElement nodeElement = node.toElement();
        if(!nodeElement.isNull()) {
            if (nodeElement.tagName() == "object") {
                qDebug() <<
"[Object]===============================";
                QDomNode childNode = nodeElement.firstChild();
```

7. The previous code continues as follows:

```
                while (!childNode.isNull()) {
                    QDomElement childNodeElement =
childNode.toElement();
                    QString name = childNodeElement.tagName();
                    if (name=="name" || name=="position" ||
name=="rotation" || name=="scale") {
                        QString text = childNodeElement.text();
                        qDebug() << name << text;
                    }
                    childNode = childNode.nextSibling();
                }
            }
            qDebug() <<
"=========================================";
        }
        node = node.nextSibling();
    }
}
```

8. Compile and run the program. Click on the `Load XML` button and select the XML file used in the first example. You should see the following output:

```
[Object]===================================
"tag" "building"
"name" "Library"
"position" "120.0,0.0,50.68"
"rotation" "0.0,0.0,0.0"
"scale" "1.0,1.0,1.0"
===================================
[Object]===================================
"tag" "building"
"name" "Town Hall"
"position" "80.2,0.0,20.5"
"rotation" "0.0,0.0,0.0"
"scale" "1.0,1.0,1.0"
===================================
[Object]===================================
"tag" "prop"
"name" "Tree"
"position" "10.46,-0.2,80.2"
"rotation" "0.0,0.0,0.0"
"scale" "1.0,1.0,1.0"
===================================
```

How it works...

Compared to `QXmlStreamReader`, the `QDomDocument` class is less straightforward when it comes to loading or saving XML data. However, `QDomDocument` does it in a strict way by making sure each element is linked to its respective parent element recursively, like in a tree structure. Unlike `QXmlStreamReader`, `QDomDocument` allows us to save data to an element created earlier, in a later time frame.

Since `QDomDocument` is not part of the Qt core library, we must add the XML module to our project manually. Otherwise, we will not be able to access `QDomDocument` and other classes related to it.

First, we load the XML file and extract its content to the `QDomDocument` class. Then, we get its document element, which acts as the root document, and obtain its direct children. We then convert each of the child nodes to `QDomElement` and obtain their tag names. By checking tag names, we are able to determine the type of data we're expecting from each element.

Since this is the first layer of elements with the tag name object, we don't expect any data from them; we repeat *step 3* again, but this time we're going to do it on the element with the tag name object and obtain all its direct children, which means the grandchildren of the document element.

Again, by checking the tag name, we're able to know what data we can expect from its children elements. If the tag name matches the ones we're expecting (in this case, name, position, rotation, and scale), we can obtain its data by calling `QDomElement::text()`.

Writing XML data using the QDomDocument class

In this example, we will learn how to write data to an XML file using the `QDomDocument` class. We will continue from the previous example and just add more code to it.

How to do it...

To learn how to save data into an XML file using the `QDomDocument` class, let's do the following:

1. Add the second button to the UI, called `Save XML`:

2. Right-click on the `Save XML` button and select **Go to slot...**. Then, pick the **clicked()** option and click **OK**. A new **clicked()** slot function will be added to your source files.

3. Write the following code within the button's `clicked()` slot function:

```
void MainWindow::on_saveXmlButton_clicked() {
    QString filename = QFileDialog::getSaveFileName(this, "Save
Xml", ".", "Xml files (*.xml)");
    QFile file(filename);
    if (!file.open(QFile::WriteOnly | QFile::Text)) {
        qDebug() << "Error saving XML file.";
        file.close();
        return;
    }
```

4. The previous code continues:

```
    QDomDocument xml("contact");

    // John Doe
    QDomElement root = xml.createElement("contact");
    root.setAttribute("category", "Family");
    xml.appendChild(root);

    QDomElement tagName = xml.createElement("name");
    root.appendChild(tagName);
    QDomText textName = xml.createTextNode("John Doe");
    tagName.appendChild(textName);
```

5. Save the `age` and `address` elements:

```
    QDomElement tagAge = xml.createElement("age");
    root.appendChild(tagAge);
    QDomText textAge = xml.createTextNode("32");
    tagAge.appendChild(textAge);

    QDomElement tagAddress = xml.createElement("address");
    root.appendChild(tagAddress);
    QDomText textAddress = xml.createTextNode("114B, 2nd Floor,
Sterling Apartment, Morrisontown");
    tagAddress.appendChild(textAddress);
```

6. Let's continue with the `phone` element. Proceed to the next contact:

```
QDomElement tagPhone = xml.createElement("phone");
root.appendChild(tagPhone);
QDomText textPhone = xml.createTextNode("0221743566");
tagPhone.appendChild(textPhone);
// Jane Smith
QDomElement root2 = xml.createElement("contact");
root2.setAttribute("category", "Friend");
xml.appendChild(root2);
```

7. Save the `name` and `age`:

```
QDomElement tagName2 = xml.createElement("name");
root2.appendChild(tagName2);
QDomText textName2 = xml.createTextNode("Jane Smith");
tagName2.appendChild(textName2);

QDomElement tagAge2 = xml.createElement("age");
root2.appendChild(tagAge2);
QDomText textAge2 = xml.createTextNode("24");
tagAge2.appendChild(textAge2);
```

8. Save the `address` and `phone`:

```
QDomElement tagAddress2 = xml.createElement("address");
root2.appendChild(tagAddress2);
QDomText textAddress2 = xml.createTextNode("13, Ave Park,
Alexandria");
tagAddress2.appendChild(textAddress2);

QDomElement tagPhone2 = xml.createElement("phone");
root2.appendChild(tagPhone2);
QDomText textPhone2 = xml.createTextNode("0025728396");
tagPhone2.appendChild(textPhone2);
```

9. Stream all the data into the XML file:

```
// Save to file
QTextStream output(&file);
output << xml.toString();
file.close();
}
```

10. Compile and run the program and click on the `Save XML` button. Enter your desired filename in the save file dialog and click **Save**.

11. Open the XML file you saved in *step 4* with any text editor and you should see something like this:

```
<!DOCTYPE contact>
<contact category="Family">
    <name>John Doe</name>
    <age>32</age>
    <address>114B, 2nd Floor, Sterling Apartment,
Morrisontown</address>
    <phone>0221743566</phone>
</contact>
```

12. We can also see the second contact under it:

```
<contact category="Friend">
    <name>Jane Smith</name>
    <age>24</age>
    <address>13, Ave Park, Alexandria</address>
    <phone>0025728396</phone>
</contact>
```

How it works...

Similar to the previous example, we first initiate the file dialog and declare a `QDomDocument` object. Then, we create the root element by calling `QDomDocument::createElement()`. Any element created from `QDomDocument` will not automatically become its direct child unless we append the newly-created element as its child.

To create the grandchildren of `QDomDocument`, simply append the newly-created elements to the root element. By utilizing the `append()` function, we can easily arrange the XML data in a tree structure without wrapping our head around it. This, in my opinion, is the advantage of using `QDomDocument` instead of `QXmlStreamReader`.

We can then add attributes to an element by calling `QDomElement::setAttribute()`. We can also create a text node by calling `QDomDocument::createTextNode()` and appending it to any of the elements in the XML structure. After we are done structuring the XML data, we can output all the data in the form of text to the `QTextStream` class and allow it to save the data into a file.

Using Google's Geocoding API

In this example, we will learn how to obtain the full address of a specific location by using Google's **Geocoding API**.

How to do it...

Let's create a program that utilizes the Geocoding API by following these steps:

1. Create a new **Qt Widgets Application** project.
2. Open `mainwindow.ui` and add a couple of text labels, input fields, and a button to make your UI to look similar to this:

3. Open your project (`.pro`) file and add the network module to your project. You can do that by simply adding the `network` text after `core` and `gui`, as shown in the following code:

```
QT += core gui network
```

4. Open `mainwindow.h` and add the following headers to the source code:

```
#include <QMainWindow>:
#include <QDebug>
#include <QtNetwork/QNetworkAccessManager>
#include <QtNetwork/QNetworkReply>
#include <QXmlStreamReader>
```

5. Declare a slot function manually and call it `getAddressFinished()`:

```
private slots:
    void getAddressFinished(QNetworkReply* reply);
```

6. Declare a private variable called `addressRequest`:

```
private:
    QNetworkAccessManager* addressRequest;
```

7. Open `mainwindow.ui` again, right-click on the **Get Address** button, and select **Go to slot...**. Then choose the **clicked()** option and press **OK**. A slot function will now be added to both the `mainwindow.h` and `mainwindow.cpp` source files.

8. Open `mainwindow.cpp` and add the following code to the class constructor:

```
MainWindow::MainWindow(QWidget *parent) :
 QMainWindow(parent),
 ui(new Ui::MainWindow) {
    ui->setupUi(this);
    addressRequest = new QNetworkAccessManager();
    connect(addressRequest, &QNetworkAccessManager::finished,
this, &MainWindow::getAddressFinished);
}
```

9. Add the following code to the `getAddressFinished()` slot function we just declared manually:

```
void MainWindow::getAddressFinished(QNetworkReply* reply) {
    QByteArray bytes = reply->readAll();
    //qDebug() << QString::fromUtf8(bytes.data(),
    bytes.size());
    QXmlStreamReader xml;
    xml.addData(bytes);
```

10. Continue to loop through the XML file to obtain the `text` element:

```
while(!xml.atEnd()) {
    if (xml.isStartElement()) {
        QString name = xml.name().toString();
        //qDebug() << name;
        if (name == "formatted_address") {
            QString text = xml.readElementText();
            qDebug() << "Address:" << text;
            return;
        }
    }
    xml.readNext();
}
```

11. Check for any error text:

```
if (xml.hasError()) {
    qDebug() << "Error loading XML:" <<
    xml.errorString();
    return;
}
qDebug() << "No result.";
}
```

12. Add the following code to the `clicked()` slot function created by Qt:

```
void MainWindow::on_getAddressButton_clicked() {
    QString latitude = ui->latitude->text();
    QString longitude = ui->longitude->text();
    QNetworkRequest request;
request.setUrl(QUrl("http://maps.googleapis.com/maps/api/geocod
e/xml?latlng=" + latitude + "," + longitude +
"&key=AIzaSyBhKayXIr2zgMW2olsxtuZ7x2QWyLo1itQ"));
    addressRequest->get(request);
}
```

13. Build and run the program and you should be able to obtain the address by inserting the longitude and latitude values and clicking the **Get Address** button:

14. Let's try with a longitude of −73.9780838 and a latitude of 40.6712957. Click the **Get Address** button and you will see the following result in the application output window:

```
Address: "180-190 7th Ave, Brooklyn, NY 11215, USA"
```

How it works...

I won't be able to tell you exactly how Google obtains the address from its backend system, but I can teach you how to request the data from Google by using `QNetworkRequest`. All you need to do is to set the URL of the network request to the URL I used in the previous source code and append both the latitude and longitude information to the URL.

After that, all we can do is wait for the response from the Google API server. We need to specify XML as the desired format when sending the request to Google; otherwise, it may return the results in JSON format. This can be done by adding the `xml` keyword within the network request URL, as highlighted here:

```
request.setUrl(QUrl("http://maps.googleapis.com/maps/api/geocode/xml?keylat
lng=" + latitude + "," + longitude +
"&key=AIzaSyBhKayXIr2zgMW2olsxtuZ7x2QWyLo1itQ"));
```

When the program receives the response from Google, the `getAddressFinished()` slot function will be called and we will be able to obtain the data sent by Google through `QNetworkReply`.

Google usually replies with a long text in XML format, which contains a ton of data we don't need. We used the `QXmlStreamReader` class to parse the data because in this case, we don't have to care about the parent-child relationship of the XML structure.

All we need is the text stored in the `formatted_address` element in the XML data. Since there is more than one element by the name of `formatted_address`, we just need to find the first one and ignore the rest. You can also do the reverse by providing an address to Google and obtain the location's coordinate from its network response.

There's more...

Google's Geocoding API is part of the Google Maps APIs web services, which provide geographical data for your map applications. Besides the Geocoding API, you can also use their **Location API**, **Geolocation API**, and **Time Zone API** to achieve your desired results.

 For more information regarding the Google Maps APIs web services, visit `https://developers.google.com/maps/web-services`.

10
Conversion Library

This chapter will cover the following recipes:

- Converting data
- Converting images
- Converting videos
- Converting currency

Introduction

Data kept within our computer environment is encoded in a variety of ways. Sometimes, it can be used directly for a certain purpose, other times, it needs to be converted into another format in order to fit the context of the task. The process of converting data from one format into another also varies depending on the source format as well as the target format.

Sometimes, the process can be very complex, especially when dealing with data that is feature-rich and sensitive, such as image or video conversion. Even a small error during the conversion process may render the file unusable.

Technical requirements

The technical requirements for this chapter include Qt 5.11.2 MinGW 32 bit, Qt Creator 4.8.2, and Windows 10.

All the code used in this chapter can be downloaded from the following GitHub repository, at `https://github.com/PacktPublishing/Qt5-CPP-GUI-Programming-Cookbook-Second-Edition/tree/master/Chapter10`.

Check out the following video to see the code in action: `http://bit.ly/2ToKfCC`

Converting data

Qt provides a set of classes and functions for easily converting between different types of data. This makes Qt more than just a GUI library; it is a complete platform for software development. The `QVariant` class, which we will be using in the following example, makes Qt even more flexible and powerful compared to the similar conversion functionalities provided by the C++ standard library.

How to do it...

Let's learn how to convert various data types in Qt by following these steps:

1. Open Qt Creator and create a new **Qt Console Application** project by going to **File | New File or Project**:

2. Open `main.cpp` and add the following headers to it:

```
#include <QCoreApplication>
#include <QDebug>
#include <QtMath>
#include <QDateTime>
#include <QTextCodec>
#include <iostream>
```

3. In the `main()` function, add the following code to convert a string into a number:

```
int numberA = 2;
QString numberB = "5";
qDebug() << "1) " << "2 + 5 =" << numberA + numberB.toInt();
```

4. Convert a number back into a string:

```
float numberC = 10.25;
float numberD = 2;
QString result = QString::number(numberC * numberD);
qDebug() << "2) " << "10.25 * 2 =" << result;
```

5. Let's see how to round down a value using `qFloor()`:

```
float numberE = 10.3;
float numberF = qFloor(numberE);
qDebug() << "3) " << "Floor of 10.3 is" << numberF;
```

6. Using `qCeil()`, we are able to round a number to the smallest integral value not smaller than its initial value:

```
float numberG = 10.3;
float numberH = qCeil(numberG);
qDebug() << "4) " << "Ceil of 10.3 is" << numberH;
```

7. Create a date-time variable by converting from a piece of date-time data written in string format:

```
QString dateTimeAString = "2016-05-04 12:24:00";
QDateTime dateTimeA = QDateTime::fromString(dateTimeAString,
"yyyy-MM-dd hh:mm:ss");
qDebug() << "5) " << dateTimeA;
```

8. Convert the date-time variable back into a string with our custom format:

```
QDateTime dateTimeB = QDateTime::currentDateTime();
QString dateTimeBString = dateTimeB.toString("dd/MM/yy hh:mm");
qDebug() << "6) " << dateTimeBString;
```

9. Call the `QString::toUpper()` function to convert a string variable into all capital letters:

```
QString hello1 = "hello world!";
qDebug() << "7) " << hello1.toUpper();
```

10. Calling `QString::toLower()` will convert the string completely into lowercase:

```
QString hello2 = "HELLO WORLD!";
qDebug() << "8) " << hello2.toLower();
```

11. The `QVariant` class provided by Qt is a very powerful data type that can be easily converted to other types without any effort from the programmer:

```
QVariant aNumber = QVariant(3.14159);
double aResult = 12.5 * aNumber.toDouble();
qDebug() << "9) 12.5 * 3.14159 =" << aResult;
```

12. This demonstrates how a single `QVariant` variable can be simultaneously converted to multiple data types without any effort from the programmer:

```
qDebug() << "10) ";
QVariant myData = QVariant(10);
qDebug() << myData;
myData = myData.toFloat() / 2.135;
qDebug() << myData;
myData = true;
qDebug() << myData;
myData = QDateTime::currentDateTime();
qDebug() << myData;
myData = "Good bye!";
qDebug() << myData;
```

13. The full source code in `main.cpp` will now look like this:

```
#include <QCoreApplication>
#include <QDebug>
#include <QtMath>
#include <QDateTime>
#include <QTextCodec>
#include <iostream>

int main(int argc, char *argv[]) {
    QCoreApplication a(argc, argv);
```

14. After that, let's add in the code to convert a string into a number, and vice versa:

```
// String to number
int numberA = 2;
QString numberB = "5";
qDebug() << "1) " << "2 + 5 =" << numberA +
numberB.toInt();

// Number to string
float numberC = 10.25;
float numberD = 2;
QString result = QString::number(numberC * numberD);
qDebug() << "2) " << "10.25 * 2 =" << result;
```

15. Write the code to convert floating-point numbers to their nearest succeeding or preceding integer number, respectively:

```
// Floor
float numberE = 10.3;
float numberF = qFloor(numberE);
qDebug() << "3) " << "Floor of 10.3 is" << numberF;

// Ceil
float numberG = 10.3;
float numberH = qCeil(numberG);
qDebug() << "4) " << "Ceil of 10.3 is" << numberH;
```

16. Convert a string into date-time format, and vice versa:

```
// Date time from string
QString dateTimeAString = "2016-05-04 12:24:00";
QDateTime dateTimeA =
QDateTime::fromString(dateTimeAString, "yyyy-MM-dd hh:mm:ss");
qDebug() << "5) " << dateTimeA;

// Date time to string
QDateTime dateTimeB = QDateTime::currentDateTime();
QString dateTimeBString = dateTimeB.toString("dd/MM/yy
hh:mm");
qDebug() << "6) " << dateTimeBString;
```

17. Continue to add code to convert strings into uppercase or lowercase characters:

```
// String to all uppercase
QString hello1 = "hello world!";
qDebug() << "7) " << hello1.toUpper();

// String to all lowercase
QString hello2 = "HELLO WORLD!";
qDebug() << "8) " << hello2.toLower();
```

18. Convert the QVariant data type into other types:

```
// QVariant to double
QVariant aNumber = QVariant(3.14159);
double aResult = 12.5 * aNumber.toDouble();
qDebug() << "9) 12.5 * 3.14159 =" << aResult;

// QVariant different types
qDebug() << "10) ";
QVariant myData = QVariant(10);
qDebug() << myData;
myData = myData.toFloat() / 2.135;
qDebug() << myData;
myData = true;
qDebug() << myData;
```

19. Convert the QVariant data type into QDateTime and QString:

```
myData = QDateTime::currentDateTime();
qDebug() << myData;
myData = "Good bye!";
qDebug() << myData;

return a.exec();
}
```

20. Compile and run the project and you should see something like this:

```
C:\Qt\Tools\QtCreator\bin\qtcreator_process_stub.exe                                    —    □    ×
1)  2 + 5 = 7
2)  10.25 * 2 = "20.5"
3)  Floor of 10.3 is 10
4)  Ceil of 10.3 is 11
5)  QDateTime(2016-05-04 12:24:00.000 Malay Peninsula Standard Time Qt::TimeSpec(LocalTime))
6)  "26/12/18 11:50"
7)  "HELLO WORLD!"
8)  "hello world!"
9) 12.5 * 3.14159 = 39.2699
10)
QVariant(int, 10)
QVariant(double, 4.68384)
QVariant(bool, true)
QVariant(QDateTime, QDateTime(2018-12-26 11:50:23.322 Malay Peninsula Standard Time Qt::TimeSpec(LocalTime)))
QVariant(QString, "Good bye!")
```

How it works...

All the data types provided by Qt, such as QString, QDateTime, and QVariant, contain functions that make conversion to other types easy and straightforward. Qt also provides its own object conversion function, qobject_cast(), which doesn't rely on the standard library. It is also more compatible with Qt and works well for converting between Qt's widget types and data types.

Qt also provides you with the QtMath class, which helps you to manipulate number variables, such as rounding up a floating point number or converting an angle from degrees to radians. QVariant is a special class that can be used to store data of all kinds of types, such as int, float, char, string, and so on. It can automatically determine the data type by examining the value stored in the variable. You can also easily convert the data into any of the types supported by the QVariant class by just calling a single function, such as toFloat(), toInt(), toBool(), toChar(), or toString().

There's more...

Be aware that each of these conversions takes computing power. Even though modern computers are extremely fast at handling these operations, you should be careful not to overdo it with a large quantity at once. If you're converting a large set of variables for complex calculations, it might slow down your computer significantly, so try to convert variables only when necessary.

Converting images

In this section, we will learn how to build a simple image converter that converts an image from one format into another. Qt supports reading and writing different types of image formats, and this support comes in the form of external DLL files due to licensing issues. However, you don't have to worry about that because as long as you include those DLL files in your project, it will work seamlessly across different formats. There are certain formats that only support reading and not writing, and some that support both.

> You can check out the full details at `http://doc.qt.io/qt-5/qtimageformats-index.html`.

How to do it...

Qt's built-in image libraries make image conversion really simple:

1. Open Qt Creator and create a new **Qt Widgets Application** project.
2. Open `mainwindow.ui` and add a line edit and push button to the canvas to select image files, a combo box to select the desired file format, and another push button to start the conversion process:

3. Double-click the combo box and a window will appear where you can edit the combo box. We will add three items to the combo box list by clicking the + button three times and renaming the items PNG, JPEG, and BMP:

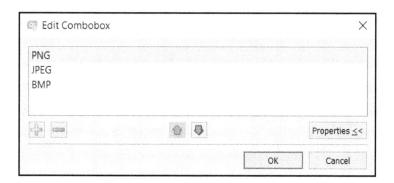

4. Right-click on one of the push buttons and select **Go to slot...**, then click the **OK** button. A slot function will be automatically added to your source files. Repeat this step for the other push button as well:

5. Let's move over to the source code. Open `mainwindow.h` and add in the following header:

```
#include <QMainWindow>
#include <QFileDialog>
#include <QMessageBox>
#include <QDebug>
```

6. Open `mainwindow.cpp` and define what will happen when the **Browse** button is clicked, which in this case is opening the file dialog to select an image file:

```
void MainWindow::on_browseButton_clicked() {
    QString fileName = QFileDialog::getOpenFileName(this, "Open
Image", "", "Image Files (*.png *.jpg *.bmp)");
    ui->filePath->setText(fileName);
}
```

7. Define what will happen when the **Convert** button is clicked:

```
void MainWindow::on_convertButton_clicked() {
    QString fileName = ui->filePath->text();
    if (fileName != "") {
        QFileInfo fileInfo = QFile(fileName);
        QString newFileName = fileInfo.path() + "/" +
fileInfo.completeBaseName();
        QImage image = QImage(ui->filePath->text());
        if (!image.isNull()) {
```

8. Check which format is being used:

```
// 0 = PNG, 1 = JPG, 2 = BMP
int format = ui->fileFormat->currentIndex();
if (format == 0) {
    newFileName += ".png";
}
else if (format == 1) {
    newFileName += ".jpg";
}
else if (format == 2) {
    newFileName += ".bmp";
}
```

9. Check whether the image has been converted:

```
qDebug() << newFileName << format;
if (image.save(newFileName, 0, -1)) {
    QMessageBox::information(this, "Success",
"Image successfully converted.");
}
else {
    QMessageBox::warning(this, "Failed", "Failed to
convert image.");
}
}
```

10. Display the message boxes:

```
else {
    QMessageBox::warning(this, "Failed", "Failed to
open image file.");
}
}
else {
    QMessageBox::warning(this, "Failed", "No file is
selected.");
}
}
```

11. Build and run the program now, and we should get a pretty simple image converter that looks like this:

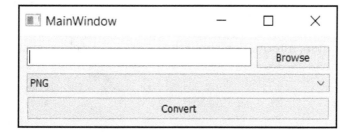

How it works...

The previous example uses the native `QImage` class from Qt, which contains functions that can access pixel data and manipulate it. It is also used to load an image file and extract its data through different decompression methods, depending on the format of the image. Once the data is extracted, you can do anything you want with it, such as display the image onscreen, manipulate its color information, resize the image, or compress it with another format and save it as a file.

We used `QFileInfo` to separate the filename from the extension so that we can amend the extension name with the new format selected by the user from the combo box. This way, we can save the newly-converted image in the same folder as the original image and automatically give it the same file name as well, except in a different format.

As long as you're trying to convert the image to a format supported by Qt, you just need to call `QImage::save()`. Internally, Qt will figure out the rest for you and output the image to the chosen format. In the `QImage::save()` function, there is a parameter that sets the image quality and another that sets the format. In this example, we just set both as the default values, which saves the image at the highest quality and lets Qt figure out the format by checking the extension stated in the output filename.

There's more...

You can also convert an image into a PDF using the `QPdfWriter` class provided by Qt. Essentially, you paint the selected image to the layout of a newly-created PDF document and set its resolution accordingly.

 For more information about the `QPdfWriter` class, visit `http://doc.qt.io/qt-5/qpdfwriter.html`.

Converting videos

In this recipe, we will create a simple video converter using Qt and FFmpeg, a leading multimedia framework that is free and open source. Although Qt supports playing video files through its widget, it does not currently support video conversion. Fear not! You can still achieve the same goal by making your program cooperate with another standalone program through the QProcess class provided by Qt.

How to do it...

Let's make a simple video converter with the following steps:

1. Download FFmpeg (static package) from http://ffmpeg.zeranoe.com/builds and extract the contents to C:/FFmpeg/.

2. Open Qt Creator and create a new **Qt Widgets Application** project by going to **File | New File or Project**.

3. Open mainwindow.ui—we're going to work on the program's user interface. Its UI is very similar to the previous example, except that we add an extra text-edit widget to the canvas, just under the combo box:

4. Double-click the combo box and a window will appear to edit the combo box. We will add three items to the combo box list by clicking the + button three times, and rename the items AVI, MP4, and MOV:

5. Right-click on one of the push buttons and select **Go to slot...**, then click the **OK** button. A slot function will then be automatically added to your source files. Repeat this step for the other push button as well.

6. Open mainwindow.h and add the following headers to the top:

```
#include <QMainWindow>
#include <QFileDialog>
#include <QProcess>
#include <QMessageBox>
#include <QScrollBar>
#include <QDebug>
```

7. Add the following pointers under the public keyword:

```
public:
    explicit MainWindow(QWidget *parent = 0);
    ~MainWindow();
    QProcess* process;
    QString outputText;
    QString fileName;
    QString outputFileName;
```

8. Add three extra slot functions under the two functions that Qt created for us previously in the *Converting images* recipe:

```
private slots:
    void on_browseButton_clicked();
    void on_convertButton_clicked();
    void processStarted();
    void readyReadStandardOutput();
    void processFinished();
```

9. Open `mainwindow.cpp` and add the following code to the class constructor:

```
MainWindow::MainWindow(QWidget *parent) :
QMainWindow(parent), ui(new Ui::MainWindow) {
    ui->setupUi(this);
    process = new QProcess(this);
    connect(process, QProcess::started, this,
MainWindow::processStarted);
    connect(process, QProcess::readyReadStandardOutput, this,
MainWindow::readyReadStandardOutput);
    connect(process, QProcess::finished, this,
    MainWindow::processFinished);
}
```

10. Define what will happen when the **Browse** button is clicked, which in this case will open up the file dialog to allow us to choose the video file:

```
void MainWindow::on_browseButton_clicked() {
    QString fileName = QFileDialog::getOpenFileName(this, "Open
Video", "", "Video Files (*.avi *.mp4 *.mov)");
    ui->filePath->setText(fileName);
}
```

11. Define what will happen if the **Convert** button is clicked. Here, we are passing the filenames and arguments to FFmpeg and then the conversion process will be handled externally by FFmpeg:

```
void MainWindow::on_convertButton_clicked() {
    QString ffmpeg = "C:/FFmpeg/bin/ffmpeg";
    QStringList arguments;
    fileName = ui->filePath->text();
    if (fileName != "") {
        QFileInfo fileInfo = QFile(fileName);
        outputFileName = fileInfo.path() + "/" +
fileInfo.completeBaseName();
```

12. Check for the file's format; specifically, whether it's `.avi`, `.mp4`, or `.mov`:

```cpp
if (QFile::exists(fileName)) {
    int format = ui->fileFormat->currentIndex();
    if (format == 0) {
        outputFileName += ".avi"; // AVI
    }
    else if (format == 1) {
        outputFileName += ".mp4"; // MP4
    }
    else if (format == 2) {
        outputFileName += ".mov"; // MOV
    }
```

13. Start the conversion using the following code:

```cpp
        qDebug() << outputFileName << format;
        arguments << "-i" << fileName << outputFileName;
        qDebug() << arguments;
process->setProcessChannelMode(QProcess::MergedChannels);
        process->start(ffmpeg, arguments);
    }
```

14. Display the message boxes:

```cpp
    else {
        QMessageBox::warning(this, "Failed", "Failed to
open video file.");
    }
}
else {
    QMessageBox::warning(this, "Failed", "No file is
selected.");
    }
}
```

15. Tell the program what to do when the conversion process has started:

```cpp
void MainWindow::processStarted() {
    qDebug() << "Process started.";
    ui->browseButton->setEnabled(false);
    ui->fileFormat->setEditable(false);
    ui->convertButton->setEnabled(false);
}
```

16. Write the slot function that gets called during the conversion process whenever FFmpeg returns an output to the program:

```
void MainWindow::readyReadStandardOutput() {
    outputText += process->readAllStandardOutput();
    ui->outputDisplay->setText(outputText);
ui->outputDisplay->verticalScrollBar()->setSliderPosition(ui->o
utputDisplay->verticalScrollBar()->maximum());
}
```

17. Define the slot function that gets called when the entire conversion process has been completed:

```
void MainWindow::processFinished() {
    qDebug() << "Process finished.";
    if (QFile::exists(outputFileName)) {
        QMessageBox::information(this, "Success", "Video
successfully converted.");
    }
    else {
        QMessageBox::information(this, "Failed", "Failed to
convert video.");
    }
    ui->browseButton->setEnabled(true);
    ui->fileFormat->setEditable(true);
    ui->convertButton->setEnabled(true);
}
```

18. Build and run the project, and you should get a simple, yet workable, video converter:

How it works...

The `QProcess` class provided by Qt is used to start external programs and communicate with them. In this case, we started `ffmpeg.exe`, located in `C:/FFmpeg/bin/`, as a process and started communicating with it. We also sent it a set of arguments to tell it what to do when it started. The arguments we used in this example are relatively basic: we only told FFmpeg the path to the source image and the output filename.

For more information regarding the argument settings available in FFmpeg, check out: `https://www.ffmpeg.org/ffmpeg.html`.

FFmpeg does more than just convert video files. You can also use it to convert audio files and images.

For more information regarding all the formats supported by FFmpeg, check out:
`https://www.ffmpeg.org/general.html#File-Formats`.

Other than that, you can also play a video or audio file by running `ffplay.exe`, located in `C:/FFmpeg/bin`, or print out the information of the video or audio file in a human-readable fashion by running `ffprobe.exe`.

Check out FFmpeg's full documentation at `https://www.ffmpeg.org/about.html`.

There's more...

There are lots of things you can do using this method. You're not limited to what Qt provides and you can break out of such limitations by carefully selecting a third-party program that provides what you need. One such example is making your own antivirus GUI by utilizing the command-line-only antivirus scanners available on the market, such as **Avira ScanCL**, **Panda Antivirus Command Line Scanner**, **SAV32CLI**, and **ClamAV**. You can build your own GUI using Qt and essentially send commands to the antivirus process to tell it what to do.

Converting currency

In this example, we will learn how to create a simple currency converter using Qt, with the help of an external service provider called **Fixer.io**.

How to do it...

Make yourself a currency converter with these simple steps:

1. Open Qt Creator and create a new **Qt Widgets Application** project from **File |
New File or Project**.

2. Open the project file (.pro) and add the network module to our project:

```
QT += core gui network
```

3. Open mainwindow.ui and remove the menu bar, toolbar, and status bar from the UI.

4. Add three horizontal layouts, a horizontal line, and a push button to the canvas. Left-click on the canvas and continue by clicking the **Lay Out Vertically** button on top of the canvas. Set the label of the push button to Convert. The UI should look something like this:

5. Add two labels to the top layout and set the text of the left one to From:, followed by the right one to To:. Add two **Line Edit** widgets to the second layout and set both their default values to 1:

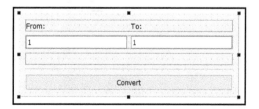

6. Select the line edit on the right and enable the **readOnly** checkbox located in the **Property** pane:

7. Set the **cursor** property to **Forbidden** so that users know it's not editable when mousing over the widget:

8. Add two combo boxes to the third layout located at the bottom. We will leave them empty for now:

9. Right-click on the **Convert** button and select **Go to slot....**. A window will pop up, asking you to select an appropriate signal. Let's keep the default **clicked()** signal as the selection and click **OK**. Qt Creator will automatically add a slot function to both `mainwindow.h` and `mainwindow.cpp`.

10. Open `mainwindow.h` and make sure the following headers are being added to the top of the source file:

```
#include <QMainWindow>
#include <QDoubleValidator>
#include <QNetworkAccessManager>
#include <QNetworkRequest>
#include <QNetworkReply>
#include <QJsonDocument>
#include <QJsonObject>
#include <QDebug>
#include <QMessageBox>
```

11. Add another slot function, called `finished()`:

```
private slots:
    void on_convertButton_clicked();
    void finished(QNetworkReply* reply);
```

12. Add two variables under the `private` label:

```
private:
    Ui::MainWindow *ui;
    QNetworkAccessManager* manager;
    QString targetCurrency;
```

13. Open the `mainwindow.cpp` file. Add several currency short codes to both combo boxes in the class constructor. Set a validator to the **Line Edit** widget on the left so that it can only accept inputs that are numbers. Initialize the network access manager and connect its `finished()` signal to our `finished()` slot function:

```
MainWindow::MainWindow(QWidget *parent) :
QMainWindow(parent), ui(new Ui::MainWindow) {
    ui->setupUi(this);
    QStringList currencies;
    currencies.push_back("EUR");
    currencies.push_back("USD");
    currencies.push_back("CAD");
    currencies.push_back("MYR");
    currencies.push_back("GBP");
```

14. We continue from the previous code and insert the currency short forms into the combo boxes. Then, we declare a new network access manager and connect its **finished** signal to our custom slot function:

```
    ui->currencyFrom->insertItems(0, currencies);
    ui->currencyTo->insertItems(0, currencies);
    QValidator *inputRange = new QDoubleValidator(this);
    ui->amountFrom->setValidator(inputRange);
    manager = new QNetworkAccessManager(this);
    connect(manager, &QNetworkAccessManager::finished, this,
&MainWindow::finished);
}
```

15. Define what will happen if the `Convert` button is clicked by the user:

```
void MainWindow::on_convertButton_clicked() {
    if (ui->amountFrom->text() != "") {
        ui->convertButton->setEnabled(false);
        QString from = ui->currencyFrom->currentText();
        QString to = ui->currencyTo->currentText();
        targetCurrency = to;
        QString url = "http://data.fixer.io/api/latest?base=" +
from + "&symbols=" + to +
"&access_key=616e8b801a222f144a9460b5e6942ca4";
```

16. Start the request by calling `get()`:

```
        QNetworkRequest request= QNetworkRequest(QUrl(url));
        manager->get(request);
    } else {
        QMessageBox::warning(this, "Error", "Please insert a
value.");
    }
}
```

17. Define what will happen when the `finished()` signal is triggered:

```
void MainWindow::finished(QNetworkReply* reply) {
    QByteArray response = reply->readAll();
    qDebug() << response;
    QJsonDocument jsonResponse =
QJsonDocument::fromJson(response);
    QJsonObject jsonObj = jsonResponse.object();
    QJsonObject jsonObj2 = jsonObj.value("rates").toObject();
    double rate = jsonObj2.value(targetCurrency).toDouble();
```

18. Continue to write the code from the preceding code, as shown in the following:

```
    if (rate == 0)
        rate = 1;
    double amount = ui->amountFrom->text().toDouble();
    double result = amount * rate;
    ui->amountTo->setText(QString::number(result));
    ui->convertButton->setEnabled(true);
}
```

19. Compile and run the project, and you should get a simple currency converter that looks like this:

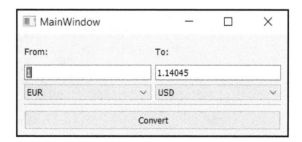

How it works...

Similar to the previous example we saw, which uses an external program to achieve a specific task, this time we used an external service provider that provided us with an open **Application Programming Interface** (**API**) that is free for all and easy to use.

This way, we don't have to think about the method used to retrieve the latest currency rate. Instead, the service provider has already done the job for us; we just have to send a polite request to ask for it. Then, we wait for the response from their server and process the data according to our intended purposes.

There are quite a few different service providers you can choose from, besides Fixer.io (`http://fixer.io`). Some are free, but come without any advanced features; some provide you with premium price. Some of these alternatives are **open exchange rates** (`https://openexchangerates.org`), **currencylayer API** (`https://currencylayer.com`), **Currency API** (`https://currency-api.appspot.com`), **XE Currency Data API** (`http://www.xe.com/xecurrencydata`), and **jsonrates** (`http://jsonrates.com`).

In the previous code, you should have noticed an access key being passed to the Fixer.io API, which is a free access key I registered for this tutorial. If you are using it for your own project, you should create an account at Fixer.io.

There's more...

Besides currency exchange rates, you can use this method to execute more advanced tasks that are perhaps too complicated to do by yourself, or are simply impossible to access unless you use the services provided by specialists, such as programmable **Short Message Service** (**SMS**) and voice services, web analytics and statistics generation, and online payment gateways. Most of these services are not free, but you can easily achieve those functions in minutes without even setting up the server infrastructure and backend system; it's definitely the cheapest and fastest way to get your product up and running without much hassle.

Accessing Databases with SQL Driver and Qt

11

The chapter will cover the following recipes:

- Setting up a database
- Connecting to a database
- Writing basic SQL queries
- Creating a login screen with Qt
- Displaying information from a database on a model view
- Advanced SQL queries

Introduction

Structured Query Language (**SQL**) is a special programming language used to manage data held in a relational database management system. A SQL Server is a database system designed to use one of the many types of SQL programming languages to manage its data.

 If you want to learn more about SQL, visit `http://www.w3schools.com/sql/sql_intro.asp`.

Technical requirements

The technical requirements for this chapter include Qt 5.11.2 MinGW 32-bit, Qt Creator 4.8.2, Windows 10, and XAMPP with MySQL.

All the code used in this chapter can be downloaded from the following GitHub link: `https://github.com/PacktPublishing/Qt5-CPP-GUI-Programming-Cookbook-Second-Edition/tree/master/Chapter11`.

Check out the following video to see the code in action: `http://bit.ly/2TptLKn`

Setting up a database

Qt supports several different types of SQL drivers in the form of plugins/add-ons. However, it's very easy to integrate these drivers into your Qt project. We will learn how to do this in the following example.

How to do it...

Let's set up our SQL Server before we dive into Qt:

1. Install and set up a MySQL Server. There are many ways you can install it. One method is to download MySQL from the official website at `http://dev.mysql.com/downloads/mysql/` and install it. After that, you also need to install MySQL Workbench from `http://dev.mysql.com/downloads/workbench/` to administrate your databases.

2. An alternative method is to install a third-party package that comes with MySQL and other useful applications, such as the Apache web server or phpMyAdmin, all in a unified installer. Examples of such packages are XAMPP, found at `https://sourceforge.net/projects/xampp/`, and AppServ, found at `https://www.appservnetwork.com/en/download/`.

3. In this example, we will install XAMPP. Open your web browser, download the XAMPP installer from `https://sourceforge.net/projects/xampp/`, and install it on your computer.

4. Open **XAMPP Control Panel** and you should see something like this:

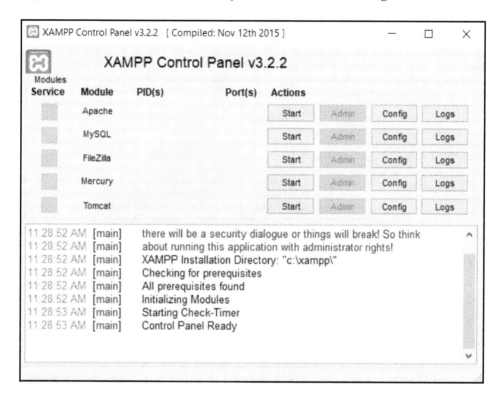

5. We need the **Apache** web server and the **MySQL** database server. Click the **Start** buttons next to the **Apache** and **MySQL** options on the control panel.

6. Once the servers have been started, open your web browser and visit `http://localhost/phpmyadmin/`. You will see a web interface by the name of **phpMyAdmin**, which looks like this:

phpMyAdmin is a web-based utility that helps you manage your MySQL databases, much like MySQL Workbench. In my opinion, **phpMyAdmin** is a lot simpler and better suited to beginners, which is why I recommend using it instead of MySQL Workbench. By default, **phpMyAdmin** automatically logs into MySQL using the default user account root, which is saved in its configuration file. We don't want to use that, for security reasons. So, let's create an account for ourselves.

7. Go to the **Users** tab, located at the top, and, once you're on that page, click **Add user account**, located at the bottom. Key in your desired username and password in the fields in the **Login Information** pane. Choose **Local** for the **Host name** option for now. At the bottom, you will see options related to **Global privileges**, check the **Check All** option and click **Go**:

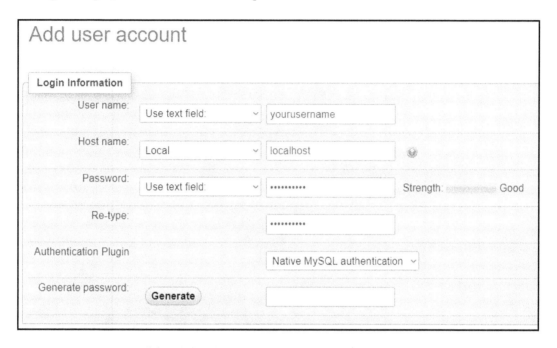

8. Go to **XAMPP Control Panel** and click **Stop** for both Apache and MySQL. Click the **Config** button in the **Apache** column and select the **phpMyAdmin** (`config.inc.php`) option; the `config.inc.php` file will be opened with your choice of text editor.

9. Search for the following line in `config.inc.php` and change the word `config` to `cookie`:

```
$cfg['Servers'][$i]['auth_type'] = 'config';
$cfg['Servers'][$i]['auth_type'] = 'cookie';
```

10. Start Apache and MySQL again by clicking the **Start** buttons. This way, we force **phpMyAdmin** to reload its configurations and apply the changes. Go to **phpMyAdmin** again from your web browser, and this time around, a login screen should appear:

11. Log into **phpMyAdmin**, then click on the **New** link located on the sidebar:

12. Key in your desired database name and press the **Create** button. Once it's been created, the database name will appear on the side bar. Click on the database name and it will take you to another page, which displays a message: **No tables found in database**. Under the message, you can create your first data table by filling in your desired table **Name** and the **Number of columns** for the table:

13. Click the **Go** button and you will be brought to another page, where you will set up the new table you're going to create. In this example, we created an `employee` table that consists of five columns of data: **id, name, age, gender**, and **married**:

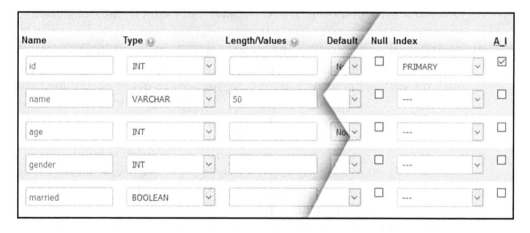

14. Click **Save** and now you will be able to see the `employee` table name appear on the side bar. We have successfully installed MySQL and set up our first database and data table.

15. We need to insert data into the database from **phpMyAdmin** so that we will be able to retrieve it in the next example. Click on the **Insert** tab while you're still in the `employee` table. You will then be taken to another page to insert new data into the `employee` table:

Column	Type	Function	Null	Value
id	int(11)			1
name	varchar(50)			John Doe
age	int(11)			42
gender	int(11)			0
married	tinyint(1)			1

16. Let's set up the SQL driver for our Qt project. Just go to your Qt installation folder and look for the `sqldrivers` folder. For example, mine is located at `C:\Qt\5.5\mingw492_32\plugins\sqldrivers`.

17. Copy the entire `sqldrivers` folder to your project's build directory. You can remove the DLL files that are not relevant to the SQL Server you're running. In our case, since we're using a MySQL Server, we can delete everything except `qsqlmysql.dll` and `qsqlmysqld.dll`. The DLL file with the letter d at the end is for **debug** builds only, while the other one is for **release** builds. Put those DLL files in their respective build directories, for example, `builds/debug/sqldrivers/qsqlmysqld.dll` for debug builds and `builds/release/sqldrivers/qsqlmysql.dll` for release builds.

18. The DLL files mentioned in the previous step are the drivers that enable Qt to communicate with different types of SQL architecture. You may also need the DLL file of the SQL client library in order for the driver to work. In our case, we need `libmysql.dll` to be located in the same directory as our program's executable. You can either get it from the installation directory of MySQL or download the `Connector/C++` package from the official website: `https://dev.mysql.com/downloads/connector/cpp/`.

How it works...

Qt provides us with SQL drivers so that we can easily connect to different types of SQL Servers without implementing them ourselves.

Currently, Qt officially supports SQLite, MySQL, ODBC, and PostgreSQL. SQL architectures that are forks from one of the supported architectures, such as MariaDB (a fork of MySQL), may still be compatible with Qt without much hassle. If you are using an architecture that isn't supported by Qt, you can still interact with your SQL database indirectly by sending an HTTP request using QNetworkAccessManager to your backend script (such as PHP, ASP, and JSP), which can then communicate with the database.

If you only need a simple file-based database and don't plan to use a server-based database, SQLite is a good choice for you.

In the *Connecting to a database* recipe, we will learn how to connect to our SQL database using Qt's SQL module.

Connecting to a database

In this recipe, we will learn how to connect our Qt 5 application to the SQL Server.

How to do it...

Connecting to SQL Server in Qt is really simple:

1. Open Qt Creator and create a new **Qt Widgets Application** project.
2. Open your project file (.pro) and add the sql module to your project, like so:

```
QT += core gui sql
```

3. Open `mainwindow.ui` and drag seven label widgets, a combo box, and a checkbox to the canvas. Set the text properties of four of the labels to `Name:`, `Age:`, `Gender:`, and `Married:`. Then, set the **objectName** properties of the rest to `name`, `age`, `gender`, and `married`. There is no need to set the object name for the previous four labels, because they're for display purposes only:

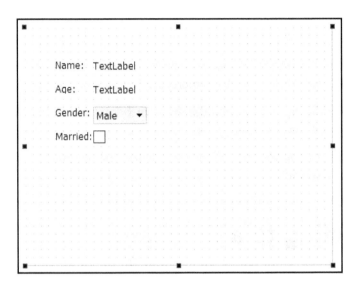

4. Open `mainwindow.h` and add the following headers below the `QMainWindow` header:

```
#include <QMainWindow>
#include <QtSql>
#include <QSqlDatabase>
#include <QSqlQuery>
#include <QDebug>
```

5. Open `mainwindow.cpp` and insert the following code into the class constructor:

```
MainWindow::MainWindow(QWidget *parent) :
QMainWindow(parent), ui(new Ui::MainWindow) {
    ui->setupUi(this);
    QSqlDatabase db = QSqlDatabase::addDatabase("QMYSQL");
    db.setHostName("127.0.0.1");
    db.setUserName("yourusername");
    db.setPassword("yourpassword");
    db.setDatabaseName("databasename");
```

6. Start the SQL query once the database connection has been opened:

```
if (db.open()) {
    QSqlQuery query;
    if (query.exec("SELECT name, age, gender, married FROM
employee")) {
        while (query.next()) {
            qDebug() << query.value(0) << query.value(1) <<
query.value(2) << query.value(3);
            ui->name->setText(query.value(0).toString());
            ui->age->setText(query.value(1).toString());
ui->gender->setCurrentIndex(query.value(2).toInt());
            ui->married->setChecked(query.value(3).toBool());
        }
    }
```

7. Print out any error texts:

```
else {
            qDebug() << query.lastError().text();
        }
        db.close();
    }
    else {
        qDebug() << "Failed to connect to database.";
    }
}
```

8. Compile and run your project now and you should get something like this:

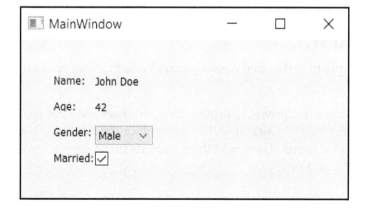

How it works...

The previous example shows you how to connect to your SQL database using the `QSqlDatabase` class derived from the SQL module. You won't be able to access any of the classes related to SQL without adding the module to your Qt project.

We must tell Qt which SQL architecture we are running by mentioning it when calling the `addDatabase()` function. Options supported by Qt are `QSQLITE`, `QMYSQL`, `QMYSQL3`, `QODBC`, `QODBC3`, `QPSQL`, and `QPSQL7`. If you encounter an error message that says **QSqlDatabase: QMYSQL driver not loaded**, you should check whether the DLL files are placed in the correct directory.

We can send our SQL statements to the database through the `QSqlQuery` class, and wait for it to return the results, which are usually either the data you requested or error messages due to invalid statements. If there is any data coming from the database server, it will all be stored in the `QSqlQuery` class. All you need to retrieve this data is to do a while loop on the `QSqlQuery` class to check for all existing records, and retrieve them by calling the `value()` function.

Writing basic SQL queries

In the previous example, we wrote our very first SQL query, which involves the `SELECT` statement. This time, we will learn how to use some other SQL statements, such as `INSERT`, `UPDATE`, and `DELETE`.

How to do it...

Let's create a simple program that demonstrates basic SQL query commands by following these steps:

1. We can use our previous project files, but there are a couple of things we need to change. Open `mainwindow.ui` and replace the labels for **Name** and **Age** with line-edit widgets. Then, add three buttons to the canvas and call them `UPDATE`, `INSERT`, and `DELETE`:

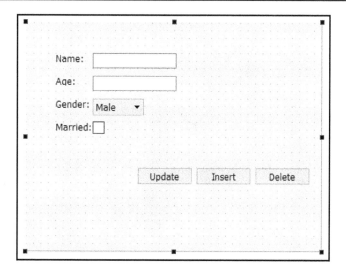

2. Open `mainwindow.h` and add the following variables under the `private` inheritance:

```
private:
    Ui::MainWindow *ui;
    QSqlDatabase db;
    bool connected;
    int currentID;
```

3. Open `mainwindow.cpp` and go to the class constructor. It is still pretty much the same as the previous example, except we store the database connection status in a `Boolean` variable called `connected`, and we also obtain the ID of the data from the database and store it to an integer variable called `currentID`:

```
MainWindow::MainWindow(QWidget *parent) :
QMainWindow(parent), ui(new Ui::MainWindow) {
    ui->setupUi(this);
    db = QSqlDatabase::addDatabase("QMYSQL");
    db.setHostName("127.0.0.1");
    db.setUserName("yourusername");
    db.setPassword("yourpassword");
    db.setDatabaseName("databasename");
    connected = db.open();
```

4. Let's make a query after we have connected to the database:

```
if (connected) {
        QSqlQuery query;
        if (query.exec("SELECT id, name, age, gender, married
FROM employee")) {
                while (query.next()) {
                        currentID = query.value(0).toInt();
                        ui->name->setText(query.value(1).toString());
                        ui->age->setText(query.value(2).toString());
        ui->gender->setCurrentIndex(query.value(3).toInt());
        ui->married->setChecked(query.value(4).toBool());
                }
        }
```

5. Print out any error messages:

```
else {
        qDebug() << query.lastError().text();
    }
}
else {
    qDebug() << "Failed to connect to database.";
}
}
```

6. Go to `mainwindow.ui` and right-click on one of the buttons we added to the canvas in *step 1*. Select **Go to slot...** and click **OK**. Repeat these steps on the other button, and now you should see three slot functions being added to both your `mainwindow.h` and `mainwindow.cpp`:

```
private slots:
    void on_updateButton_clicked();
    void on_insertButton_clicked();
    void on_deleteButton_clicked();
```

7. Open `mainwindow.cpp` and we will declare what the program will do when we click on the **Update** button:

```
void MainWindow::on_updateButton_clicked() {
    if (connected) {
        if (currentID == 0) {
            qDebug() << "Nothing to update.";
        }
        else {
            QString id = QString::number(currentID);
            QString name = ui->name->text();
```

```
                QString age = ui->age->text();
                QString gender =
QString::number(ui->gender->currentIndex());
                QString married =
QString::number(ui->married->isChecked());
```

8. Make an **UPDATE** query, like so:

```
                qDebug() << "UPDATE employee SET name = '" + name +
"', age = '" + age + "', gender = " + gender + ", married = " +
married + " WHERE id = " + id;
                QSqlQuery query;
                if (query.exec("UPDATE employee SET name = '" +
name + "', age = '" + age + "', gender = " + gender + ",
married = " + married + " WHERE id = " + id)) {
                    qDebug() << "Update success.";
                }
```

9. Print out the last error message, if any:

```
        else {
                qDebug() << query.lastError().text();
            }
        }
    } else {
        qDebug() << "Failed to connect to database.";
    }
}
```

10. Declare what will happen when the INSERT button is clicked:

```
void MainWindow::on_insertButton_clicked() {
    if (connected) {
        QString name = ui->name->text();
        QString age = ui->age->text();
        QString gender =
QString::number(ui->gender->currentIndex());
        QString married =
QString::number(ui->married->isChecked());
        qDebug() << "INSERT INTO employee (name, age, gender,
married) VALUES ('" + name + "','" + age + "', " + gender + ","
+ married + ")";
```

11. Make an `INSERT` query, like so:

```
QSqlQuery query;
if (query.exec("INSERT INTO employee (name, age, gender,
married) VALUES ('" + name + "','" + age + "', " + gender + "," +
married + ")")) {
        currentID = query.lastInsertId().toInt();
        qDebug() << "Insert success.";
    } else {
        qDebug() << query.lastError().text();
    }
} else {
    qDebug() << "Failed to connect to database.";
}
}
```

12. Declare what will happen when the `Delete` button is clicked:

```
void MainWindow::on_deleteButton_clicked() {
    if (connected) {
        if (currentID == 0) {
            qDebug() << "Nothing to delete.";
        } else {
            QString id = QString::number(currentID);
            qDebug() << "DELETE FROM employee WHERE id = " +
id;

            QSqlQuery query;
            if (query.exec("DELETE FROM employee WHERE id = " +
id)) {
                currentID = 0;
                qDebug() << "Delete success.";
            } else {
                qDebug() << query.lastError().text();
            }
        }
    } else {
        qDebug() << "Failed to connect to database.";
    }
}
```

13. Call `QSqlDatabase::close()` at the class destructor to properly terminate the SQL connection before exiting the program:

```
MainWindow::~MainWindow() {
    db.close();
    delete ui;
}
```

14. Compile and run the program now and you should be able to select the default data from the database. Then, you can choose to update it or delete it from the database. You can also insert new data into the database by clicking the `Insert` button. You can use phpMyAdmin to check whether the data is being altered correctly:

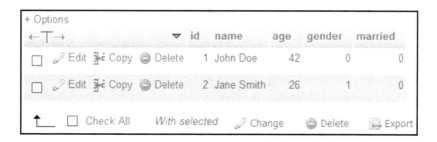

How it works...

It's very important to check whether the database is connected before we proceed to send a SQL query to the database. Therefore, we keep that status in a variable and use it to check before sending out any queries. This, however, is not recommended for complex programs that are kept open for long periods of time, as the database might get disconnected during those periods, and a fixed variable may not be accurate. In that case, it's better to check the actual status by calling `QSqlDatabase::isOpen()`.

The `currentID` variable is used to save the ID of the current data you obtained from the database. When you want to update the data or delete it from the database, this variable is crucial for letting the database know what data you're trying to update or delete. If you set your database table correctly, MySQL will treat each item of data as a unique entry, so you can be sure that no repeated ID will be produced in the database when new data is being saved.

After inserting new data into the database, we call `QSqlQuery::lastInsertId()` to obtain the ID of the new data and save it as a `currentID` variable so that it becomes the current data that we can update or delete from the database. It is a good habit to test your SQL queries on phpMyAdmin before using them in Qt. You can instantly find out whether your SQL statements are correct or incorrect, instead of waiting for your project to be built, trying it out, then rebuilding it. As programmers, we must work in the most efficient way. Work hard, and work smart.

Creating a login screen with Qt

In this recipe, we will learn how put our knowledge to use and create a functional login screen using Qt and MySQL.

How to do it…

Create your first functional login screen by following these steps:

1. Open a web browser and go to phpMyAdmin. We will create a new data table called `user`, which looks like this:

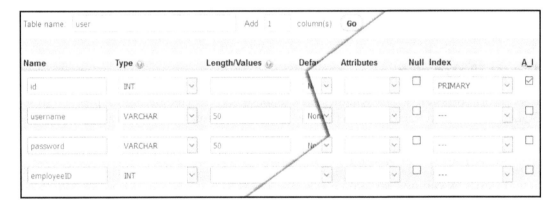

2. Let's insert our first item of data into the newly-created table and set `employeeID` to the ID of an existing employee. This way, the user account we create will be linked to the data of one of the employees:

3. Open Qt Creator and create a new **Qt Widgets Application** project. We will start off with `mainwindow.ui`. Place a stacked widget on the canvas and make sure it contains two pages. Then, set up the two pages in the stacked widget like this:

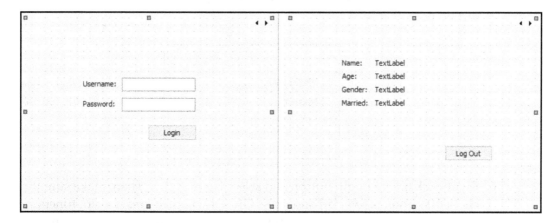

4. On the first page of the stacked widget, click the Edit Tab Order icon on top of the widget so that you can adjust the order of the widgets in your program:

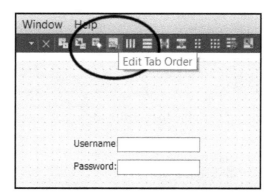

5. Once you click the Edit Tab Order icon, you will see some numbers appear on top of each widget in the canvas. Make sure the numbers look as they do in the screenshot that follows. Otherwise, click on the numbers to change their order. We only do this for the first page of the stacked widget; it's okay to keep the second page as it is:

6. Right-click on the **Login** button and select **Go to slot...**. Then, make sure the **clicked()** option is selected and press **OK**. Qt will then create a slot function for you in your project source files. Repeat this step for the **Log Out** button as well.

7. Open `mainwindow.h` and add the following headers after the `#include <QMainWindow>` line:

```
#include <QMainWindow>
#include <QtSql>
#include <QSqlDatabase>
#include <QSqlQuery>
#include <QMessageBox>
#include <QDebug>
```

8. Add the following variable to `mainwindow.h`:

```
private:
    Ui::MainWindow *ui;
    QSqlDatabase db;
```

9. Open `mainwindow.cpp` and put this code in the class constructor:

```
MainWindow::MainWindow(QWidget *parent) :
QMainWindow(parent),
ui(new Ui::MainWindow) {
    ui->setupUi(this);
    ui->stackedWidget->setCurrentIndex(0);
    db = QSqlDatabase::addDatabase("QMYSQL");
    db.setHostName("127.0.0.1");
    db.setUserName("yourusername");
    db.setPassword("yourpassword");
    db.setDatabaseName("databasename");
```

```
        if (!db.open()) {
            qDebug() << "Failed to connect to database.";
        }
    }
```

10. Define what will happen if the **Login** button is clicked:

```
void MainWindow::on_loginButton_clicked() {
    QString username = ui->username->text();
    QString password = ui->password->text();
    QSqlQuery query;
    if (query.exec("SELECT employeeID from user WHERE username
= '" + username + "' AND password = '" + password + "'")) {
        if (query.size() > 0) {
            while (query.next()) {
                QString employeeID = query.value(0).toString();
                QSqlQuery query2;
```

11. Make a SQL query:

```
        if (query2.exec("SELECT name, age, gender, married FROM
employee WHERE id = " + employeeID)) {
            while (query2.next()) {
                QString name = query2.value(0).toString();
                QString age = query2.value(1).toString();
                int gender = query2.value(2).toInt();
                bool married = query2.value(3).toBool();
                ui->name->setText(name);
                ui->age->setText(age);
```

12. We continue the preceding code, in which we set the `gender` and `married` texts before switching the stacked widget to its second page:

```
                if (gender == 0)
                    ui->gender->setText("Male");
                else
                    ui->gender->setText("Female");
                if (married)
                    ui->married->setText("Yes");
                else
                    ui->married->setText("No");
                ui->stackedWidget->setCurrentIndex(1);
            }
        }
    }
}
```

13. Print an error message if the login fails:

```
else {
    QMessageBox::warning(this, "Login failed", "Invalid
username or password.");
    }
} else {
    qDebug() << query.lastError().text();
}
}
```

14. Define what will happen if the **Log Out** button is clicked:

```
void MainWindow::on_logoutButton_clicked() {
    ui->stackedWidget->setCurrentIndex(0);
}
```

15. Close the database when the main window is closed:

```
MainWindow::~MainWindow() {
    db.close();
    delete ui;
}
```

16. Compile and run the program and you should be able to log in with the dummy account. After you have logged in, you should be able to see the dummy employee information linked to the user account. You can also log out by clicking on the **Log Out** button:

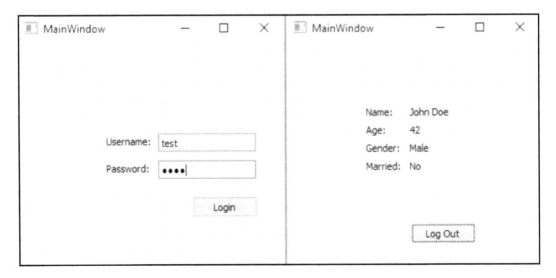

How it works...

In this example, we select data from the user table that matches the username and password that we inserted into the text fields. If nothing is found, it means we have provided an invalid username or password. Otherwise, obtain the employeeID data from the user account and do another SQL query to look for information from the employee table that matches the employeeID variable. Then, display the data according to the UI of your program.

We must set the widget order in the **Edit Tab Order** mode so that when the program has started, the first widget that gets focused on is the username line-edit widget. If the user presses the *Tab* key on the keyboard, the focus should switch to the second widget, which is the password line edit. An incorrect widget order will ruin the user experience and drive away any potential users. Make sure that the **echoMode** option of the password line edit is set to Password. That setting will hide the actual password inserted into the line edit and replace it with dot symbols for security purposes.

Displaying information from a database on a model view

In this recipe, we will learn how to display multiple sets of data obtained from our SQL database on a model view in our program.

How to do it...

Follow these steps to display information from a database on a model view widget:

1. We will be using the database table called employee, which we used in the previous example, *Creating a login screen with Qt*. This time, we need a lot more data in the employee table. Open up your web browser and log into your phpMyAdmin control panel.

Add data for a few more employees so that we can display it later in our program:

2. Open Qt Creator, create a new **Qt Widgets Application** project, and then add the **SQL module** to your project.

3. Open `mainwindow.ui` and add a **table widget** (not a table view) from **Item Widget** (Item-Based) under the **Widget box pane**. Select the main window on the canvas and click on either the Lay Out Vertically or Lay Out Horizontally button to make the table widget stick to the size of the main window, even when it's resized:

4. Double-click on the table widget and a window will then appear. Under the **Columns** tab, add five items by clicking on the + button in the top-left corner. Name the items ID, Name, Age, Gender, and Married. Click **OK** when you're done:

5. Right-click on the table widget and select **Go to slot...** in the pop-up menu. Scroll all the way down, select the **itemChanged(QTableWidgetItem*)** option in the pop-up window, and press **OK**. A slot function will be created in both your source files.

6. Open `mainwindow.h` and add these private variables to the `MainWindow` class:

```
private:
    Ui::MainWindow *ui;
    bool hasInit;
    QSqlDatabase db;
```

7. Add the following class headers to `mainwindow.h`:

```
#include <QtSql>
#include <QSqlDatabase>
#include <QSqlQuery>
#include <QMessageBox>
#include <QDebug>
#include <QTableWidgetItem>
```

8. Open `mainwindow.cpp` – we're going to write tons of code there. We need to declare what will happen when the program is started. Add the following code to the constructor of the `MainWindow` class:

```
MainWindow::MainWindow(QWidget *parent) :
QMainWindow(parent),
ui(new Ui::MainWindow) {
    hasInit = false;
    ui->setupUi(this);
    db = QSqlDatabase::addDatabase("QMYSQL");
```

```
db.setHostName("127.0.0.1");
db.setUserName("yourusername");
db.setPassword("yourpassword");
db.setDatabaseName("databasename");
ui->tableWidget->setColumnHidden(0, true);
```

9. The SQL query code looks like this:

```
if (db.open()) {
    QSqlQuery query;
    if (query.exec("SELECT id, name, age, gender, married
FROM employee")) {
        while (query.next()) {
            qDebug() << query.value(0) << query.value(1) <<
query.value(2) << query.value(3) << query.value(4);
            QString id = query.value(0).toString();
            QString name = query.value(1).toString();
            QString age = query.value(2).toString();
            int gender = query.value(3).toInt();
            bool married = query.value(4).toBool();
```

10. Create several `QTableWidgetItem` objects:

```
ui->tableWidget->setRowCount(ui->tableWidget->rowCount() + 1);
            QTableWidgetItem* idItem = new
QTableWidgetItem(id);
            QTableWidgetItem* nameItem = new
QTableWidgetItem(name);
            QTableWidgetItem* ageItem = new
QTableWidgetItem(age);
            QTableWidgetItem* genderItem = new
QTableWidgetItem();
            if (gender == 0)
                genderItem->setData(0, "Male");
            else
                genderItem->setData(0, "Female");
            QTableWidgetItem* marriedItem = new
QTableWidgetItem();
            if (married)
                marriedItem->setData(0, "Yes");
            else
                marriedItem->setData(0, "No");
```

11. Move those objects to the table widget:

```
ui->tableWidget->setItem(ui->tableWidget->rowCount() - 1, 0,
idItem);
ui->tableWidget->setItem(ui->tableWidget->rowCount() - 1, 1,
nameItem);
ui->tableWidget->setItem(ui->tableWidget->rowCount() - 1, 2,
ageItem);
ui->tableWidget->setItem(ui->tableWidget->rowCount() - 1, 3,
genderItem);
ui->tableWidget->setItem(ui->tableWidget->rowCount() - 1, 4,
marriedItem);
            }
          hasInit = true;
        } else {
            qDebug() << query.lastError().text();
        }
      } else {
          qDebug() << "Failed to connect to database.";
      }
  }
```

12. Declare what will happen when an item of the table widget has been edited. Add the following code to the `on_tableWidget_itemChanged()` slot function:

```
void MainWindow::on_tableWidget_itemChanged(QTableWidgetItem
*item) {
    if (hasInit) {
        QString id = ui->tableWidget->item(item->row(),
0)->data(0).toString();
        QString name = ui->tableWidget->item(item->row(),
1)->data(0).toString();
        QString age =
QString::number(ui->tableWidget->item(item->row(),
2)->data(0).toInt());
        ui->tableWidget->item(item->row(), 2)->setData(0, age);
        QString gender;
        if (ui->tableWidget->item(item->row(),
3)->data(0).toString() == "Male") {
            gender = "0";
        } else {
            ui->tableWidget->item(item->row(), 3)->setData(0,
"Female");
            gender = "1";
        }
        QString married;
        if (ui->tableWidget->item(item->row(),
4)->data(0).toString() == "No") {
```

```
                          married = "0";
                    } else {
                          ui->tableWidget->item(item->row(), 4)->setData(0,
            "Yes");
                          married = "1";
                    }
                    qDebug() << id << name << age << gender << married;
                    QSqlQuery query;
                    if (query.exec("UPDATE employee SET name = '" + name +
            "', age = '" + age + "', gender = '" + gender + "', married =
            '" + married + "' WHERE id = " + id)) {
                          QMessageBox::information(this, "Update Success",
            "Data updated to database.");
                    } else {
                          qDebug() << query.lastError().text();
                    }
              }
        }
```

13. Close the database at the class destructor:

```
MainWindow::~MainWindow() {
    db.close();
    delete ui;
}
```

14. Compile and run the example now and you should get something like this:

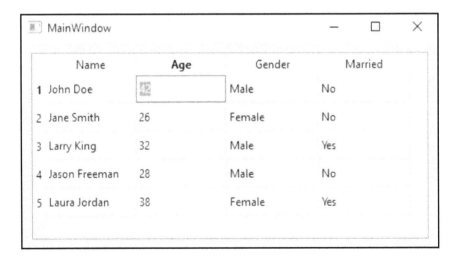

How it works...

The table widget is similar to the one you see in spreadsheet applications such as Microsoft Excel and OpenOffice Calc. In contrast with other types of model viewers, such as list view or tree view, table view (or table widget) is a two-dimensional model viewer, which displays data in the form of rows and columns.

The main difference between a table view and a table widget in Qt is that a table widget is built on top of a table view class, which means a table widget is easier to use and more suitable for beginners. However, a table widget is less flexible and tends to be less scalable than a table view, which is not the best choice if you want to customize your table.

After retrieving data from MySQL, we created a `QTableWidgetItem` item for each of the data items and set which column and row should be added to the table widget. Before adding an item to the table widget, we must increase the row count of the table by calling `QTableWidget::setRowCount()`. We can also get the current row count of the table widget by simply calling `QTableWidget::rowCount()`.

The first column from the left is hidden from view because we only use it to save the ID of the data so that we can use it to update the database when one of the data items in its row has changed. The `on_tableWidget_itemChanged()` slot function will be called when the data in one of the cells has changed. It will not only get called when you edit the data in the cell, but also when the data is first added to the table after being retrieved from the database. To ensure that this function is only triggered when we edit the data, we use a Boolean variable called `hasInit` to check whether we have done the initialization process (adding the first batch of data to the table). If `hasInit` is false, ignore the function call.

To prevent users from entering a totally irrelevant type of data, such as inserting letters into a numerical-only data cell, we manually check whether the data is anything close to what we'd expected when it's being edited. Revert it to a default value if it doesn't come close to anything considered valid. This is, of course, a simple hack, which does the job but is not the most professional method. Alternatively, you can try to create a new class that inherits the `QItemDelegate` class and define how your model view should behave. Then, call `QTableWidget::setItemDelegate()` to apply the class to your table widget.

Advanced SQL queries

By following this recipe, you will learn how to use advanced SQL statements such as INNER JOIN, COUNT, LIKE, and DISTINCT.

How to do it...

You can do a lot more than just performing simple queries on the SQL database. Let's follow these steps to learn how:

1. We need to add a few tables to our database before we can dive into the programming part. Open your web browser and access **phpMyAdmin**. We need several tables for this example to work:

2. I will show you the structure of each of the tables required for this project and the dummy data inserted into the tables for **testing**. The first table is called branch, which is used to store the IDs and names of different branches of the dummy company:

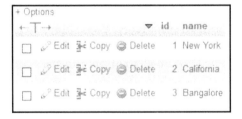

3. Secondly, we have the `department` table, which stores the IDs and names of different departments of the dummy company, which is also linked to the `branch` data by the branch IDs:

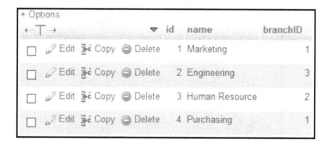

4. We also have an `employee` table, which stores information on all the employees in the dummy company. This table is similar to the one we used in the previous examples, except it has two extra columns, `birthday` and `departmentID`:

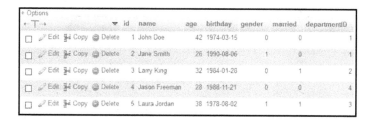

5. We also have a table called `log`, which contains dummy records of the login time for each employee. The `loginTime` column can be a `timestamp` or `date-time` variable type:

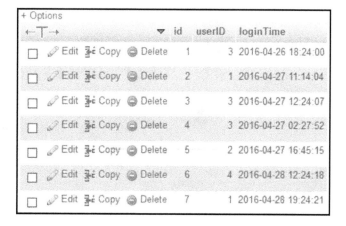

6. We have the `user` table that we also used in the previous examples:

7. Open Qt Creator. This time, instead of choosing **Qt Widgets Application**, we create a **Qt Console Application**:

8. Open your project file (`.pro`) and add the `sql` module to your project:

```
QT += core sql
QT -= gui
```

9. Open `main.cpp` and add the following header files to the top of the source file:

```
#include <QSqlDatabase>
#include <QSqlQuery>
#include <QSqlError>
#include <QDate>
#include <QDebug>
```

10. Add the following function to display employees who are more than 30 years old:

```
void filterAge() {
    qDebug() << "== Employees above 30 year old =============";
    QSqlQuery query;
    if (query.exec("SELECT name, age FROM employee WHERE age > 30")) {
        while (query.next()) {
            qDebug() << query.value(0).toString() << query.value(1).toString();
        }
    } else {
        qDebug() << query.lastError().text();
    }
    qDebug() << "\n";
}
```

11. Add the following function to display the department and branch information of each employee:

```
void getDepartmentAndBranch() {
    qDebug() << "== Get employees' department and branch =============";
    QSqlQuery query;
    if (query.exec("SELECT myEmployee.name, department.name, branch.name FROM (SELECT name, departmentID FROM employee) AS myEmployee INNER JOIN department ON department.id = myEmployee.departmentID INNER JOIN branch ON branch.id = department.branchID")) {
        while (query.next()) {
            qDebug() << query.value(0).toString() << query.value(1).toString() << query.value(2).toString();
        }
    } else {
```

```
                qDebug() << query.lastError().text();
        }
        qDebug() << "\n";
}
```

12. Add the following function, which displays employees who are working in the New York branch and are under 30 years old:

```
void filterBranchAndAge() {
    qDebug() << "== Employees from New York and age below 30
=============";
    QSqlQuery query;
    if (query.exec("SELECT myEmployee.name, myEmployee.age,
department.name, branch.name FROM (SELECT name, age,
departmentID FROM employee) AS myEmployee INNER JOIN department
ON department.id = myEmployee.departmentID INNER JOIN branch ON
branch.id = department.branchID WHERE branch.name = 'New York'
AND age < 30")) {
        while (query.next()) {
            qDebug() << query.value(0).toString() <<
query.value(1).toString() << query.value(2).toString() <<
query.value(3).toString();
        }
    } else {
        qDebug() << query.lastError().text();
    }
    qDebug() << "\n";
}
```

13. Add the following function, which counts the total number of female employees in the dummy company:

```
void countFemale() {
    qDebug() << "== Count female employees =============";
    QSqlQuery query;
    if (query.exec("SELECT COUNT(gender) FROM employee WHERE
gender = 1")) {
        while (query.next()) {
            qDebug() << query.value(0).toString();
        }
    } else {
        qDebug() << query.lastError().text();
    }
    qDebug() << "\n";
}
```

14. Add the following function, which filters the employee list and only displays those whose names start with `Ja`:

```
void filterName() {
    qDebug() << "== Employees name start with 'Ja'
=============";
    QSqlQuery query;
    if (query.exec("SELECT name FROM employee WHERE name LIKE
'%Ja%'")) {
        while (query.next()) {
            qDebug() << query.value(0).toString();
        }
    } else {
        qDebug() << query.lastError().text();
    }
    qDebug() << "\n";
}
```

15. Add the following function, which displays employees who have birthdays in `August`:

```
void filterBirthday() {
    qDebug() << "== Employees birthday in August
=============";
    QSqlQuery query;
    if (query.exec("SELECT name, birthday FROM employee WHERE
MONTH(birthday) = 8")) {
        while (query.next()) {
            qDebug() << query.value(0).toString() <<
query.value(1).toDate().toString("d-MMMM-yyyy");
        }
    } else {
        qDebug() << query.lastError().text();
    }
    qDebug() << "\n";
}
```

16. Add the following function, which checks who logged into the dummy system on `27 April 2019` and displays their names on the terminal:

```
void checkLog() {
    qDebug() << "== Employees who logged in on 27 April 2019
=============";
    QSqlQuery query;
    if (query.exec("SELECT DISTINCT myEmployee.name, FROM
(SELECT id, name FROM employee) AS myEmployee INNER JOIN user
ON user.employeeID = myEmployee.id INNER JOIN log ON log.userID
= user.id WHERE DATE(log.loginTime) = '2019-04-27'")) {
```

```
            while (query.next()) {
                qDebug() << query.value(0).toString();
            }
        } else {
            qDebug() << query.lastError().text();
        }
        qDebug() << "\n";
    }
```

17. In the `main()` function, connect the program to the MySQL database and call all the functions that we defined in the previous steps. Close the database connection and we're done:

```
int main(int argc, char *argv[]) {
    QCoreApplication a(argc, argv);
    QSqlDatabase db = QSqlDatabase::addDatabase("QMYSQL");
    db.setHostName("127.0.0.1");
    db.setUserName("reonyx");
    db.setPassword("reonyx");
    db.setDatabaseName("testing");
    if (db.open()) {
        filterAge();
        getDepartmentAndBranch();
        filterBranchAndAge();
        countFemale();
        filterName();
        filterBirthday();
        checkLog();
        db.close();
    } else {
        qDebug() << "Failed to connect to database.";
    }
    return a.exec();
}
```

18. Compile and run the project and you should see a terminal window that displays the filtered results:

How it works...

A console application does not have GUI and only shows you a text display in a terminal window. This is usually used in a backend system, as it uses fewer resources compared to a widget application. We used it in this example because it's faster to display the result, without the need to place any widgets in the program, which we don't need in this case.

We separated the SQL queries into different functions so that it's easier to maintain the code and it doesn't become too messy. Do note that, in C++, the functions have to be located before the main() function, or they will not be able to be called by main().

There's more...

The INNER JOIN statement used in the preceding example joins two tables together and selects all rows from both tables, as long as there is a match between the columns in both tables. There are many other types of JOIN statements that you can use in MySQL (and some other types of SQL architecture), such as LEFT JOIN, RIGHT JOIN, and FULL OUTER JOIN.

The following diagram shows the different types of **JOIN** statements and their effects:

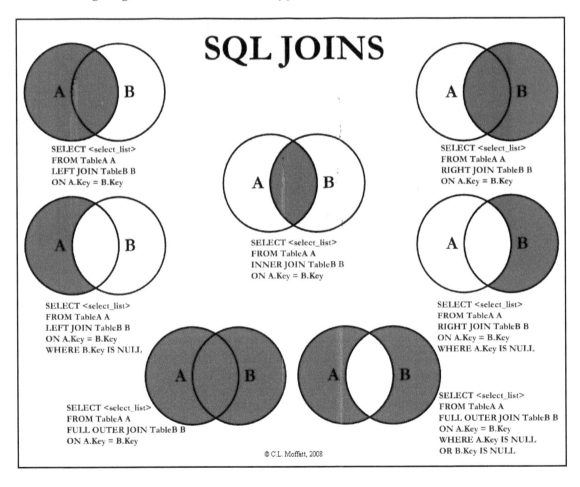

The following bullet points explain the LIKE and DISTINCT statements, which we used in our example code in this recipe:

- The LIKE statement is normally used to search for a string variable in the database without the full word. Notice that there are two % symbols, located before and after the search keyword.
- The DISTINCT statement used in the previous example filters out results that have the exact same variable. For example, without the DISTINCT statement, you will see two versions of Larry King appear in the terminal because there are two records of him logging into the system on the same day. By adding the DISTINCT statement, MySQL will eliminate one of the results and ensure every result is unique.
- You may be wondering what d-MMMM-yyyy stands for and why we used it in the preceding example. That is actually an expression supplied to the QDateTime class in Qt to display the date-time result using a given format. In this case, it will change the date-time data that we get from MySQL, 2019-08-06, to the format that we specified, resulting in 6-August-2019.

For more information, check out Qt's documentation at http://doc.qt.io/qt-5/qdatetime.html#toString, which has the full list of expressions that can be used to determine the format of the date and time string.

Develop Web Applications using Qt WebEngine **12**

In this chapter, we will cover the following recipes:

- Introducing Qt WebEngine
- Using WebView and web settings
- Embedding Google Maps in your project
- Calling C++ functions from JavaScript
- Calling JavaScript functions from C++

Introduction

Qt includes a module called **Qt WebEngine** that allows us to embed a web browser widget into our program and use it to display web pages or local HTML content. Prior to version 5.6, Qt used another similar module called **Qt WebKit**, which is now deprecated and has since been replaced by the Chromium-based WebEngine module. Qt also allows communication between JavaScript and C++ code through the **WebChannel**, which enables us to make use of this module in a much more effective fashion.

Technical requirements

The technical requirements for this chapter include Qt 5.11.2 MSVC 2017 64-bit, Qt Creator 4.8.2, and Windows 10.

All the code used in this chapter can be downloaded from the GitHub repository for this chapter, at https://github.com/PacktPublishing/Qt5-CPP-GUI-Programming-Cookbook-Second-Edition/tree/master/Chapter12.

Check out the following video to see the code in action: http://bit.ly/2ToK3Do

Introducing Qt WebEngine

In this example project, we will explore the basic features of the WebEngine module in Qt and try building a simple working web browser. Since Qt 5.6, Qt's **WebKit** module has been deprecated and replaced by the **WebEngine** module, which is based on Google's Chromium engine.

How to do it...

First, let's set up our WebEngine project:

1. Download and install Microsoft Visual Studio if you do not have it installed on your computer. At the moment, Qt's WebEngine module only works with the Visual C++ compiler and not others, such as MinGW or Clang. This might change in the future, but it all depends on whether Qt developers want to make port it to other compilers or not. You can download the latest **Visual Studio** from https://www.visualstudio.com.

2. Make sure that the Qt version you installed on your computer supports the **Visual C++ compiler**. You can add the **MSVC 2015 64-bit** component to your Qt installation using Qt's maintenance tool. Also, make sure that you have installed the **Qt WebEngine** component in your Qt version:

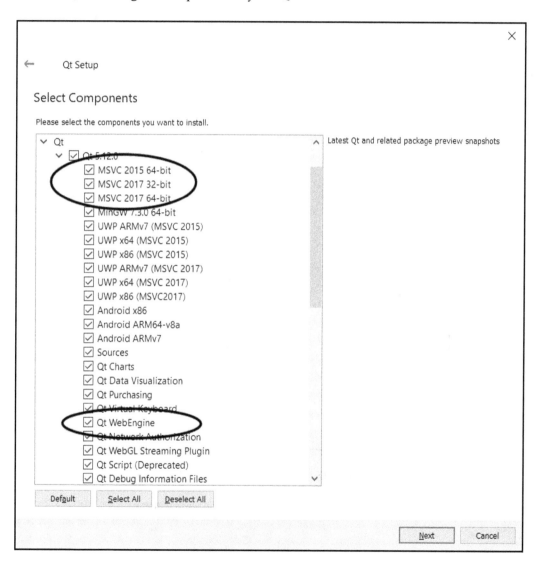

3. Open up Qt Creator and create a new **Qt Widgets Application** project. Select a kit that uses the Visual C++ compiler:

4. Open up your project file (`.pro`) and add the following modules to your project:

```
QT += core gui webengine webenginewidgets
```

5. Open up `mainwindow.ui` and remove the **menuBar, mainToolBar,** and **statusBar** objects, as we don't need those in this project:

6. Place two horizontal layouts on the canvas, then place a line edit widget and a push button for the layout at the top:

7. Select the canvas and click on the Lay Out Vertically button located at the top of the editor:

8. The layouts will expand and follow the size of the main window. The line edit will also expand horizontally, based on the width of the horizontal layout:

9. Add two buttons to the left side of the line edit. We'll use these two buttons to move backward and forward between page histories. Add a **Progress Bar** widget at the bottom of the main window so that we can find out whether the page has finished loading or is still in progress. We don't have to worry about the horizontal layout in the middle at this point, as we'll be adding the webview to it later at *step 16* using C++ code, and the space will be occupied:

10. Right-click on one of the buttons and select **Go to slot...**, then select **clicked()** and click **OK**. A slot function will be automatically created for you in `mainwindow.h` and `mainwindow.cpp`. Repeat this step for all the other buttons as well.

11. Right-click on the line edit and select **Go to slot...**, then select **returnPressed()** and click **OK**. Another slot function will now be automatically created for you in `mainwindow.h` and `mainwindow.cpp`.

12. Let's hop over to `mainwindow.h`. The first thing we need to do is to add the following header to `mainwindow.h`:

```
#include <QtWebEngineWidgets/QtWebEngineWidgets>
```

13. Declare the `loadUrl()` function under the class destructor:

```
public:
    explicit MainWindow(QWidget *parent = 0);
    ~MainWindow();
    void loadUrl();
```

14. Add a custom slot function called `loading()` to `mainwindow.h`:

```
private slots:
    void on_goButton_clicked();
    void on_address_returnPressed();
    void on_backButton_clicked();
    void on_forwardButton_clicked();
    void loading(int progress);
```

15. Declare a `QWebEngineView` object and call it `webview`:

```
private:
    Ui::MainWindow *ui;
    QWebEngineView* webview;
```

16. Open the `mainwindow.cpp` file and initiate the WebEngine view. Add it to the second horizontal layout and connect its `loadProgress()` signal to the `loading()` slot function we just added to `mainwindow.h`:

```
MainWindow::MainWindow(QWidget *parent) :
QMainWindow(parent),
ui(new Ui::MainWindow) {
    ui->setupUi(this);
    webview = new QWebEngineView;
    ui->horizontalLayout_2->addWidget(webview);
    connect(webview, QWebEngineView::loadProgress, this,
MainWindow::loading);
}
```

17. Declare what will happen when the `loadUrl()` function is called:

```
void MainWindow::loadUrl() {
    QUrl url = QUrl(ui->address->text());
    url.setScheme("http");
    webview->page()->load(url);
}
```

18. Call the `loadUrl()` function when the **Go** button is clicked or when the *Enter* key is pressed:

```
void MainWindow::on_goButton_clicked() {
    loadUrl();
}
void MainWindow::on_address_returnPressed() {
    loadUrl();
}
```

19. As for the other two buttons, we'll ask the `webview` to load the previous page or the next page if it is available in the history stack:

```
void MainWindow::on_backButton_clicked() {
    webview->back();
}
void MainWindow::on_forwardButton_clicked() {
    webview->forward();
}
```

20. Change the value of `progressBar` when the web page is being loaded:

```
void MainWindow::loading(int progress) {
    ui->progressBar->setValue(progress);
}
```

21. Build and run the program now and you will get a very basic but functional web browser:

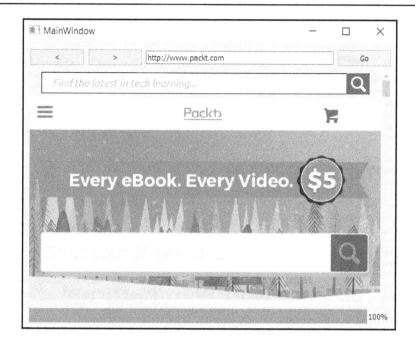

How it works...

The old webview system was based on Apple's WebKit engine and only available in Qt 5.5 and its predecessor. Since 5.6, WebKit has been completely abandoned by Qt and replaced with Google's Chromium engine. The API has been completely changed and therefore all the code related to Qt WebKit will not work correctly once migrated to 5.6. If you're new to Qt, it's recommended you skip WebKit and learn the WebEngine API since it is becoming the new standard in Qt.

 If you have used Qt's WebKit in the past, this webpage teaches you how to port your old code over to Web Engine: `https://wiki.qt.io/Porting_from_QtWebKit_to_QtWebEngine`.

In *step 16*, we connected the `loadProgress()` signal that belongs to the webview widget to the `loading()` slot function. The signal will be called automatically when the webview is loading the web page you requested by calling `QWebEnginePage::load()` in *step 17*. You can also connect the `loadStarted()` and `loadFinished()` signals if you need to.

In *step 17*, we used the `QUrl` class to convert the text obtained from the line edit to URL format. By default, the address we inserted will lead to the local path if we do not specify the URL scheme (HTTP, HTTPS, FTP, and so on). We may not be able to load the page if, say, we gave it `packtpub.com` instead of `http://packtpub.com`. Therefore, we manually specify a URL scheme for it by calling `QUrl::setScheme()`. This will ensure the address is properly formatted before passing it to the webview.

There's more...

If you're running Qt 5.6 or later versions, and for some reason you need the WebKit module for your project (usually for maintaining an old project), you can obtain the module code from GitHub and build it by yourself: `https://github.com/qt/qtwebkit`.

Using WebView and web settings

In this recipe, we will dive deeper into the features available in Qt's WebEngine and explore the settings that we can use to customize our WebView. We will use the source files from the previous example and add more code to it.

How to do it...

Let's explore some of the basic features of the Qt WebEngine:

1. Open `mainwindow.ui` and add a vertical layout under the progress bar. Add a **Plain Text Edit** widget (under the **Input Widgets** category) and a push button to the vertical layout. Change the display of the push button to `Load HTML` and set the **plaintext** property of the **Plain Text Edit** widget to the following:

```
<Img
src="https://www.google.com/images/branding/googlelogo/1x/googl
elogo_color_272x92dp.png"></img>
<h1>Hello World!</h1>
<h3>This is our custom HTML page.</h3>
<script>alert("Hello!");</script>
```

This is how it should look after you have added the code on top of the **Plain Text Edit**:

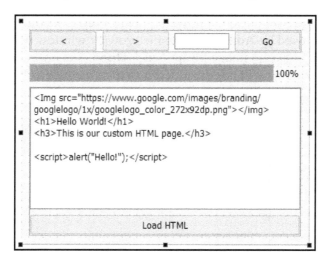

2. Go to **File | New File or Project**. A window will pop up and ask you to choose a file template. Select **Qt Resource File** under the **Qt** category and click on the **Choose...** button. Type in your desired filename and click **Next**, followed by **Finish**:

3. Open the resource file we just created by right-clicking on it in the **Projects** pane and selecting the **Open in Editor** option. Once the file is opened by the editor, click on the **Add** button, followed by **Add Prefix**. Set the prefix as / and click **Add**, followed by **Add Files**. The file browser window will appear and we will select the tux.png image file and click **Open**. The image file is now added to our project, where it will be embedded into the executable file (.exe) once it's compiled:

4. Open mainwindow.h and add the following headers to it:

```
#include <QMainWindow>
#include <QtWebEngineWidgets/QtWebEngineWidgets>
#include <QDebug>
#include <QFile>
```

5. Make sure the following functions and pointers have been declared in mainwindow.h:

```
public:
    explicit MainWindow(QWidget *parent = 0);
    ~MainWindow();
    void loadUrl();
private slots:
    void on_goButton_clicked();
    void on_address_returnPressed();
    void on_backButton_clicked();
    void on_forwardButton_clicked();
    void startLoading();
    void loading(int progress);
    void loaded(bool ok);
    void on_loadHtml_clicked();
```

```
private:
    Ui::MainWindow *ui;
    QWebEngineView* webview;
```

6. Open `mainwindow.cpp` and add the following code to the class constructor:

```
MainWindow::MainWindow(QWidget *parent) :
QMainWindow(parent),
ui(new Ui::MainWindow) {
    ui->setupUi(this);
    webview = new QWebEngineView;
    ui->horizontalLayout_2->addWidget(webview);
//webview->page()->settings()->setAttribute(QWebEngineSettings:
:JavascriptEnabled, false);
//webview->page()->settings()->setAttribute(QWebEngineSettings:
:AutoLoadImages, false);
    //QString fontFamily =
webview->page()->settings()->fontFamily(QWebEngineSettings::Ser
ifFont);
    QString fontFamily =
webview->page()->settings()->fontFamily(QWebEngineSettings::San
sSerifFont);
    int fontSize =
webview->page()->settings()->fontSize(QWebEngineSettings::Minim
umFontSize);
    QFont myFont = QFont(fontFamily, fontSize);
webview->page()->settings()->setFontFamily(QWebEngineSettings::
StandardFont, myFont.family());
```

7. Load the image file and place it on the webview:

```
QFile file(":://tux.png");
if (file.open(QFile::ReadOnly)) {
    QByteArray data = file.readAll();
    webview->page()->setContent(data, "image/png");
} else {
    qDebug() << "File cannot be opened.";
}
connect(webview, QWebEngineView::loadStarted, this,
MainWindow::startLoading());
connect(webview, QWebEngineView::loadProgress, this,
MainWindow::loading(int));
connect(webview, QWebEngineView::loadFinished, this,
MainWindow::loaded(bool)));
}
```

8. The `MainWindow::loadUrl()` function stays the same as in the previous example in the *Introducing Qt WebEngine* section, which sets the URL scheme to HTTP before loading the page:

```
void MainWindow::loadUrl() {
    QUrl url = QUrl(ui->address->text());
    url.setScheme("http");
    webview->page()->load(url);
}
```

9. The same goes for the following functions, which also remain the same as the previous example in the *Introducing Qt WebEngine* section:

```
void MainWindow::on_goButton_clicked() {
    loadUrl();
}
void MainWindow::on_address_returnPressed() {
    loadUrl();
}
void MainWindow::on_backButton_clicked() {
    webview->back();
}
void MainWindow::on_forwardButton_clicked() {
    webview->forward();
}
```

10. Add both the `MainWindow::startLoading()` and `MainWindow::loaded()` slot functions, which will be called by the `loadStarted()` and `loadFinished()` signals. These two functions basically show the progress bar when a page is starting to load, and hide the progress bar when the page has finished loading:

```
void MainWindow::startLoading() {
    ui->progressBar->show();
}
void MainWindow::loading(int progress) {
    ui->progressBar->setValue(progress);
}
void MainWindow::loaded(bool ok) {
    ui->progressBar->hide();
}
```

11. Call `webview->loadHtml()` to convert the plain text to HTML content when the **Load HTML** button is clicked:

```
void MainWindow::on_loadHtml_clicked() {
    webview->setHtml(ui->source->toPlainText());
}
```

12. Build and run the program and you should see something like the following:

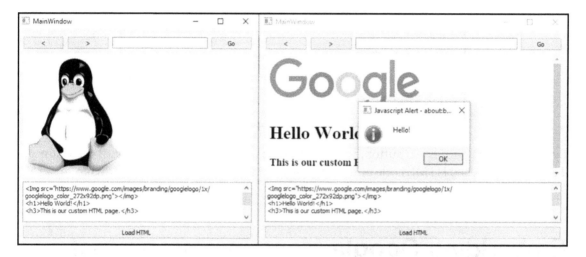

How it works...

In this example, we used C++ to load an image file and set it as the WebView's default content (instead of a blank page). We could achieve the same result by loading a default HTML file with an image at startup.

Some of the code in the class constructor has been commented out. You can remove the double slashes, //, and see the difference it makes – the JavaScript alert will no longer appear (since JavaScript is disabled) and images will no longer appear in your webview.

Another thing you can try is to change the font family from
`QWebEngineSettings::SansSerifFont` to `QWebEngineSettings::SerifFont`. You
will notice a slight difference in the font as it appears in the webview:

By clicking the `Load HTML` button, we ask the WebView to treat the content of the **Plain
Text Edit** widget as HTML code and load it as an HTML page. You can use this to make a
simple HTML editor powered by Qt!

Embedding Google Maps in your project

In this recipe, we will learn how to embed **Google Maps** in our project through Qt's
WebEngine module. This example doesn't focus much on Qt and C++, but rather on the
Google Maps API in HTML code.

How to do it...

Let's create a program that displays Google Maps by following these steps:

1. Create a new **Qt Widgets Application** project and remove the **statusBar**,
   menuBar, and **mainToolBar**.
2. Open your project file (`.pro`) and add the following modules to your project:

   ```
   QT += core gui webengine webenginewidgets
   ```

3. Open `mainwindow.ui` and add a vertical layout to the canvas. Then, select the canvas and click the Lay Out Vertically button on top of the canvas. You will get the following:

4. Open `mainwindow.cpp` and add the following headers to the top of the source code:

```
#include <QtWebEngineWidgets/QWebEngineView>
#include <QtWebEngineWidgets/QWebEnginePage>
#include <QtWebEngineWidgets/QWebEngineSettings>
```

5. Add the following code to the `MainWindow` constructor:

```
MainWindow::MainWindow(QWidget *parent)  :
QMainWindow(parent),
ui(new Ui::MainWindow) {
    ui->setupUi(this);
    QWebEngineView* webview = new QWebEngineView;
    QUrl url = QUrl("qrc:/map.html");
    webview->page()->load(url);
    ui->verticalLayout->addWidget(webview);
}
```

6. Go to **File** | **New File or Project** and create a Qt resource file (.qrc). We will add an HTML file to our project, called map.html:

7. Open map.html with your favorite text editor. It's not recommended to open an HTML file using Qt Creator, as it does not provide any color-coding for HTML syntax.

8. Start writing the HTML code by declaring the important tags, such as <html>, <head>, and <body>:

```
<!DOCTYPE html>
<html>
    <head>
    </head>
    <body ondragstart="return false">
    </body>
</html>
```

9. Add a <div> tag to the body and set its ID as map-canvas:

```
<body ondragstart="return false">
    <div id="map-canvas" />
</body>
```

10. Add the following code to the head of the HTML document:

```
<meta name="viewport" content="initial-scale=1.0, user-
scalable=no" />
<style type="text/css">
    html { height: 100% }
    body { height: 100%; margin: 0; padding: 0 }
    #map-canvas { height: 100% }
</style>
<script type="text/javascript"
src="https://maps.googleapis.com/maps/api/js?key=YOUR_KEY_HERE&
libraries=drawing"></script>
```

11. Add the following code, also to the head of the HTML document, beneath the code we inserted in the previous step:

```
<script type="text/javascript">
    var map;
    function initialize() {
        // Add map
        var mapOptions = {
            center: new google.maps.LatLng(40.705311,
-74.2581939), zoom: 6
        };
        map = new google.maps.Map(document.getElementById("map-
canvas"),mapOptions);
        // Add event listener
        google.maps.event.addListener(map, 'zoom_changed',
function() {
            //alert(map.getZoom());
        });
```

12. Create a marker and place it on the map:

```
        // Add marker
        var marker = new google.maps.Marker({
            position: new google.maps.LatLng(40.705311,
-74.2581939), map: map, title: "Marker A",
        });
        google.maps.event.addListener (marker, 'click', function()
{
            map.panTo(marker.getPosition());
        });
        marker.setMap(map);
```

13. Add a polyline to the map:

```
// Add polyline
var points = [ new google.maps.LatLng(39.8543, -73.2183),
new google.maps.LatLng(41.705311, -75.2581939), new
google.maps.LatLng(40.62388, -75.5483) ];
var polyOptions = {
    path: points,
    strokeColor: '#FF0000',
    strokeOpacity: 1.0,
    strokeWeight: 2
};
historyPolyline = new google.maps.Polyline(polyOptions);
historyPolyline.setMap(map);
```

14. Add a polygon shape:

```
// Add polygon
var points = [ new google.maps.LatLng(37.314166, -75.432),
new google.maps.LatLng(40.2653, -74.4325), new
google.maps.LatLng(38.8288, -76.5483) ];
var polygon = new google.maps.Polygon({
    paths: points,
    fillColor: '#000000',
    fillOpacity: 0.2,
    strokeWeight: 3,
    strokeColor: '#fff000',
});
polygon.setMap(map);
```

15. Create a drawing manager and apply it to the map:

```
// Setup drawing manager
var drawingManager = new
google.maps.drawing.DrawingManager();
drawingManager.setMap(map);
    }
    google.maps.event.addDomListener(window, 'load', initialize);
</script>
```

16. Compile and run the project. You should see the following:

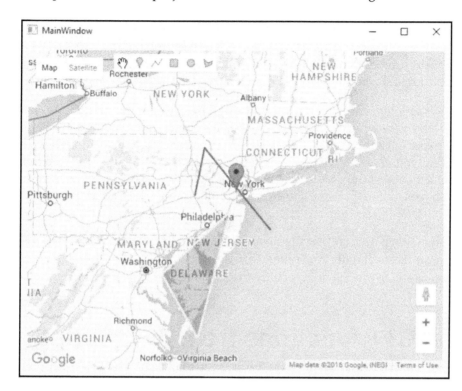

How it works...

Google allows you to embed Google Maps in a web page using their JavaScript library, called the **Google Maps API**. Through Qt's WebEngine module, we can embed Google Maps in our C++ project by loading an HTML file to our webview widget, which uses the Google Maps API. The only downside of this method is that we cannot load the map when there is no internet connection.

The Google API can be called by your website as Google allows it. Choose the free API if your plan is for heavier traffic.

Go to `https://console.developers.google.com` to get a free key and replace `YOUR_KEY_HERE` in the JavaScript source path with the API key you obtained from Google.

We must define a `<div>` object, which serves as a container for the map. Then, when we initialize the map, we specify the ID of the `<div>` object so that the Google Maps API knows which HTML element to look for when embedding the map. By default, we set the center of the map to the coordinates of New York and set the default zoom level to 6. Then, we add an event listener that gets triggered when the zoom level of the map changes. Remove the double slashes, `//`, from the code to see it in action.

After that, we added a marker to the map through JavaScript. The marker also has an event listener attached to it, which will trigger the `panTo()` function when the marker is clicked. It basically pans the map view to the marker that has been clicked. Although we have added the drawing manager to the map (the icon buttons beside the **Map** and **Satellite** buttons), which allows users to draw any type of shape on top of the map, it's also possible to add the shapes manually using JavaScript, similar to how we added the marker in *step 12*, in the *How to do it...* section.

Lastly, you may have noticed that the headers are added to `mainwindow.cpp` instead of `mainwindow.h`. This is totally fine unless you are declaring class pointers in `mainwindow.h`—then you have to include those headers in it.

Calling C++ functions from JavaScript

In this recipe, we will learn how put our knowledge to use and create a functional login screen using Qt and MySQL.

How to do it...

Let's learn how to call C++ functions from JavaScript using the following steps:

1. Create a **Qt Widgets Application** project. Open the project file (`.pro`) and add the following modules to the project:

   ```
   QT += core gui webengine webenginewidgets
   ```

2. Open `mainwindow.ui` and delete the **mainToolBar**, **menuBar**, and **statusBar**, as we don't need any of these in this example program.

3. Add a vertical layout to the canvas, then select the canvas and click on the Lay Out Vertically button on top of the canvas. Add a text label to the top of the vertical layout and set its text to `Hello!`. Make its font bigger by setting its **styleSheet** property as follows:

```
font: 75 26pt "MS Shell Dlg 2";
```

This is how it look like after we applied the font properties to our style sheet:

4. Go to **File | New File or Project** and create a resource file. Add an empty HTML file and all the JavaScript files, CSS files, font files, and so on that belong to **jQuery**, **Boostrap**, and **Font Awesome** to your project resources:

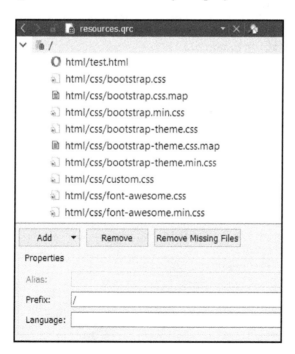

5. Open your HTML file, which in this case is called `test.html`. Link all the necessary JavaScript and CSS files to the HTML source code, between the `<head>` tags:

```
<!DOCTYPE html>
<html>
    <head>
        <script
src="qrc:///qtwebchannel/qwebchannel.js"></script>
        <script src="js/jquery.min.js"></script>
        <script src="js/bootstrap.js"></script>
        <link rel="stylesheet" type="text/css"
href="css/bootstrap.css">
        <link rel="stylesheet" type="text/css" href="css/font-
awesome.css">
    </head>
    <body>
    </body>
</html>
```

6. Add the following JavaScript to the `<head>` element, wrapped between the `<script>` tags:

```
<script>
    $(document).ready(function() {
        new QWebChannel(qt.webChannelTransport,
function(channel) {
            mainWindow = channel.objects.mainWindow;
        });
        $("#login").click(function(e) {
            e.preventDefault();
            var user = $("#username").val();
            var pass = $("#password").val();
            mainWindow.showLoginInfo(user, pass);
        });
```

7. Print `Good bye!` when clicking on the `changeText` button with the following code:

```
$("#changeText").click(function(e) {
    e.preventDefault();
    mainWindow.changeQtText("Good bye!");
});
});
</script>
```

8. Add the following code to the `<body>` element:

```
<div class="container-fluid">
    <form id="example-form" action="#" class="container-fluid">
        <div class="form-group">
            <div class="col-md-12"><h3>Call C++ Function from
Javascript</h3></div>
            <div class="col-md-12">
                <div class="alert alert-info" role="alert">
                    <i class="fa fa-info-circle"></i>
                    <span id="infotext">Click "Login" to send
username and password variables to C++. Click "Change Cpp Text"
to change the text label on Qt GUI.</span>
                </div>
            </div>
```

9. Continuing from the previous code, this time, we create the input fields for `username` and `password`, with two buttons at the bottom called `Login` and `Change Cpp Text`:

```
            <div class="col-md-12">
                <label>Username:</label>
                <input id="username" type="text"><p />
            </div>
            <div class="col-md-12">
                <label>Password:</label> <input id="password"
type="password"><p />
            </div>
            <div class="col-md-12">
                <button id="login" class="btn btn-success"
type="button"><i class="fa fa-check"></i> Login</button>
<button id="changeText" class="btn btn-primary" type="button">
<i class="fa fa-pencil"></i> Change Cpp Text</button>
            </div>
        </div>
    </form>
</div>
```

10. Open `mainwindow.h` and add the following public functions to the `MainWindow` class:

```
public:
    explicit MainWindow(QWidget *parent = 0);
    ~MainWindow();
    Q_INVOKABLE void changeQtText(QString newText);
    Q_INVOKABLE void showLoginInfo(QString user, QString pass);
```

11. Open `mainwindow.cpp` and add the following headers to the top of the source code:

```
#include <QtWebEngineWidgets/QWebEngineView>
#include <QtWebChannel/QWebChannel>
#include <QMessageBox>
```

12. Add the following code to the `MainWindow` constructor:

```
MainWindow::MainWindow(QWidget *parent) :
QMainWindow(parent),
ui(new Ui::MainWindow) {
    qputenv("QTWEBENGINE_REMOTE_DEBUGGING", "1234");
    ui->setupUi(this);
    QWebEngineView* webview = new QWebEngineView();
    ui->verticalLayout->addWidget(webview);
    QWebChannel* webChannel = new QWebChannel();
    webChannel->registerObject("mainWindow", this);
    webview->page()->setWebChannel(webChannel);
    webview->page()->load(QUrl("qrc:///html/test.html"));
}
```

13. Declare what happens when `changeQtText()` and `showLoginInfo()` are called:

```
void MainWindow::changeQtText(QString newText) {
    ui->label->setText(newText);
}
void MainWindow::showLoginInfo(QString user, QString pass) {
    QMessageBox::information(this, "Login info", "Username is "
+ user + " and password is " + pass);
}
```

14. Compile and run the program; you should see something similar to the following screenshot. If you click on the **Change Cpp Text** button, the word **Hello!** at the top will change to **Goodbye!** If you click on the **Login** button, a message box will appear and show you exactly what you typed in the **Username** and **Password** input fields:

How it works...

In this example, we used two JavaScript libraries: jQuery, and Bootstrap. We also used an iconic font package called Font Awesome. These third-party add-ons were used to make the HTML user interface more interesting and responsive to different screen resolutions. We also used jQuery to detect the document's ready status, as well as to obtain the values of the input fields.

 You can download jQuery from `https://jquery.com/download`, Bootstrap from `http://getbootstrap.com/getting-started/#download`, and Font Awesome from `http://fontawesome.io`.

Qt's WebEngine uses a mechanism called **WebChannel**, which enables peer-to-peer communication between the C++ program and the HTML page. The WebEngine module provides a JavaScript library that makes integration a lot easier. The JavaScript is embedded in your project's resource by default, so you don't need to import it into your project manually. You just have to include it in your HTML page by calling the following:

```
<script src="qrc:///qtwebchannel/qwebchannel.js"></script>
```

Once you have included `qwebchannel.js`, you can initialize the `QWebChannel` class and assign the Qt object we registered earlier in C++ to a JavaScript variable.

In C++, this is done as follows:

```
QWebChannel* webChannel = new QWebChannel();
webChannel->registerObject("mainWindow", this);
webview->page()->setWebChannel(webChannel);
```

Then in JavaScript, this is done as follows:

```
new QWebChannel(qt.webChannelTransport, function(channel) {
    mainWindow = channel.objects.mainWindow;
});
```

You may be wondering what this line means:

```
qputenv("QTWEBENGINE_REMOTE_DEBUGGING", "1234");
```

Qt's WebEngine uses the remote debugging method to check for JavaScript errors and other problems. The number `1234` defines the port number you want to use for remote debugging.

Once you have enabled remote debugging, you can access the debugging page by opening up a Chromium-based web browser, such as **Google Chrome** (this will not work in **Firefox** and other browsers), and type in `http://127.0.0.1:1234`. You will then see a page that looks like this:

The first page will display all the HTML pages that are currently running in your program, which in this case is `test.html`. Click on the page link and it will take you to another page for inspection. You can use this to check for CSS errors, JavaScript errors, and missing files. Note that you should disable remote debugging once your program is bug-free and ready for deployment. This is because remote debugging takes time to initialize and will increase your program's startup time.

If you want to call a C++ function from JavaScript, you must place the `Q_INVOKABLE` macro in front the function's declaration; otherwise, it will not work:

```
Q_INVOKABLE void changeQtText(QString newText);
```

Calling JavaScript functions from C++

In the previous recipe, we learned how to call C++ functions from JavaScript through Qt's **WebChannel** system. In this example, we will try to do the reverse: call JavaScript functions from C++ code.

How to do it...

We can call JavaScript functions from C++ through the following steps:

1. Create a new **Qt Widgets Application** project and add the `webengine` and `webenginewidgets` modules to your project.

2. Open `mainwindow.ui` and remove the **mainToolBar**, **menuBar**, and **statusBar**.

3. Add a vertical layout and a horizontal layout to the canvas. Select the canvas and click Lay Out Vertically. Make sure the horizontal layout is located at the bottom of the vertical layout.

4. Add two push buttons to the horizontal layout; one is called **Change HTML Text** and the other is called **Play UI Animation**. Right-click on one of the buttons and click **Go to slot...**. A window will pop up and ask you to pick a signal. Select the **clicked()** option and click **OK**. Qt will automatically add a slot function to your source code. Repeat this step for the other button:

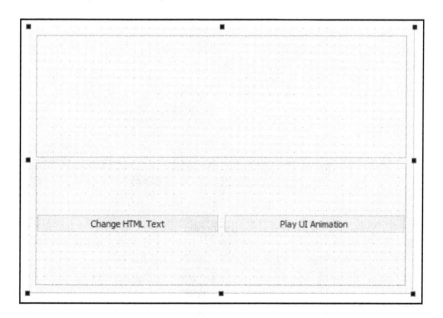

5. Open `mainwindow.h` and add the following headers to it:

```
#include <QtWebEngineWidgets/QWebEngineView>
#include <QtWebChannel/QWebChannel>
#include <QMessageBox>
```

6. Declare the class pointer of a `QWebEngineView` object called `webview`:

```
public:
    explicit MainWindow(QWidget *parent = 0);
    ~MainWindow();
    QWebEngineView* webview;
```

7. Open `mainwindow.cpp` and add the following code to the `MainWindow` constructor:

```
MainWindow::MainWindow(QWidget *parent) :
QMainWindow(parent),
ui(new Ui::MainWindow) {
    //qputenv("QTWEBENGINE_REMOTE_DEBUGGING", "1234");
    ui->setupUi(this);
    webview = new QWebEngineView();
    ui->verticalLayout->addWidget(webview);
    QWebChannel* webChannel = new QWebChannel();
    webChannel->registerObject("mainWindow", this);
    webview->page()->setWebChannel(webChannel);
    webview->page()->load(QUrl("qrc:///html/test.html"));
}
```

8. Define what will happen when the `changeHtmlText` button and the `playUIAnimation` button are clicked:

```
void MainWindow::on_changeHtmlTextButton_clicked() {
    webview->page()->runJavaScript("changeHtmlText('Text has
been replaced by C++!');");
}

void MainWindow::on_playUIAnimationButton_clicked() {
    webview->page()->runJavaScript("startAnim();");
}
```

9. Let's create a resource file for our project by going to **File** | **New File or Project**. Select **Qt Resource File** under the **Qt** category and click **Choose....** Insert your desired filename and click **Next**, followed by **Finish**.

10. Add an empty HTML file and all the required add-ons (jQuery, Bootstrap, and Font Awesome) to the project resources. Add the `tux.png` image file to the resources file as well, as we'll be using it in a short while in *step 14*.

11. Open the HTML file we just created and add it to the project resources; in our case, it's called `test.html`. Add the following HTML code to the file:

```html
<!DOCTYPE html>
<html>
    <head>
        <script
src="qrc:///qtwebchannel/qwebchannel.js"></script>
        <script src="js/jquery.min.js"></script>
        <script src="js/bootstrap.js"></script>
        <link rel="stylesheet" type="text/css"
href="css/bootstrap.css">
        <link rel="stylesheet" type="text/css" href="css/font-
awesome.css">
    </head>
    <body>
    </body>
</html>
```

12. Add the following JavaScript code, which is wrapped within the `<script>` tags, to the `<head>` element of our HTML file:

```javascript
<script>
    $(document).ready(function() {
        $("#tux").css({ opacity:0, width:"0%", height:"0%" });
        $("#listgroup").hide();
        $("#listgroup2").hide();
        new QWebChannel(qt.webChannelTransport,
function(channel) {
            mainWindow = channel.objects.mainWindow;
        });
    });
    function changeHtmlText(newText) {
        $("#infotext").html(newText);
    }
```

13. Define the `startAnim()` function:

```javascript
function startAnim() {
    // Reset
    $("#tux").css({ opacity:0, width:"0%", height:"0%" });
    $("#listgroup").hide();
    $("#listgroup2").hide();
    $("#tux").animate({ opacity:1.0, width:"100%",
height:"100%" }, 1000, function() {
        // tux animation complete
        $("#listgroup").slideDown(1000, function() {
            // listgroup animation complete
```

```
                           $("#listgroup2").fadeIn(1500);
                   });
               });
           }
       </script>
```

14. Add the following code to the `<body>` element of our HTML file:

```
<div class="container-fluid">
    <form id="example-form" action="#" class="container-fluid">
        <div class="form-group">
            <div class="col-md-12"><h3>Call Javascript Function
from C++</h3></div>
            <div class="col-md-12">
                <div class="alert alert-info" role="alert"><i
class="fa fa-info-circle"></i> <span id="infotext"> Change this
text using C++.</span></div>
            </div>
            <div class="col-md-2">
                <img id="tux" src="tux.png"></img>
            </div>
```

15. Continue writing the following code to which we've added a list:

```
<div class="col-md-5">
    <ul id="listgroup" class="list-group">
        <li class="list-group-item">Cras justoodio</li>
        <li class="list-group-item">Dapibus acfacilisis in</li>
        <li class="list-group-item">Morbi leorisus</li>
        <li class="list-group-item">Porta acconsectetur ac</li>
        <li class="list-group-item">Vestibulum ateros</li>
    </ul>
</div>
<div id="listgroup2" class="col-md-5">
    <a href="#" class="list-group-item active">
        <h4 class="list-group-item-heading">Item heading</h4>
        <p class="list-group-item-text">Cras justo odio</p>
    </a>
```

16. The code continues as we add the remaining items to the second list:

```
                <a href="#" class="list-group-item">
                    <h4 class="list-group-item-heading">Item
heading</h4>
                    <p class="list-group-item-text">Dapibus ac
facilisis in</p>
                </a>
                <a href="#" class="list-group-item">
```

```
                            <h4 class="list-group-item-heading">Item
heading</h4>
                            <p class="list-group-item-text">Morbi leo
risus</p>
                    </a>
                </div>
            </div>
        </form>
    </div>
```

17. Build and run the program; you should get a similar result to that in the
following screenshot. When you click on the **Change HTML Text** button, the
information text is located within the top panel. If you click on the **Play UI
Animation** button, the penguin image, alongside the two sets of widgets, will
appear one after the other, with different animations:

How it works...

This example is similar to the previous one in the *Calling C++ functions from JavaScript* section. Once we have included the **WebChannel** JavaScript library and initiated the `QWebChannel` class, we can call any of the JavaScript functions from C++ by calling `webview->page()->runJavascript("jsFunctionNameHere();")`. Don't forget to apply the web channel created in C++ to the WebView's page as well; otherwise, it will not be able to communicate with the `QWebChannel` class in your HTML file.

By default, we change the CSS properties of the penguin image and set its opacity to `0`, width to `0%`, and height to `0%`. We also hide the two list groups by calling the `hide()` jQuery function. When the **Play UI Animation** button is clicked, we repeat the steps again just in case the animations have been played before (that is, the same button has been clicked before), then we hide them again in order for the animations to be replayed.

One powerful feature of jQuery is that you can define what happens after an animation finishes, which allows us to play the animations in sequence. In this example, we started with the penguin image and interpolated its CSS properties to a targeted setting within a second (1,000 milliseconds). Once that's done, we start another animation, which makes the first list group slide from top to bottom in one second. After that, we run the third animation, which makes the second list group fade in from nowhere within 1.5 seconds.

To replace the information text located in the top panel, we created a JavaScript function called `changeHtmlText()`; within the function itself, and we got the HTML element by referring to its ID and calling `html()` to change its contents.

Performance Optimization 13

In this chapter, we will cover the following recipes:

- Optimizing form and C++
- Profiling and optimizing QML
- Rendering and animation

Introduction

Qt 5 is known for its optimized performance. However, performance issues may still occur if your code is poorly written. There are many ways we can identify these issues and fix them before releasing the software to our users.

Technical requirements

The technical requirements for this chapter include Qt 5.11.2 MinGW 32 bit, Qt Creator 4.8.2, and Windows 10.

All of the code that's used in this chapter can be downloaded from the following GitHub link: https://github.com/PacktPublishing/Qt5-CPP-GUI-Programming-Cookbook-Second-Edition/tree/master/Chapter13.

Check out the following video to see the code in action: http://bit.ly/2FrX5Ls

Optimizing form and C++

It's very important to learn how to optimize your form-based Qt 5 applications that are built with C++. The best way to do that is to learn how to measure and compare different methods that are used and decide which one works the best for you.

How to do it...

Let's get started by following these steps:

1. Let's create a `Qt Widgets Application` project and open up `mainwindow.cpp`. After that, add the following headers to the top of the source code:

```
#include <QPushButton>
#include <QGridLayout>
#include <QMessageBox>
#include <QTime>
#include <QDebug>
```

2. Create a `QGridLayout` object and set its parent as `centralWidget`:

```
MainWindow::MainWindow(QWidget *parent) : QMainWindow(parent),
ui(new Ui::MainWindow)
{
    ui->setupUi(this);
    QGridLayout *layout = new QGridLayout(ui->centralWidget);
```

3. Create a `QTime` object. We will be using this to measure the performance of our next operation:

```
QTime* time = new QTime;
time->start();
```

4. We will use two loops to fill in 600 push buttons to our grid layout and connect all of them to a lambda function when clicked. We will then measure the elapsed time and print out the result, as follows:

```
for (int i = 0; i < 40; ++i) {
    for (int j = 0; j < 15; ++j) {
        QPushButton* newWidget = new QPushButton();
        newWidget->setText("Button");
        layout->addWidget(newWidget, i, j);
        connect(newWidget, QPushButton::clicked,
        [this]() {
            QMessageBox::information(this, "Clicked", "Button
has been clicked!");
        });
    }
}
qDebug() << "Test GUI:" << time->elapsed() << "msec";
```

5. If we build and run the project now, we will see that a window fills with lots of buttons on it. When we click on one of them, a message box will pop up on the screen. It only took around nine milliseconds on my computer to create and lay out all of the 600 buttons on the main window. There is also no performance issue when we move the window around or resize it, which is quite impressive. It proves that Qt 5 can handle this pretty well. However, please be aware that your users might be using older machines, and you might want to be extra careful when designing your user interface:

6. Let's add a style sheet to each of the buttons, like so:

```
QPushButton* newWidget = new QPushButton();
newWidget->setText("Button");
newWidget->setStyleSheet("background-color: blue; color:
white;");
layout->addWidget(newWidget, i, j);
```

7. Build and run the program again. This time, it took roughly 75 milliseconds to set up the GUI. This means that the style sheet does have some impact on the performance of your program:

8. Once you are done with that, let's do some performance tests on different types of C++ containers. Open up `main.cpp` and add the following headers:

```cpp
#include "mainwindow.h"
#include <QApplication>
#include <QDebug>
#include <QTime>
#include <vector>
#include <QVector>
```

9. Create a `testArray()` function before the `main()` function:

```cpp
int testArray(int count) {
    int sum = 0;
    int *myarray = new int[count];
```

```
        for (int i = 0; i < count; ++i)
            myarray[i] = i;
        for (int j = 0; j < count; ++j)
            sum += myarray[j];
        delete [] myarray;
        return sum;
    }
```

10. Create another function called `testVector()`, as follows:

```
    int testVector(int count) {
        int sum = 0;
        std::vector<int> myarray;
        for (int i = 0; i < count; ++i)
            myarray.push_back(i);
        for (int j = 0; j < count; ++j)
            sum += myarray.at(j);
        return sum;
    }
```

11. Once you are done with that, proceed to create yet another function called `testQtVector()`:

```
    int testQtVector(int count) {
        int sum = 0;
        QVector<int> myarray;
        for (int i = 0; i < count; ++i)
            myarray.push_back(i);
        for (int j = 0; j < count; ++j)
            sum += myarray.at(j);
        return sum;
    }
```

12. Inside the `main()` function, define a `QTime` object and an integer variable called `lastElapse`:

```
    int main(int argc, char *argv[]) {
        QApplication a(argc, argv);
        MainWindow w;
        w.show();

        QTime* time = new QTime;
        time->start();
        int lastElapse = 0;
```

13. We will call the three functions we created in the previous steps to test their performance:

```
int result = testArray(100000000);
qDebug() << "Array:" << (time->elapsed() - lastElapse) <<
"msec";
lastElapse = time->elapsed();

int result2 = testVector(100000000);
qDebug() << "STL vector:" << (time->elapsed() - lastElapse) <<
"msec";
lastElapse = time->elapsed();

int result3 = testQtVector(100000000);
qDebug() << "Qt vector:" << (time->elapsed() - lastElapse) <<
"msec";
lastElapse = time->elapsed();
```

14. Build and run the program now; we will see the performance difference of these containers. On my computer, the array took 650 milliseconds to execute, STL vector took roughly 3,830 milliseconds, and Qt vector took around 5,400 milliseconds to execute. As a result, the array is still the container that yields the best performance, despite its lack of features compared to the other two. Surprisingly, Qt's own vector class works slightly slower than the vector container provided by the C++ standard library.

How it works...

When creating a Qt Widgets Application project, try to do the following to improve performance:

- Avoid adding too many pages to a stacked widget and filling them with widgets, as Qt needs to find all of them recursively during the rendering process and event handling, which will highly impact the program's performance.
- Do note that the QWidget class uses the Raster Engine, a software render to render the widgets instead of using GPU. However, it is lightweight enough to keep the performance good most of the time. Alternatively, you should consider using QML for your program's GUI instead, since it is fully hardware accelerated.

- Turn off **mouseTracking**, **tabletTracking**, and other event catching for your widgets if they do not need it. These trackings and catchings cost extra CPU usage to your program:

- Keep your style sheets as simple as possible. A large style sheet needs a longer time for Qt to parse the information into the rendering system, which will also impact performance.
- Different C++ containers produce different speeds, as we showed in the preceding example. Surprisingly, Qt's vector container is slightly slower than STL's (the C++ standard library) vector container. Overall, the good old C++ array is still the fastest, but does not provide sorting functionality. Use what is best for your requirements.
- For large operations, use asynchronous methods whenever possible as it will not stall the main process and keep your program running smoothly.
- Multi-threading is really good for running different operations in parallel event loops. However, it can also become quite ugly if not done right, for example, creating and destroying threads frequently, or inter-thread communications that are not planned well.
- Try to avoid using the web engine unless absolutely necessary. This is because embedding a full web browser on your program is really heavy and overkill, especially for a small application. You can consider using QML instead of making a hybrid application if you want to create user interface-centric software.
- By doing performance tests like we did in the preceding example project, you can easily determine which method is the best choice for your project and how to make your program perform better.

Profiling and optimizing QML

The QML engine in Qt 5 took advantage of hardware acceleration to make its rendering capability and performance superior to the old widgets user interface. However, it does not mean that you should not care about optimization; that is because small performance issues may snowball into bigger problems over time and causing damage to your product's reputation.

How to do it...

Follow these steps to start profiling and optimizing a QML application:

1. Let's create a **Qt Quick Application - Empty** project:

2. Then, go to **Analyze** | **QML Profiler** and run the **QML Profiler** tool:

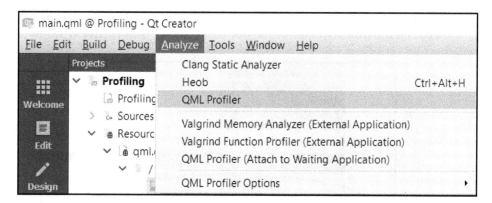

3. Your Qt Quick project will then be ran by the **QML Profiler**. The **QML Profiler** window will also appear under the code editor. Click the **Stop** button located at the top bar of the **QML Profiler** window after the program is passed your test point, which in this case, successfully created the empty window:

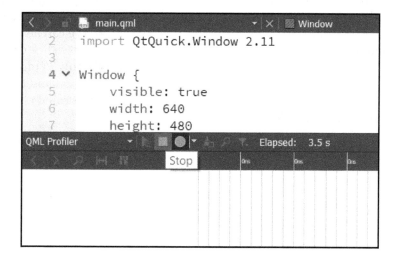

4. After you stop the profiler analysis, a timeline will be displayed on the **Timeline** tab under the **QML Profiler** window. There are three tabs that you can switch between, namely **Timeline**, **Flame Graph**, and **Statistics**. You can switch between the different tabs at the bottom of the **QML Profiler** window:

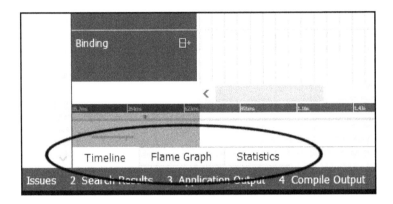

5. Let's check out the timeline tab. We can see five different categories under the timeline display: **Scene Graph**, **Memory Usage**, **Compiling**, **Creating**, and **Binding**. These categories give us an overview of the different stages and processes of our program throughout its execution. We can also see that there are some colorful bars being displayed on the timeline. Let's click on one of the bars under the **Creating** category that says **QtQuick.Window/Window**. Once clicked, we will be able to see the total duration for this operation and the location of the code displayed on the rectangular window, which is located at the top of the **QML Profiler** window:

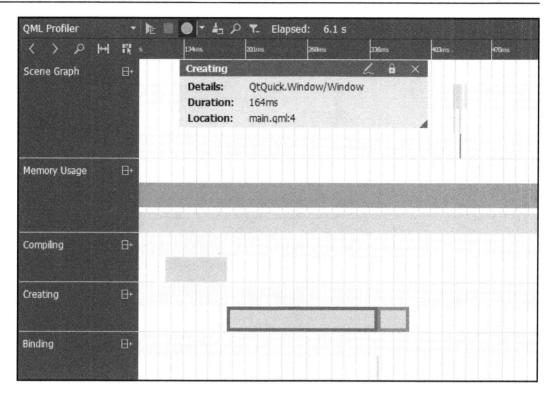

6. Once you are done with that, let's move on and open up the **Flame Graph** tab instead. Under the **Flame Graph** tab, you will see the visualization of the total time, memory, and allocation of your application in the form of percentages. You can switch between total time, memory, and allocation by clicking on the selection box that's located at the top-right corner of the **QML Profiler** window:

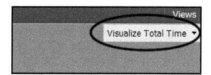

7. Not only that, you will also see the percentage value displayed on your QML code editor:

```
~25.2%   1   import QtQuick 2.11
         2   import QtQuick.Window 2.11
         3
~74.8%   4 ∨ Window {
         5       visible: true
         6       width: 640
         7       height: 480
         8       title: qsTr("Hello World")
         9   }
        10
```

8. Open up the **Statistic** category under the **QML Profiler** window. This tab is basically showing us information about the processes in table form:

Location	Type	Time in Percer	Total Time	Self Time in P	Self Time	Calls	Mean Time
<program>		100.00 %	265ms	0.00 %	0ns	1	265ms
main.qml:4	Creating	74.76 %	198ms	74.76 %	198ms	2	99.2ms
main.qml:0	Compiling	25.23 %	66.9ms	25.23 %	66.9ms	1	66.9ms
<bytecode>	Binding	0.01 %	24.6µs	0.01 %	24.6µs	1	24.6µs

Caller	Type	Total Time	Calls	Caller Description
<program>		198ms	2	Main Program

Timeline   Flame Graph   Statistics

How it works...

This is similar to what we did in the previous example project that uses C++ and widgets except, this time, it is being automatically analyzed by the QML Profiler tool that's provided by Qt 5.

The QML Profiler not only produces the total time used for running a specific process, but it also displays the memory allocation, the execution timeline of your application, and other information that gives you insight into the performance of your software.

By looking at the data that was analyzed by the QML Profiler, you will be able to find out which part of your code slows down the program, allowing you to fix any problems quickly.

There are some rules that you need to be aware of when writing QML to avoid performance bottlenecks. For instance, type conversion can sometimes be expensive, especially between types that are not closely matched (string to number, for example). Small issues like this will likely snowball into bottlenecks when your project grows larger over time.

Other than that, try not to use id for an item lookup multiple times in the block of code that is being run often, as in the following example:

```
Item {
    width: 400
    height: 400
    Rectangle {
        id: rect
        anchors.fill: parent
        color: "green"
    }
    Component.onCompleted: {
        for (var i = 0; i < 1000; ++i) {
            console.log("red", rect.color.r);
            console.log("green", rect.color.g);
            console.log("blue", rect.color.b);
            console.log("alpha", rect.color.a);
        }
    }
}
```

Instead, we can use a variable to cache the data and avoid multiple look-ups on the same item over and over again:

```
Component.onCompleted: {
    var rectColor = rect.color;
    for (var i = 0; i < 1000; ++i) {
        console.log("red", rectColor.r);
        console.log("green", rectColor.g);
        console.log("blue", rectColor.b);
        console.log("alpha", rectColor.a);
    }
}
```

Besides, if you change the property of a binding expression, especially in a loop, Qt will be forced to re-evaluate it repeatedly. This will cause some performances issue. Instead of doing this, the user should follow the next code snippet:

```
Item {
    id: myItem
    width: 400
    height: 400
    property int myValue: 0
    Text {
        anchors.fill: parent
        text: myItem.myValue.toString()
    }
    Component.onCompleted: {
        for (var i = 0; i < 1000; ++i) {
            myValue += 1;
        }
    }
}
```

Instead, we can use a temporary variable for storing the data of myValue, then apply the final result back to myValue once the loop has been completed:

```
Component.onCompleted: {
    var temp = myValue;
    for (var i = 0; i < 1000; ++i) {
        temp += 1;
    }
    myValue = temp;
}
```

Consider using an anchor to position your UI items instead of using bindings. Item positioning with bindings is really slow and inefficient, although it allows for maximum flexibility.

Rendering and animation

When it comes to an application that renders graphics and animation, good performance is critical. Users can easily notice any performance issue when the graphics are not animating smoothly on screen. In the following example, we will look at how we can further optimize a graphics-heavy Qt Quick application.

How to do it...

To learn how to render animation in QML, follow this example:

1. Create a **Qt Quick Application - Empty** project. Then, right-click on the **Resources** icon under our project panel and add `tux.png` into our project's resource:

2. Open up `main.qml` and change the window size to `650 x 650`. We will also add `id` to the `Window` item and name it `window`:

```
Window {
    id: window
    visible: true
    width: 650
    height: 650
```

3. Add the following code inside the `Window` item:

```
property int frame: 0;
onAfterRendering: { frame++; }

Timer {
    id: timer
    interval: 1000
    running: true
    repeat: true
    onTriggered: { frame = 0; }
}
```

4. Right after that, add `Repeater` and `Image` under it:

```
Repeater {
    model: 10
    delegate:
        Image {
            id: tux
            source: "tux.png"
```

```
sourceSize.width: 50
sourceSize.height: 60
width: 50
height: 60
smooth: false
antialiasing: false
asynchronous: true
```

5. We will proceed and add the following code:

```
property double startX: Math.random() * 600;
property double startY: Math.random() * 600;
property double endX: Math.random() * 600;
property double endY: Math.random() * 600;
property double speed: Math.random() * 3000 + 1000;

RotationAnimation on rotation{
    loops: Animation.Infinite
    from: 0
    to: 360
    duration: Math.random() * 3000 + 1000;
}
```

6. Once you are done with that, add the following code at the bottom of the previous code:

```
SequentialAnimation {
    running: true
    loops: Animation.Infinite
    ParallelAnimation {
        NumberAnimation {
            target: tux
            property: "x"
            from: startX
            to: endX
            duration: speed
            easing.type: Easing.InOutQuad

    }
```

7. The preceding code animates the x property of the image. We need another NumberAnimation property to animate the y property:

```
NumberAnimation {
    target: tux
    property: "y"
    from: startY
    to: endY
    duration: speed
    easing.type: Easing.InOutQuad
    }
}
```

8. After that, we repeat the entire code of the ParallelAnimation, except this time, we swap the from and to values, like so:

```
ParallelAnimation {
    NumberAnimation {
        target: tux
        property: "x"
        from: endX
        to: startX
        duration: speed
        easing.type: Easing.InOutQuad
    }
```

9. The same goes for NumberAnimation for the y property:

```
NumberAnimation {
    target: tux
    property: "y"
    from: endY
    to: startY
    duration: speed
    easing.type: Easing.InOutQuad
    }
}
```

10. Then, we add a `Text` item for displaying the frame rate of our application:

```
Text {
    property int frame: 0
    color: "red"
    text: "FPS: 0 fps"
    x: 20
    y: 20
    font.pointSize: 20
```

11. Let's add `Timer` under `Text` and update the frame rate display on every second:

```
Timer {
    id: fpsTimer
    repeat: true
    interval: 1000
    running: true
    onTriggered: {
        parent.text = "FPS: " + frame + " fps"
    }
}
}
```

12. If we build and run the program now, we will be able to see several penguins moving around the screen with a steady **60 fps**:

13. Let's go back to our code and change the `model` property of the `Repeater` item to `10000`. Build and run the program again; you should see that your window is full of moving penguins and that the frame rate has significantly dropped to roughly **29 fps**, which is not too bad, considering the amount of penguins we have:

14. Then, go back to our source code and comment out both of the `sourceSize` properties. We also set the `smooth` and `antialiasing` properties to `false`, while setting the `asynchronous` property to `false`:

```
Image {
    id: tux
    source: "tux.png"
    //sourceSize.width: 50
    //sourceSize.height: 60
    width: 50
```

```
height: 60
smooth: true
antialiasing: true
asynchronous: false
```

15. Let's build and run the program again. This time, the frame rate dropped slightly to **22 fps**, but the penguins look smoother and are of a better quality, even when moving:

How it works...

The QML engine that powers Qt Quick applications are very optimized and powerful when it comes to rendering animated graphics on screen. However, there are still some tips that we can follow to make it even faster.

Try and make use of the built-in features provided by Qt 5 instead of implementing your own, such as `Repeater`, `NumberAnimation`, and `SequentialAnimation`. This is because Qt 5 developers have put great effort into optimizing these features so that you don't have to.

The `sourceSize` properties tell Qt to resize the image before loading it into memory so that large images do not use more memory than necessary.

The `smooth` property, when enabled, tells Qt to filter the image to make look it smoother when scaled or transformed from its natural size. It will not make any difference if the image is rendered at the same as its `sourceSize`. This property will impact the performance of your application on some older hardware.

The `antialiasing` property tells Qt to remove the aliasing artifacts around the edge of the image and make it look smoother. This property will also impact the performance of your program.

The `asynchronous` property tells Qt to load the image under a low priority thread, which means that your program will not stall when loading a huge image file.

We used the frame rate for indicating the performance of our program. Since `onAfterRendering` always gets called on every frame, we can then accumulate the `frame` variable on every render. Then, we used `Timer` to reset the `frame` value every second. Finally, we displayed the value on screen using a `Text` item.

Other Books You May Enjoy

If you enjoyed this book, you may be interested in these other books by Packt:

Hands-On Design Patterns with C++
Fedor G. Pikus

ISBN: 9781788832564

- Recognize the most common design patterns used in C++
- Understand how to use C++ generic programming to solve common design problems
- Explore the most powerful C++ idioms, their strengths, and drawbacks
- Rediscover how to use popular C++ idioms with generic programming
- Understand the impact of design patterns on the program's performance

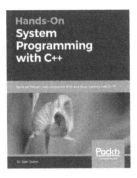

Hands-On System Programming with C++
Dr. Rian Quinn

ISBN: 9781789137880

- Understand the benefits of using C++ for system programming
- Program Linux/Unix systems using C++
- Discover the advantages of Resource Acquisition Is Initialization (RAII)
- Program both console and file input and output
- Uncover the POSIX socket APIs and understand how to program them
- Explore advanced system programming topics, such as C++ allocators
- Use POSIX and C++ threads to program concurrent systems
- Grasp how C++ can be used to create performant system applications

Leave a review - let other readers know what you think

Please share your thoughts on this book with others by leaving a review on the site that you bought it from. If you purchased the book from Amazon, please leave us an honest review on this book's Amazon page. This is vital so that other potential readers can see and use your unbiased opinion to make purchasing decisions, we can understand what our customers think about our products, and our authors can see your feedback on the title that they have worked with Packt to create. It will only take a few minutes of your time, but is valuable to other potential customers, our authors, and Packt. Thank you!

Index

SVG files
  shapes, exporting to 108, 110, 111, 113
SVG graphics
  reference 114

T

table widget 337
TCP client
  creating 183, 184, 185, 186, 187, 188
TCP networking 183
TCP server
  creating 176, 177, 178, 179, 180, 182
texture
  using, in OpenGL 159, 160, 161, 162
threads
  data, sharing between 212, 214, 216
  using 204
  worker threads 207
three.js
  reference 173
touch-driven application
  developing 237, 239, 240, 242, 243
transitions
  in QML 92
Transmission Control Protocol (TCP) 176, 182

U

UDP networking 183
UI events
  with signals and slots mechanism 61, 62, 63,
    64, 65, 67, 68
User Datagram Protocol (UDP) connection 182

V

Vector3d animation 95
Vertex Array Object (VAO) 150
Vertex Buffer Object (VBO) 150

vertex shader 149
videos
  converting 297, 298, 299, 300, 302
Visual C++ compiler 351
Visual Studio
  download link 350

W

WebChannel 349, 375
WebEngine project
  setting up 350, 352, 353, 354, 355, 356, 357
widget properties
  animating, animators used 96, 97, 98
  customizing 32, 34, 35, 36
widget sub-controls
  customizing 32, 34, 35, 36
window
  creating, that continuously changes background
    color 92, 93, 94, 95
worker threads 207

X

XAMPP
  reference 310
XE Currency Data API
  reference 308
XML 263
XML data
  processing, QDomDocument class used 274,
    276, 277
  processing, stream reader used 264, 265, 266,
    267, 268
  writing, QDomDocument class used 277, 278,
    280
  writing, Stream Writer used 270, 271, 273
XML format
  reference 270